KT-495-728

Your Garden in the City

HOW TO PLAN IT,

Your Garden in the City

BUILD IT, AND GROW IT

by Jack Kramer

Drawings by: Adrian Martinez
Robert Johnson
Michael Valdez

A HERBERT MICHELMAN BOOK   CROWN PUBLISHERS, INC.,   NEW YORK

Printed in the United States of America

Published simultaneously in Canada by
General Publishing Company Limited

Library of Congress Cataloging in
Publication Data
Kramer, Jack
Your garden in the city.
"A Herbert Michelman book."
Bibliography: p.

Includes index.
1. Gardening. 2. Gardens—Design. 3. Garden
structures—Design and construction. Title.
SB453.K74   1982   635.9   81-12519
                                 AACR2
ISBN: 0-517-544849

Book design by Deborah Bailey Kerner

10 9 8 7 6 5 4 3 2 1
First Edition

CONTENTS

PART I

PLANNING

A beautiful garden does not happen by itself. It takes planning, construction, planting, and care. The initial energy and cost may seem excessive but once the green oasis in the city is complete it is well worth the expenditure of time and money. Indeed, it can be a solace to the soul and provide beauty to the eye.

Careful planning, as well as using the space you have to the greatest advantage, eliminates much work and saves time. Whether you want a backyard garden, a roof greenery, or a patio or terrace retreat, there are ways of accomplishing your garden in the city.

In the following chapters we look at ways to use your space for many types of gardens.

Entrance garden in
Chicago, Illinois.

1

Location & Design

LOCATION

The two things that most hinder successful gardening—air pollution and excessive shade—are ever present in the city, where you especially need a sylvan setting, more so than in the country, where nature lends a helping hand. A fantastic garden in an urban environment provides delightful enjoyment and keen satisfaction in working with the elements. Today's city garden can be a jewel, if you know enough about plants and their relationship to the environment. City gardening involves design and construction planning, careful plant selection, and perseverance to keep plants healthy and growing, in spite of pollution and less than favorable light conditions.

There are many places within your property (no matter how small they may be) where you can create a desirable garden. Consider ground-level areas: front,

This small backyard garden is a beautiful retreat in the city turmoil; there is a place for plants and a place to sit and relax—and escape. Some plants are in the ground but most greenery is arranged in planters or in containers. Note the balance and design of the landscape material—both vertical and horizontal accents. (Photograph by C. D. Luckhart)

This city garden on a narrow lot in Chicago, Illinois, is low maintenance and includes a man-made pond. Plants are mainly native specimens and sculptural shrubs are the mainstay of the plan. (Photograph by Matsumoto)

rear, and side—which would be best for the garden? (You must handle each area differently.) What about a lovely garden on the roof? If you are an apartment dweller, a patio or terrace can be ideal for a handsome, small greenery.

To start planning, make an inventory of what available space you have for growing plants. Then consider *carefully* the area. Are there any outstanding vistas worth keeping? Or does concrete abound on all sides? (What surrounds the garden is as important as what goes into it.) Do not overlook any disadvantages, such as winds and overly sunny exposures. You must cope intelligently with them.

What about the orientation of the garden? Pay attention to how the sun strikes your property; without sufficient light, good plant growth can be difficult (but not impossible). Usually, a southern exposure is the warmest and most satisfying for outdoor living and plants, but a northern exposure is fine for lots of shade-tolerant plants. If the site is confining, consider installing interesting levels or terraces, which add dimension and depth to your garden. If you have a city skyline view, frame it dramatically with trees and shrubs. If you have no view at all, which is so often the case, develop dramatic interests within the boundaries of the garden to decorate, distract, and form a picture: specimen plantings, standards, and espaliers. Sculpture, fountains, and gazebos are other novel ways of keeping the eye within the confines of the garden.

DESIGN

In colonial America the garden was merely a place to grow flowers. In the United States today the garden is a way of life, our extra living space. But because the average city property is even smaller than it was ten years ago and the cost of land has risen so much, the city garden demands different approaches from those taken in the past. New structural and synthetic materials, new plants, and new ways of growing plants make today's city gardening an exciting adventure.

The informal or natural theme depends upon asymmetrical balance, that is, no pairs of trees or shrubs, no straight lines or borders. It is a continuous flow of plant material. Today's city garden depends upon a certain

On a narrow city lot this gardener's choice is cut flowers and dahlias and lilies, which creates a profusion of color. Most of the plants are in the ground. (Photograph by C. D. Luckhart)

amount of both formal and informal qualities. Climate and the nature of the location also affect what qualities you should stress.

Some gardeners suggest you start a city garden with random plantings, filling in with more plant material later. Others, and I am one, strongly urge you to *plan* the garden before you start, especially for those places where every inch of space counts. Why not create a totally harmonious scene rather than a hodgepodge of plants?

Although design and planning do take time in the beginning, they save money and work later. It is far better to plant what will grow in your garden rather than experiment with plants that may need replacing later. And if you want a terrace, patio, or small pool, you have to reserve space at the start for these garden features. Later, when plants are in place and growing, it is expensive, messy, and time-consuming to have to dig up and replant your garden.

Containers and planters, flower beds, and vegetables fit in even the smallest garden. You can have vegetables—tomatoes, cucumbers, and squash—in tubs if you do not have extensive ground. And diminutive flower beds can yield beautiful cut flowers for indoors.

Formal and Informal Gardens

Through the centuries people have tried to beautify their surroundings by gardening. The famous Hanging Gardens of Babylon were built around 600 B.C. The wealthy Persians and Egyptians built their houses around open courtyards, and the Greeks blended grand architecture and symmetry in the city with detailed landscaping: flower beds, pools, stately trees, and potted

Even a few trees and shrubs and some seasonal plants in decorative pots can make a city garden— this is a fine example of a low-maintenance retreat. (Photograph by C. D. Luckhart)

plants. The Romans were skillful gardeners, designing many still-famous garden pavilions. However, gardening and landscaping truly blossomed with the building of Italian and French villas and palaces and country manors in England in the eighteenth century. These were huge, symmetrical, and beautiful formal gardens, but they were impractical. Later, when houses and grounds became smaller, the British restyled gardening and produced the more natural city garden, ending formality.

The average city lot is too small to accommodate

Shade-loving plants and ground covers create a lush green backyard garden in San Francisco, California. Such a garden almost takes care of itself. (Photograph by Matthew Barr)

either a formal or an informal garden. The formal plan is like a mirror: one side reflects the other, creating symmetry. The resulting geometric pattern can be pleasing when it suits the house, but generally you need much land, which is impossible with city property.

The informal or natural landscape also has drawbacks. You must have old trees and shrubs, which often are not on city plots. Neglected city gardens are usually in poor shape, and a keen eye is necessary to observe and save any remnants of trees or shrubs. Occasionally, careful pruning and cutting can transform plant materials into useful trees or shrubs, but restoring them to health takes time.

GROUND-LEVEL GARDENS

Ground-level gardens are popular because, as part of the home, they can make a small house appear larger, especially if the windows are opened to bring in the outdoors. Use small flowering trees, handsome evergreens, and screening hedges. And do not forget to plant easy-maintenance ground covers massed together to create a carpet of greenery. Concentrate on spring bulbs planted early; they impart seasonal color and are superb in any situation. Incorporate a small paved area as a place for chairs and tables. And a paved floor with just a few container plants can be a low-maintenance yet handsome garden.

The front garden borders the street and provides direct access to the home. Here privacy is a critical factor. Often, as with typical brownstones, the garden is either below the sidewalk level in an areaway or two to three feet above it. A sunken garden can be a quiet entrance to the lower unit, with a tree for shade and some potted plants (with fencing for security) bringing a most attractive touch of green to the lower unit. When the garden is above the sidewalk, a retaining wall can provide the necessary privacy.

The rear or backyard area is usually the most popular space for the typical urban garden. Here is where you can use your ingenuity to create a closed, yet open landscape, even in the smallest area.

If the rear property has parking or outbuildings, consider a side-yard garden. These narrow areas are more suitable for plants than you might think, and this garden spot can be viewed from your windows. With proper plant selection side gardens can be dramatic. Strive for an intimate, cozy scene.

GARDENS IN THE SKY

Balcony and roof gardens are always a challenge. A balcony is generally an awkward, small area, and the

garden on top of a building is subject to wind and scorching sun. Yet you can create a bright green scene in each area. Use tall plants in tubs on the sides to screen you from neighbors and to create a feeling of enclosure; use smaller plants and flowers in pots to give the excitement of color. However, do not fence yourself in.

Roof gardens can be both elegant and stunning. Do not let surrounding wires or poles bother you; with careful planning you can camouflage them. Generally, there is more space to work with here than in ground gardens, and the garden on top of the world is unique. You can

This rooftop retreat is strictly a container garden; there is little in-ground planting or planters. It is an easy maintenance garden requiring little time and care. (Photograph by Matthew Barr)

A rooftop garden with a grand vista—always a pleasure to be in. The plants are in wooden planters and almost anything can be grown in this garden. (Photograph by Matthew Barr)

handle potential sun and wind problems by using shade screens, canopies, awnings, trees, and so on. You need to know something about building construction for this garden: What is the roofing material? Will the structure support a garden? How will the drainage be handled? Is the roof of a good quality so that leaks and repairs will not be a problem? How do you get to the garden from the floor below?

This small deck garden overlooks the street; note how the owners used hanging plants as screens. A pleasant city-escape place. (Photograph by Matthew Barr)

PLANNING ON PAPER

Planning on paper saves much unnecessary labor later. You do not have to draw a ground plan to scale; merely make a sketch. Using your sketch as a guide, mark the location of the house and its boundary lines on graph paper, letting each square equal one foot. Draw the

Dahlias predominate in this city garden in the air, and a handsome lath house shelters begonias—the owners' passion. (Photograph by C. D. Luckhart)

outline of the house and include steps, walks, driveways, trees, and shrubs.

To determine the ground slope, stretch a string across the plot. (Use a mason's level on the string.) Measure the distance between the ground and the string to determine how much of a grade exists. On the graph paper record the high and low areas and how much the grade drops. Put in sun, shade, and north-exposure designations. Study the composition: If all the present features are on the graph paper, start planning the garden.

Lay a sheet of tracing paper over the graph paper. First sketch traffic patterns on the tracing paper. Draw rough sizes and shapes desired for outdoor objects:

terrace, garden beds, planters, new trees and shrubs, play and service areas, and so on. The shapes drawn should start to relate to one another. (Start again with a new piece of tracing paper if you are not satisfied.) Consider all things carefully. Remember that many plants in city gardens are in planters, boxes, tubs, and pots, so carefully study the types of containers available (do-it-yourself containers and commercial ones) to know what to use (see chapter 5).

Once you have a satisfactory sketch, make a detailed design. Be sure to include the exact measurements of the house and lot, outdoor objects, and existing plant material. Decide how much construction will be necessary in the garden—fences, terraces, walls—and how much planting will be needed.

From the following basic patterns you can draw any number of combinations of forms.

Rectangular or square patterns. These forms are the easiest and most natural; they are usually projections of the house form. Working with a uniform module (a space continually repeated) simplifies a plan. The module can be 3 × 4 feet or any other suitable size. You can pave the patio with 3 × 4-foot blocks, use stepping-stones of the same size, and plant islands and beds that will relate to the same module. Thus, every design line will be in proportion and visually pleasing. Your pattern will be simple but concisely organized.

Acute or obtuse angles or triangles. These shapes reflect the angular form of the house and site, provide a focal point for the eye, and give a sense of space and direction.

Circular forms. Circular forms add interest to the pattern. When properly balanced with straight lines, they present an attractive picture.

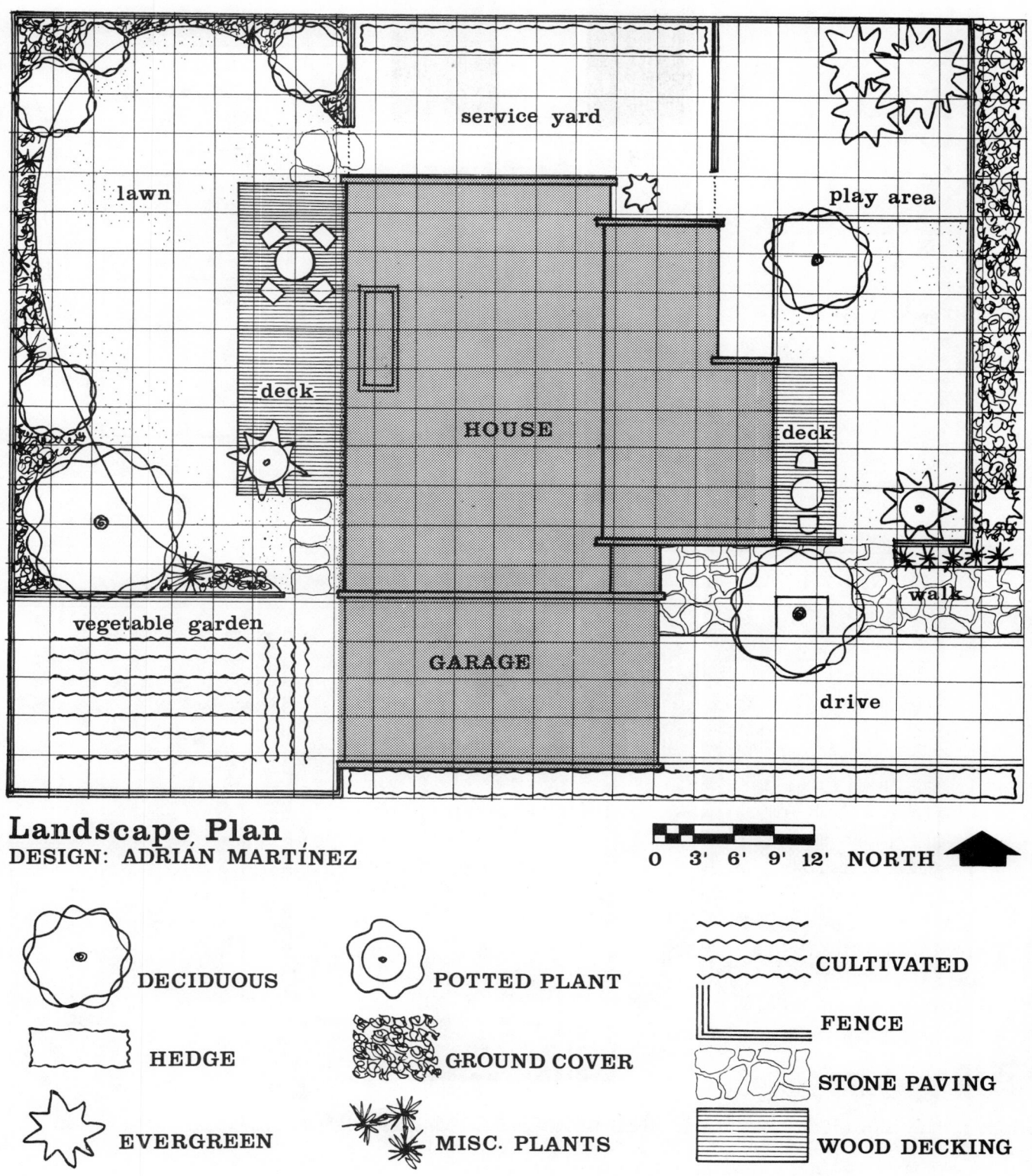

Landscape Plan
DESIGN: ADRIÁN MARTÍNEZ

0 3' 6' 9' 12' NORTH

Landscape Symbols

DECIDUOUS   POTTED PLANT   CULTIVATED

HEDGE   GROUND COVER   FENCE

           STONE PAVING

EVERGREEN   MISC. PLANTS   WOOD DECKING

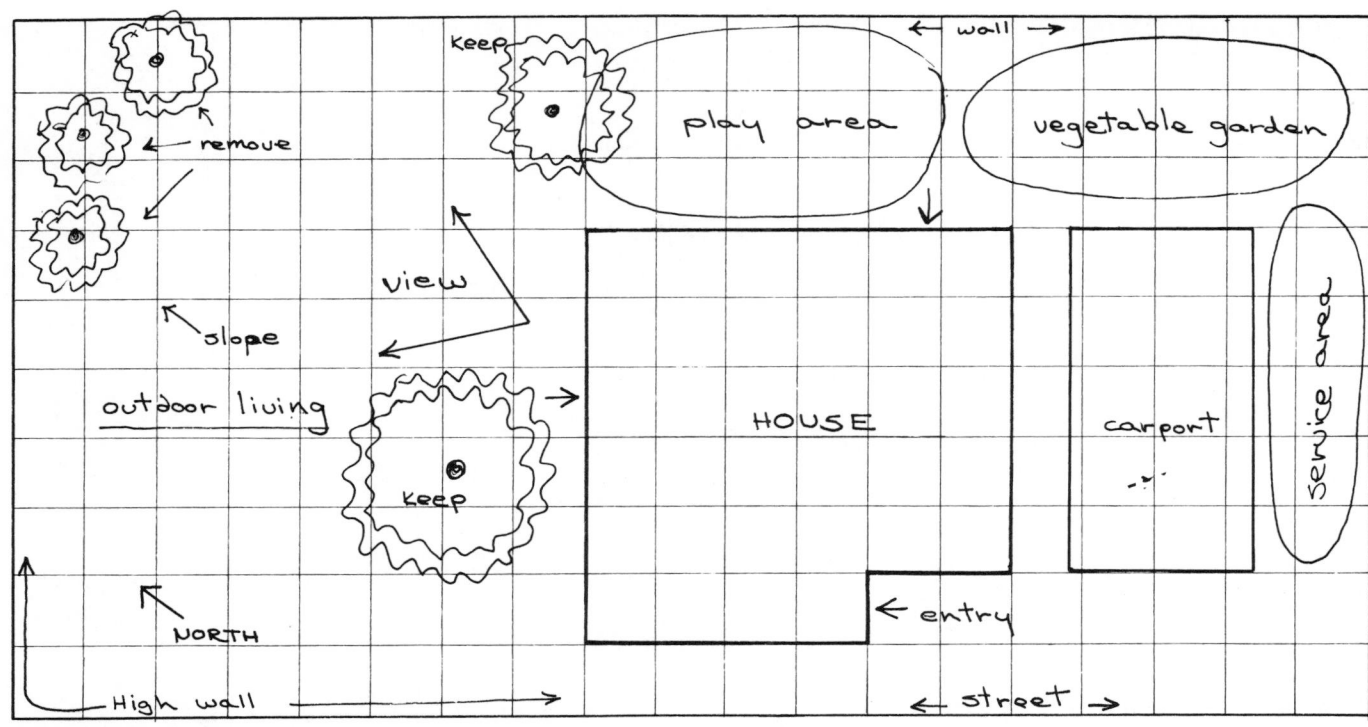

(a) **PRELIMINARY PLAN** site conditions, existing & proposed areas

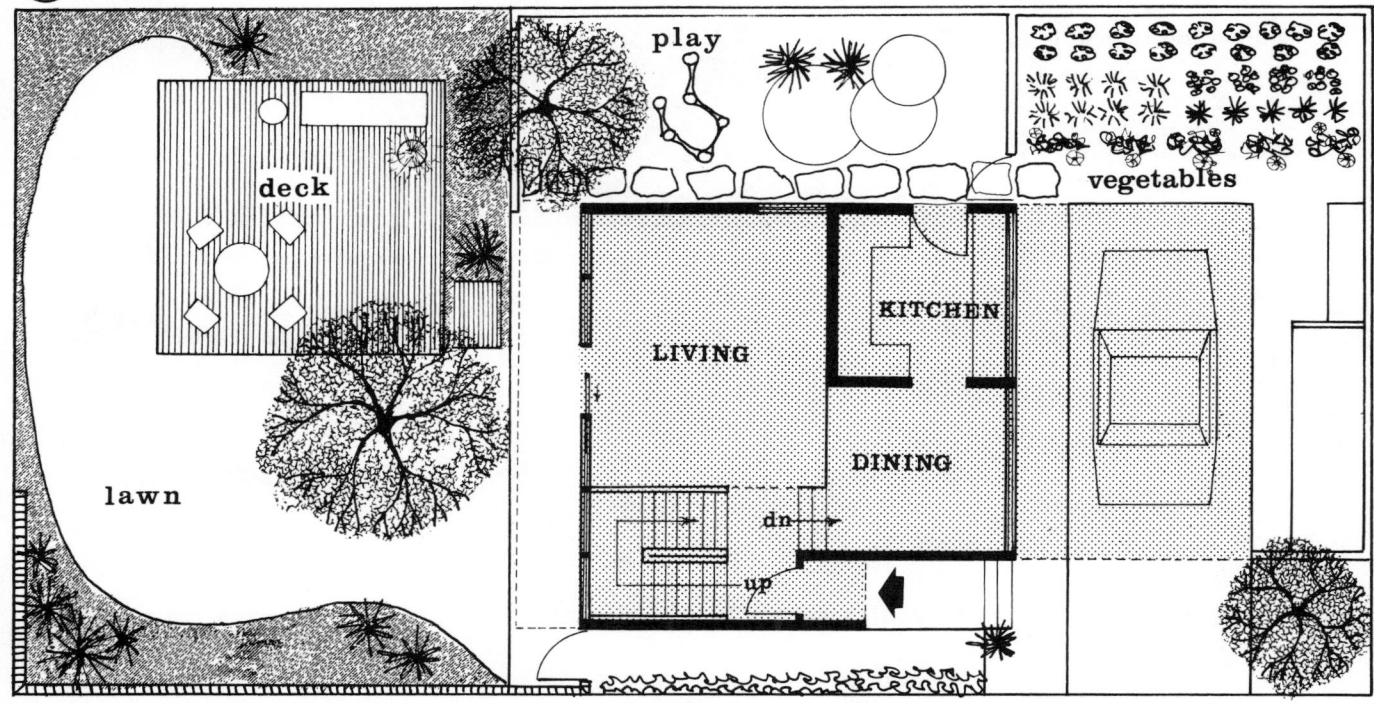

(b) **FINISHED PLAN** area development, planting

Making a Landscape Plan

Free curves. These curving and sweeping lines have an ever-changing radius, producing richness in motion when skillfully used with the geometric forms.

Scale, Proportion, Unity, and Rhythm

Plants have spreading or horizontal, round or globular, weeping or trailing, vertical (pyramidal) or columnar form. The *form* of a plant is vitally important; unless you know what the plant will look like when it is mature, selecting form is a guessing game. When you select plants, try to visualize the plant fully grown. Some species lose their symmetrical form with age, and others lose their lower branches as they get older.

Scale and proportion are the keys to an attractive setting.

Scale is the visual relationship of the size of each form to the size of every other form and to the design as a whole. You must establish an appealing scale between the garden and the dwelling. For example, a large plant can link the garden to the house or apartment. Creating an illusion of space with plant materials is an exciting part of city gardening.

Proportion is the harmonious relationship of one part of the garden to another part and to the whole garden. A large paved terrace and a small lawn can be in proportion; on another site the patio can be small and the lawn large. Making both areas the same size is a mistake because there is no interest; one element does not complement the other. Balance vertical forms with several horizontal elements.

Unity is a blending of all plants so that they become a whole. You do not want unrelated masses insulting the eye. Well-chosen plants of related forms, colors, and

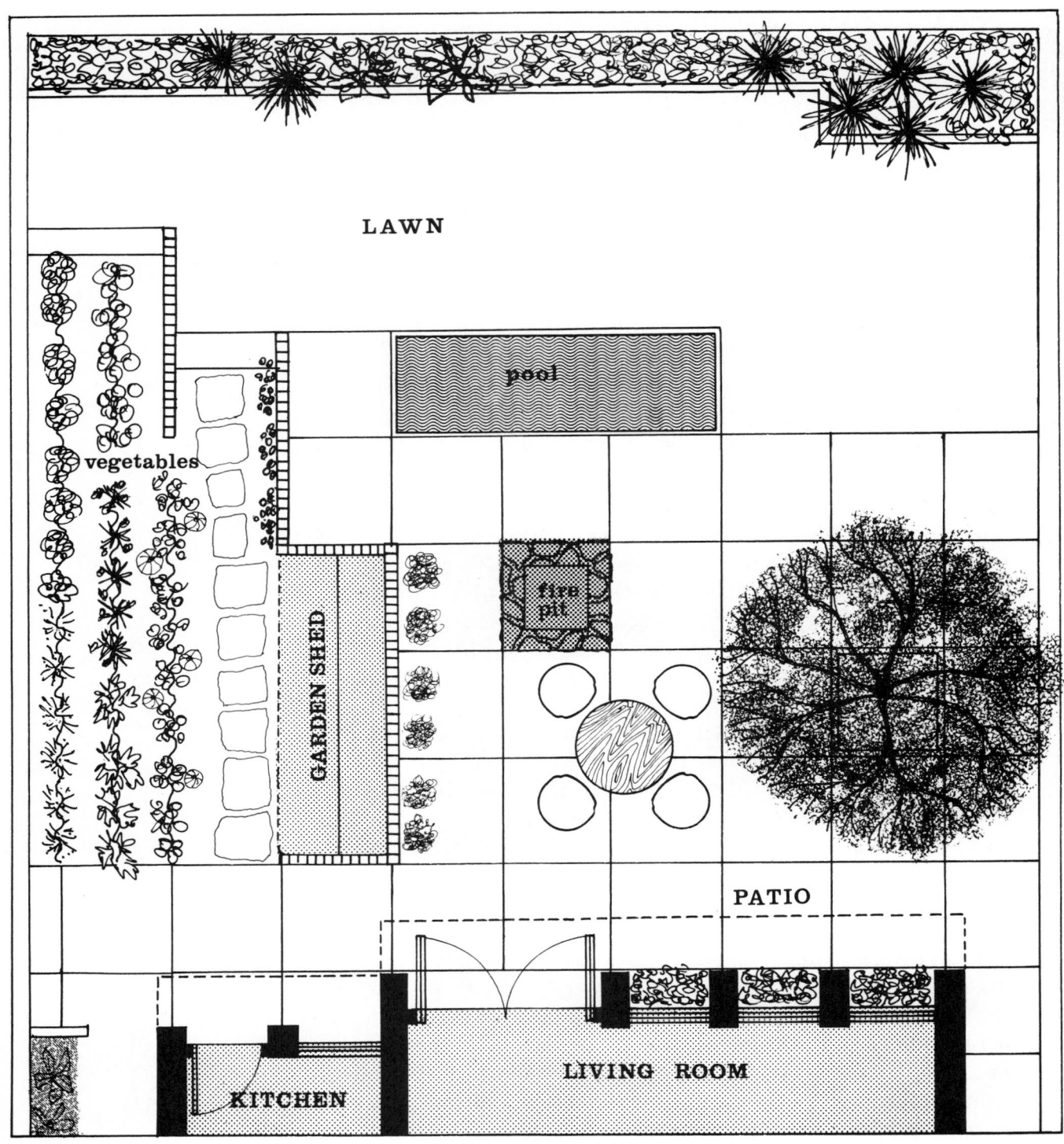

design: adrián martínez

Form in the Garden: Rectangular

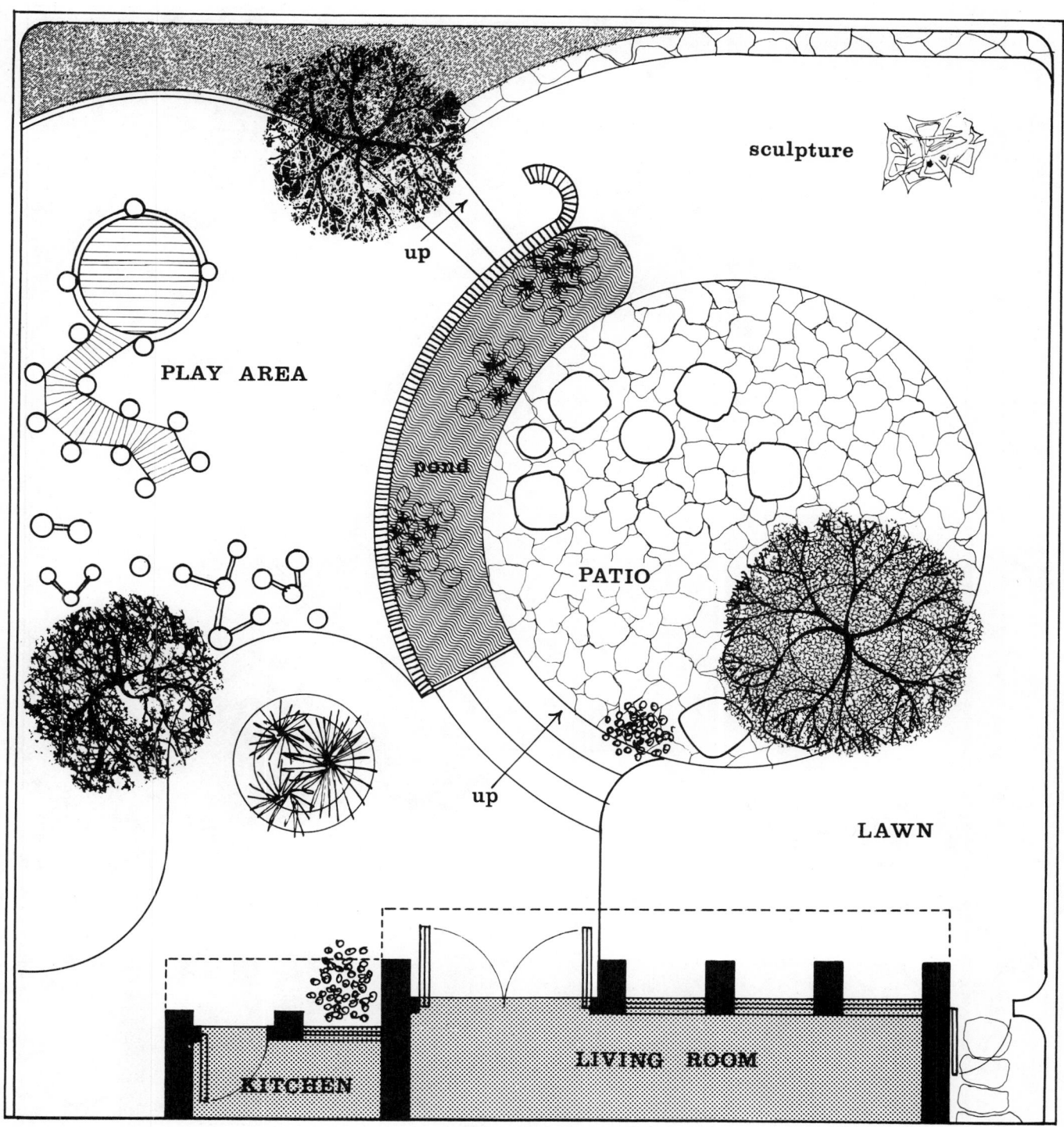

PLAY AREA

sculpture

pond

PATIO

up

up

LAWN

KITCHEN

LIVING ROOM

design: adrián martínez

Form in the Garden: Circular

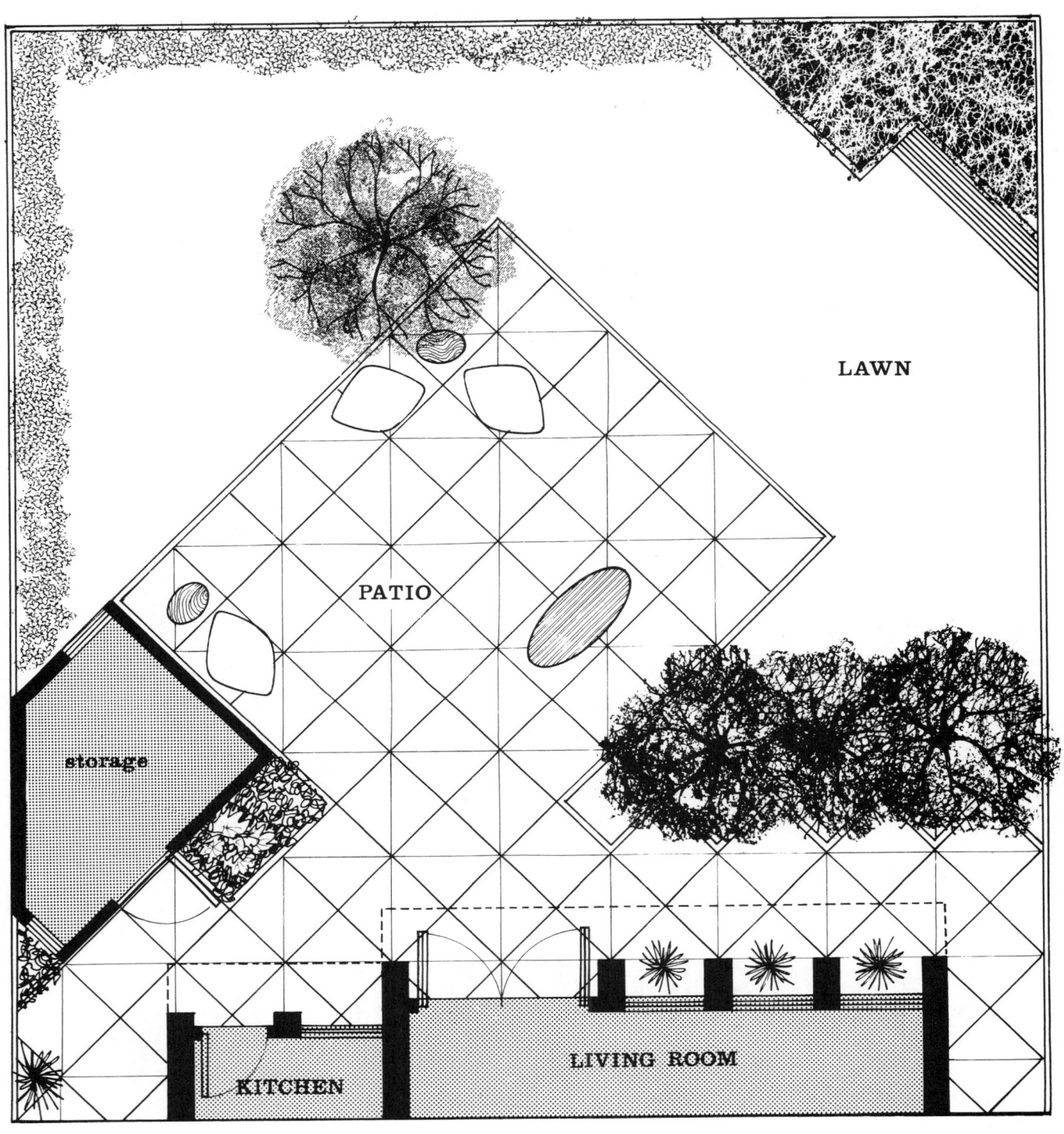

design: adrián martínez

Form in the Garden: Triangular

textures achieve the unity every attractive garden needs.

Rhythm is repeating the same group of plants to give a sense of movement and balance. The plants should be of similar size, form, and emphasis for use as one feature.

Scale, proportion, unity, and rhythm are all interrelated, each factor depending upon the other. Generally, if you get the scale and proportion right, unity and rhythm fall into place.

CONSTRUCTION

Whether you have a backyard garden or a roof greenery, a side-yard haven or a private garden court, in each area some construction will be necessary to make the garden glow: planter boxes, walls, fences. Many city gardens are essentially container gardens—plants in boxes and pots of various shapes, sizes, colors, and materials—especially roof gardens, which are almost completely installed by hand.

In yards you can plant directly into the soil, so containers are not that important (unless the soil is so bad that you *should* plant in containers). But you will need fences and screens. And usually a small patio involves construction, including floors and edgings. Thus, when you plan your garden you should know something about carpentry and wood, masonry and walls, and general "how-to" outdoor building. All this information is presented in chapters 4, 5, and 6.

2

Gardens In The Ground

Gardens at ground level can be an entrance, atrium, side yard, or backyard. Even a small space of 10 × 10 feet can be enough for a pleasant green retreat. And you can make such gardens look larger by planting more in the ground than in containers, although containers do have their place in these areas.

First, notice just what exists already in the area you will be using for a garden. Are there a few trees, some shrubs? Can you use these plants as the starting point, or will you have to install a completely new garden? (A new garden will cost you a fortune.) If you are renting and want to recondition the soil, ask your manager or the property owner if he will share in the expense of beautifying the property. If he refuses, plan on seasonal potted plants.

Now consider how much sunshine the area will receive daily. High buildings immediately to the east of your building will cut off sun and air circulation in the

One planter filled with flowers can make an entrance garden—a pleasant sight for visitors. In such situations it is best to use only one or two kinds of plants but mass them for effect. (Photogragh by Matthew Barr)

garden. Remember, to have flowers, a lawn, or flowering shrubs, you need at least three to four hours of daily sunshine, preferably morning sun, which means a southern or southeastern exposure. If your exposure is northern, work with the challenge: Plan an all-green garden or a shade garden.

Next, check the soil in the garden area. If it is dry and caked, it has no nutritional value for plants. You will have to invest several hundred dollars for fresh topsoil if you want any kind of plant to grow. A 10 × 20-foot area can need 10 to 12 yards of topsoil, and at an average cost of $7.85 per square yard, this can run into money.

Do not forget to investigate fences, doors, and gates to a yard area you are thinking of using. What condition are the items in? Can you use them at all? How much money and time will it take to restore them to working order, if necessary? Finally, look *up* at the rest of the building. How many apartments are above you? Will

Planter beds at right guide the visitor to this house, and the entrance garden is simple but attractive. (Photograph by Matthew Barr)

they block out light? What about smoke or soot from nearby chimneys, passing cars and trucks, and so on? Air pollution has to be reckoned with because many plants react adversely to it. If pollution is a problem in your section of the city, you may have to settle for fewer plants—those that can tolerate the conditions.

ENTRANCE GARDENS

Often a building is set back from the street, creating empty space in front. Usually the area is not large, but it can be a place for a garden. The problem in this situation is that the garden is visible to all passersby. You can build a wall to create a courtyard-entry garden, but this is expensive and creates a closed-in feeling many people object to. A better idea is to use shrubs as barriers, to give definition.

You must carefully plan the entrance garden; often gardens grown strictly for display do not work well. It is hard to keep plants in prime condition all the time, and because this is where guests get their first impressions of the home, you want your small-space garden to look just right. A good solution, one most frequently used, is to maintain a small lawn or ground cover area and then concentrate color around it. These plant borders are called *drifts*. Use hedges and trees to define the property.

Annuals and perennials work best. Place plants in groups of five to ten of the same species, planted fairly close together. Add more plants if you have space. Always use three to five areas of color that complement each other. A single drift of plants looks like an isolated attempt at flower gardening left unfinished. Several drifts or areas of color create balance and proportion.

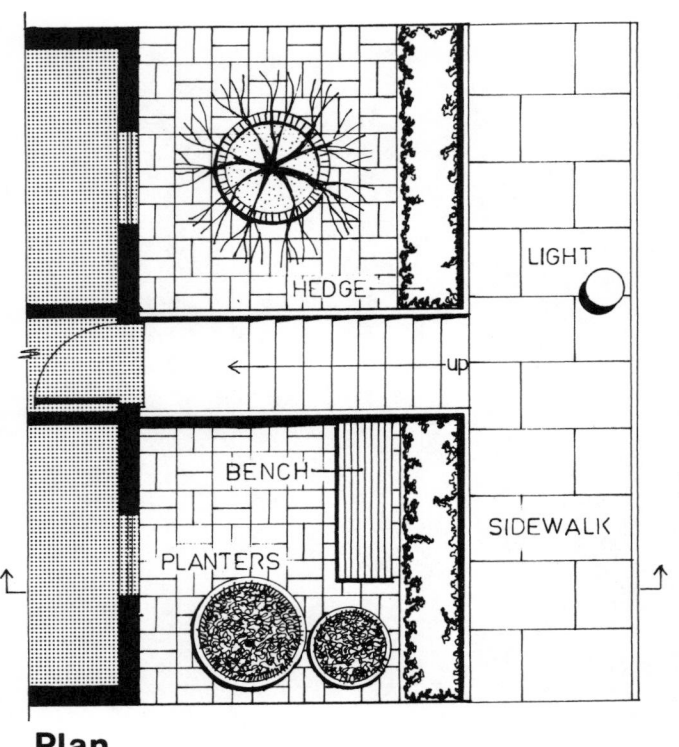

Plan

LIGHT

HEDGE

up

SIDEWALK

BENCH

PLANTERS

Section **Below Sidewalk Level**

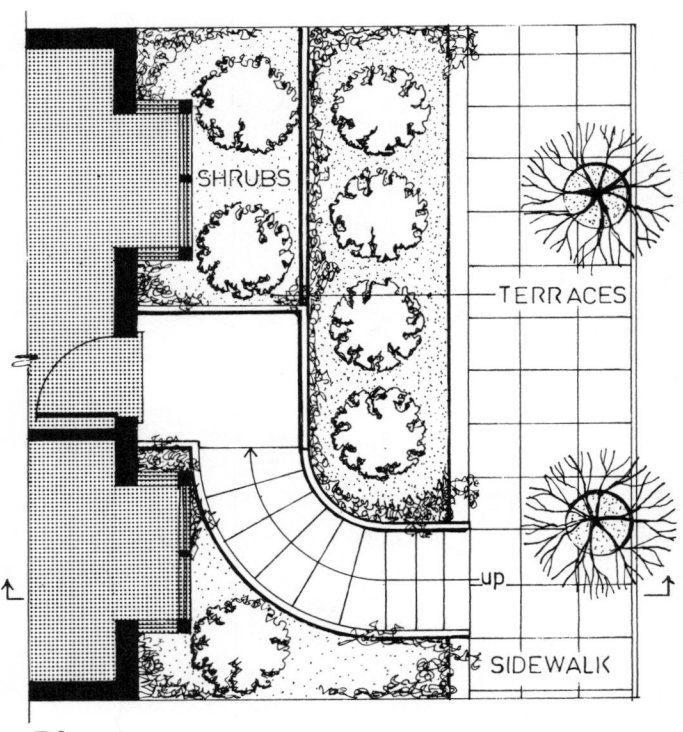

Plan

SHRUBS

TERRACES

up

SIDEWALK

Section

Above Sidewalk Level

DESIGNS: ADRIÁN MARTÍNEZ

City Front Yards

The areas of flowers should be close to the building or far away, near the street side, but never midway in the center. Flowers situated midway on the property create an unappealing sawed-in-half look. Balance is the key word here. Put plants either at the rear or the front, with the carpet of green lawn or ground cover creating a unified look. The trees and shrubs serve as vertical accents.

ATRIUM GARDENS

The atrium garden is in the center of the building, an open court surrounded by the walls or windows. It is a good solution in cities, where you want privacy. Good layout is the secret to an attractive atrium. Because of the atrium's position, plants are always on display, so careful planning is necessary. Use plants that look good and require low maintenance.

For a successful atrium, use the walls of the interior court for trelliswork and grow vines. This helps eliminate the bare look that sometimes occurs. Select plants as if they were pieces of furniture; this is the place for lovely roses in containers, perhaps some fuchsias and dramatic specimen plants. Several small trees and graceful shrubs complete the scene.

In an atrium, unlike an entrance garden, you can put flower beds in the center and leave paths around them. Or you can spot drifts of plants in one corner, having three or four drifts in one area. Balance this scene with a few container plants in other corners. Always leave room for access to the building and plenty of space for paths to get around the garden.

The atrium is an open, airy spot where plants are

This atrium garden is resplendent with begonias, and there is a mass of color throughout the area. The atrium adjoins the living room and is a handsome place to stroll in. (Photograph by C. D. Luckhart)

sparse and the statement is made by the unused or *negative* area. A crowded garden can be attractive, but be sure to allow space for you and your activities.

The surface of the atrium is very important, so be sure to make selections carefully. There are several alternatives. For example, you can grow a lawn or put in ground cover, with suitable paths of gravel. This works well and looks good. Other possibilities are patio-type floors or hard surfacing, but I find these areas less appealing than lawn or ground covers. You can also use loose fill materials like pea gravel or small-grade fir bark as a covering.

SIDE-YARD GARDENS

Side-yard gardens offer a great opportunity for gardeners with small areas. This neglected space, usually quite narrow, dark, uncluttered, and unattended, can add immeasurable beauty to the average home if it is properly utilized.

I pointed out earlier that it takes very little space to create an adequate garden. That is true even if the side yard is very narrow. The average home and some condominiums have a surprising amount of usable footage running along both sides.

If your side yard fits the dimensions of a balcony, and adequate sunlight is available, then our section on balcony gardening in Chapter 3 can be easily adapted to your needs. However, if either or both of your side yards is in shade, as is often the case in urban developments, use shade-tolerant plants. These may give a predominately green effect, but this does not mean drabness.

An attractive side-yard garden can be accomplished with only a few plants. It is the brick terrace that makes this area so inviting. (Photograph by Roger Scharmer)

Green is an often overlooked or even misused color. Its full potential is rarely realized. Many gardeners consider green plants useful almost solely for backdrop, but in a side yard they can provide a colorful study in hue and texture. Evergreens and shrubs are the obvious choices for narrow spaces because they require little maintenance. Green plants come in a variety of *shades* of green: yellow, blue, and lush dark green, and others in between. You can add contrast by growing plants with rough bark alongside those with smooth bark. Add visual appeal by growing plants with satin-textured leaves coupled with plants bearing rough dark-green velvet leaves. Or spindle-shaped leaves with broad ones—the number of possible combinations is huge.

Two things you should consider when planning your side garden are the view from inside the building and the amount of sunlight coming in from the outside. Tall,

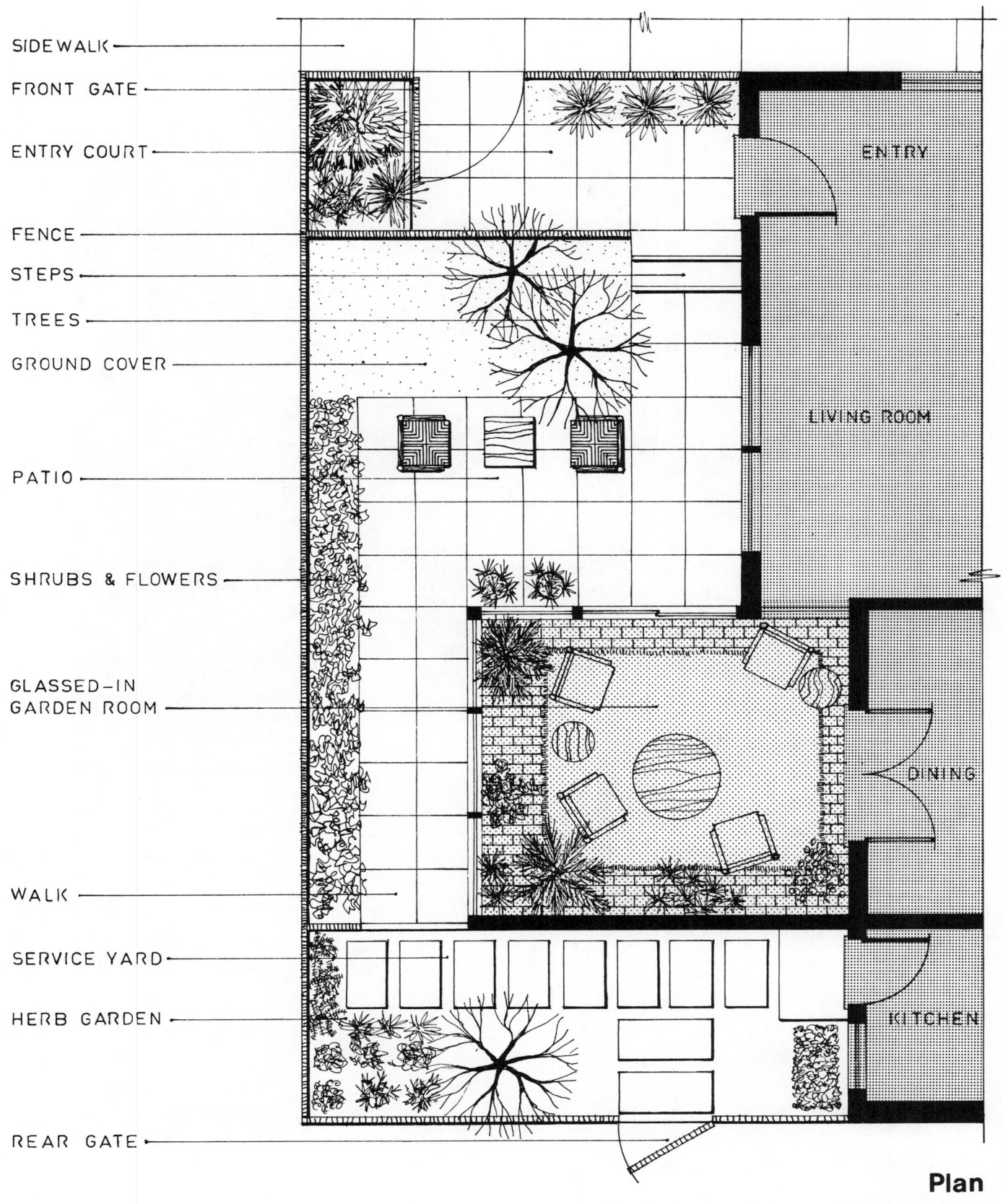

SIDEWALK

FRONT GATE

ENTRY COURT

FENCE

STEPS

TREES

GROUND COVER

PATIO

SHRUBS & FLOWERS

GLASSED-IN
GARDEN ROOM

WALK

SERVICE YARD

HERB GARDEN

REAR GATE

ENTRY

LIVING ROOM

DINING

KITCHEN

Plan

DESIGN: ADRIÁN MARTÍNEZ

Side Yard

A lush green effect is achieved in this small side-yard area—plants are massed for a green effect. (Photograph by C. D. Luckhart)

narrow shrubs or vines on a trellis planted close to a window may look very handsome from the inside, but they can also decrease the amount of sunlight entering a room, making it gloomy. Plan for both the view and the sun by varying the height of the planting.

BACKYARD GARDENS

The typical city backyard that dates from the early 1900s probably has an oblong or square central bed, such as the one I had when I rented an apartment in Chicago. This central bed usually has a lawn in the center, with straight, narrow, concrete walks around it. In its day, this was considered a neat and proper town garden.

Today we lean more toward the informal type of garden, with its freedom from strict design guidelines. A garden should be personal and relate to the building. Its use is also of prime importance: Is it going to be merely a lovely green picture to view, or are you going to use it for a retreat or a place to relax in?

The backyard site is generally small and often narrow. However, it is easy to work within these limitations. A simple but cohesive design will create the most happy expression of plants and land. To achieve a measure of success, the garden must be an extension of the house, almost like another room even though it is outside.

The atrium and entrance gardens are usually limiting in what you can grow, but the backyard offers enough space for all kinds of gardens. A cutting garden along one side works well. Or a vegetable garden and special rose garden, for example, can be accommodated in the

A working gardener's backyard complete with potting bench and stands. Four planters and some container plants create the garden. (Photograph by Matthew Barr)

backyard site. Planning is important, but it is not paramount as long as you stay within the realm of good design. Remember: scale, proportion, unity, and rhythm.

To achieve good design, always *repeat plant material;* that is, if you have a clump of perennials in one corner, put in two more clumps nearby to balance the scene. Repetition of plant material is the key to the basic elements of design. But too much repetition can ruin the effect.

If trees and shrubs are not already growing on the property, put them in because a few good specimens of

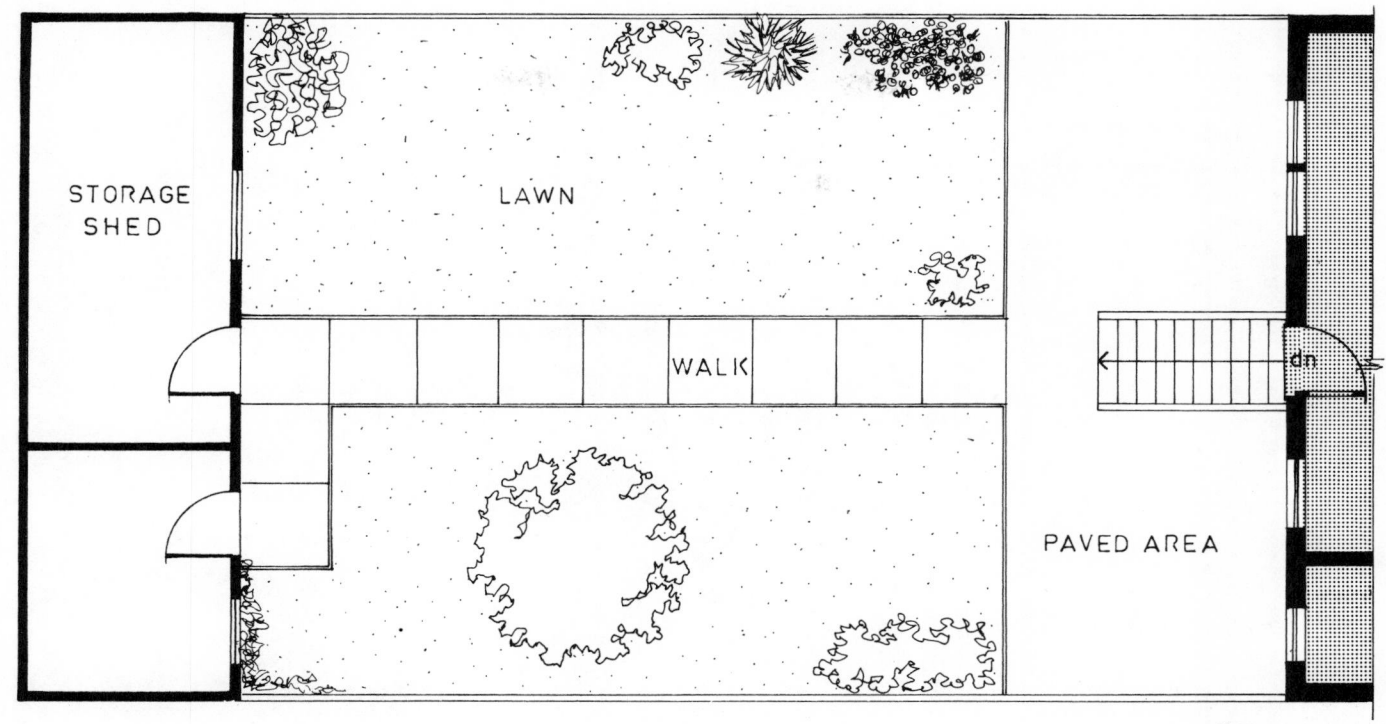

"Before"

"After"

DESIGN : ADRIÁN MARTÍNEZ

Typical City Backyard

HOUSE INTERIOR

FENCE

POTTED PLANTS

BUILT-IN SEAT

FLOWERS

POOL

STONE PAVED PATIO

TERRACED PLANTERS

TREE

SHRUBS

GATE

POTTING & STORAGE SHED

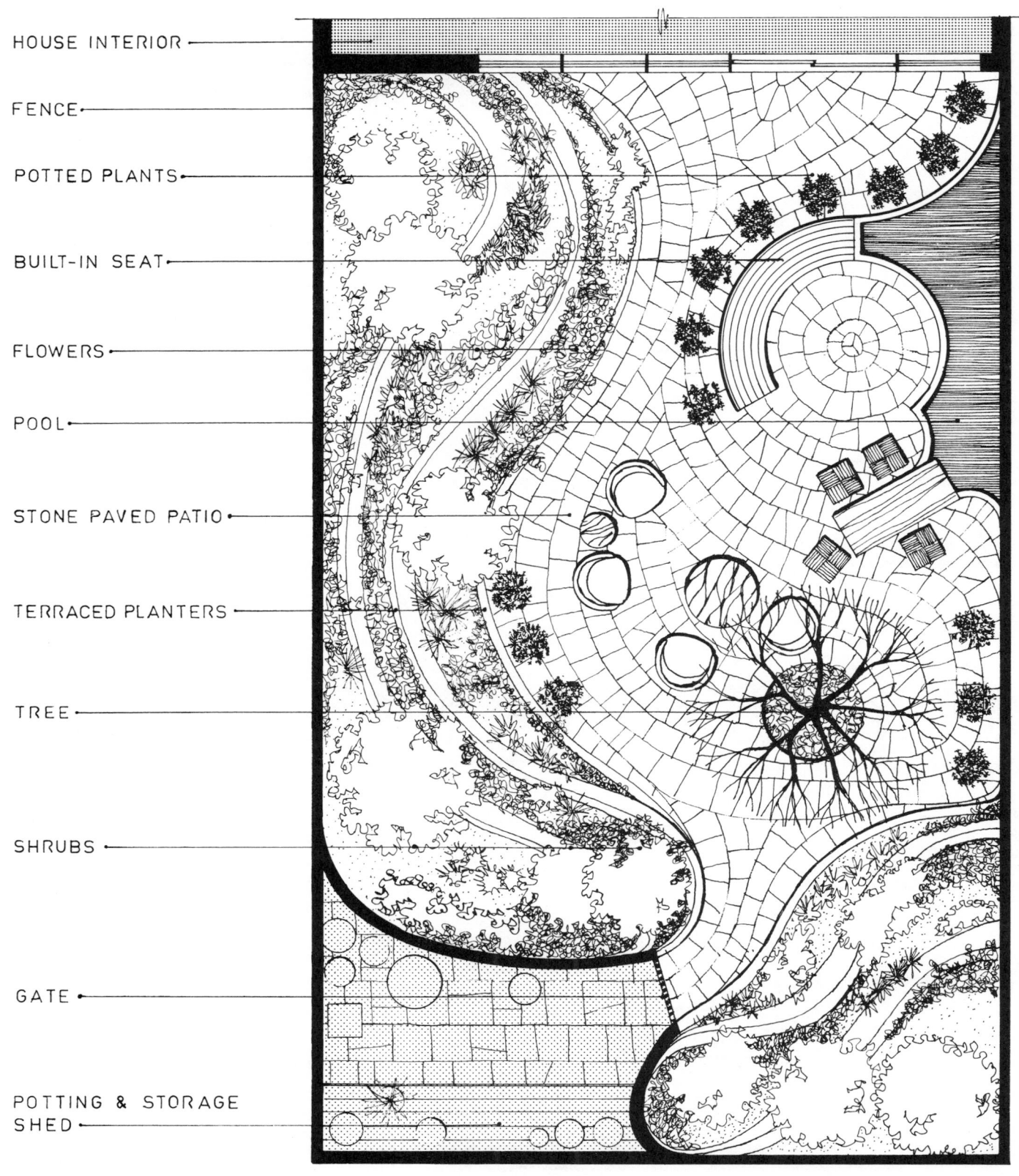

Plan: 25' x 40' lot

DESIGN: ADRIÁN MARTÍNEZ

Narrow Backyard

trees and shrubs form the backbone of any garden. Not many of these vertical accents are needed—a few trees and perhaps six good shrubs will do the job admirably. Then you can select your flower garden if you want one and install a lawn or a vegetable site. The possibilities in the backyard garden are limitless; what you select depends upon what pleases you.

PATIO AND TERRACE GARDENS

Many times the site for the garden (whether it is in front or back) can be enhanced by installing a patio or terrace arrangement. By adding a handsomely paved floor you create an additional living space—it is here you can enjoy morning coffee or simply sit and relax. In a patio or terrace setup you will not need many plants—a few work fine to create a peaceful scene. The patio or terrace is really partly a garden and partly a place to sit down, so some appropriate patio furniture is necessary. Whether small or large, for lounging or for cooking, for growing plants or for viewing the city, a terrace or patio is a big plus in living.

Many factors dictate the size and placement of the outdoor room. Weather is important. The patio that bakes in the sun most of the day offers little pleasure for daytime use. And a patio in constant wind is not a comfortable place for plants or people. We cannot change the position of the sun or stop the wind, but we can modify these elements. Screens, fences, trees, and shrubs offer shade, protection, and privacy.

A south patio basks in sun; in chilly climates it can be a blessing, but in arid regions it is likely to become an annoyance. A west patio is ideal in morning and eve-

ning, but during the day it may become uncomfortably warm. A patio that faces east is often ideal; it has morning sun, but in the afternoon it is cool and shady. Northern exposures need not be neglected. Many plants thrive in shade.

Generally most patios are in the rear of the house, where there is ample space and privacy and where we can use a free hand to complement nature. However, rear patios are not obligatory. There are many fine front patios screened by fences from the street. Terraces alongside the house—long and narrow—have their uses,

This handsome city terrace in New York uses a few trees and much brick to make it inviting. The garden is lush green but maintenance is minimal. (Photograph by Molly Adams)

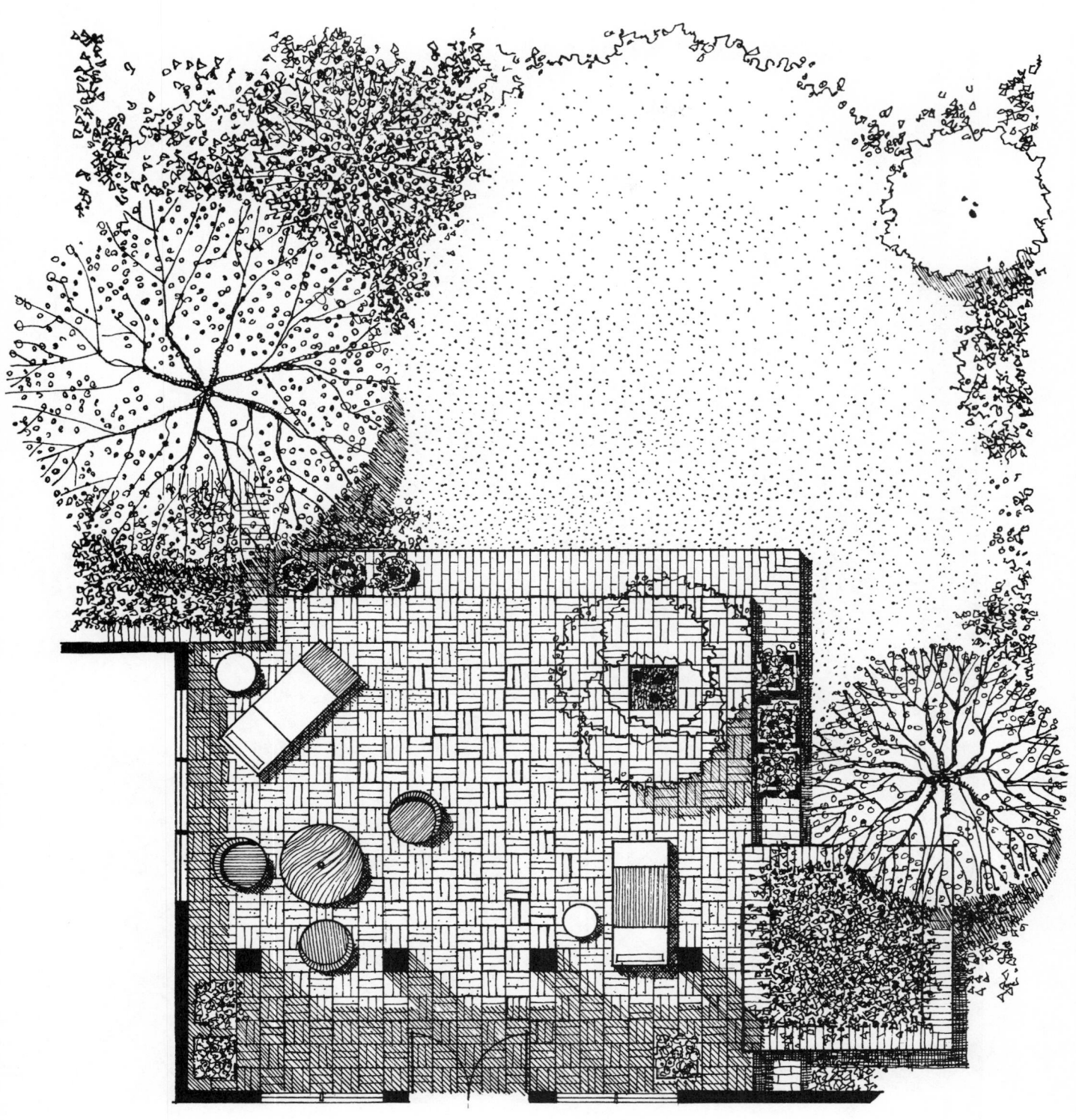

PATIO ARRANGEMENT
FOR AN L-SHAPED HOUSE

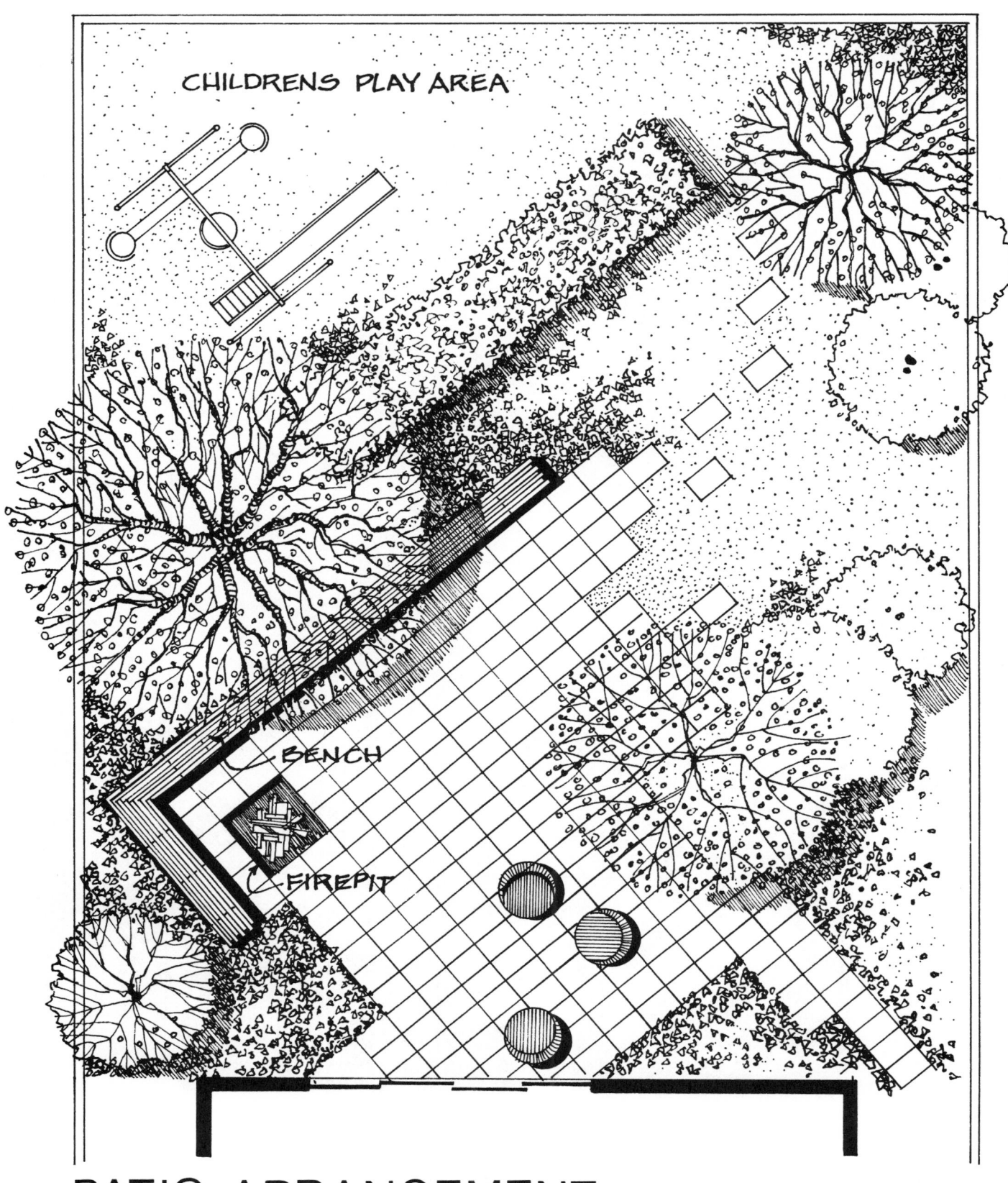

CHILDRENS PLAY AREA

BENCH

FIREPIT

PATIO ARRANGEMENT ON A NARROW LOT

too. If cleverly designed, they can be very handsome.

The enclosed court, or atrium, surrounded by the house, is well known, and it has many advantages. From all rooms it offers a pleasant view. It gives protection from wind for plants and people. And with a roof the court becomes a conservatory, a splendid place for all kinds of tropical plants.

Floor Considerations

Industry has given us a wide selection of materials for outdoor flooring. Because the selection is large, choose carefully. Select a paving that is in character with your home. Choose it for durability and service.

Although a patio floor may be grass or cinders, more often it is brick, concrete, or flagstone. But if low-cost surfacing is necessary or if the floor is to be temporary, use a loose-fill material such as wood chips, lava rock, or crushed bricks.

Before making your final decision about the patio floor, ask yourself these questions:

1. Will the paving be able to withstand weather and heat?

2. Will it be easy to maintain?

3. Is the floor comfortable to walk on? Is it so rough that it might injure children's knees?

4. Does water sink through the paving, or does it flow off in sheets, making it slippery?

5. Should the paving be light in color or dark? Light paving creates a glare; dark paving stores up heat.

6. And finally, in selecting paving, think about the cost and the installation fee. Can you do it yourself, or will it be necessary to hire a paving contractor or masonry firm? (See Chapter 4.)

3

Gardens in the Sky

If you rent or own a typical upper-story city apartment, flat, or condominium, where do you find room for a garden? And when you do find the room, what limitations do you face? Will the landlord let you use the backyard, roof, balcony, patio, or deck for plants? How much money do you want to invest in plants, containers, and support structures? All these factors have to be considered, but dealing with them soundly will reward you with a green cityscape. With today's overcrowded city conditions, there is a new interest in gardening because it is a unique and pleasant way of adding a garden to the home when outdoor land is limited. A small city garden high up and properly planned is a retreat in the midst of brick and concrete. Gardening in the sky is a challenge because you are dealing with a set of design rules and attitudes different from those for ground gardening. Many factors contribute to the success of a garden in the sky—whether tiny balconies, decks, and patios, or spacious and costly penthouse roofs

Although small, this balcony deck garden, provides a green screen of beauty; hanging containers hold many kinds of trailing plants. (Photograph by Matthew Barr)

or terraces—and more careful thought about construction and selection of plants is necessary than when planning ground gardens.

BALCONY AND DECK GARDENS

The advent of the modern apartment building introduced the novelty of the balcony and deck (and the little patio on the ground floor). These areas, of concrete or

Replete with hot tub, this California deck garden uses only a few plants to make it an appealing scene. There is hardly any maintenance here and yet the area is green and inviting. (Photograph by Werner)

wood, are usually long and narrow, windy, and hard to cope with. However, they can be pleasant areas for a few potted and hanging plants and perhaps a tree.

Put seasonal flowering plants (for color) in ornamental containers; instead of using one large pot, group several small ones for a lush display. And do not overlook trailing plants in hanging baskets (hang them away from windy areas) for added decoration. Even a pair of lovely *Asparagus sprengeri* adds a note of lacy loveliness to an area, and at eye level such plants are impressive sights. Plant vines and tailers in wooden planters and use them to cover bare walls and railings or for privacy from nearby neighbors. Also grow vines flat against a wall or on a trellis in espalier fashion to conserve space and yet bring leafy green into the picture. Vines demand more pruning and trimming than other plants, but they are worth every effort because

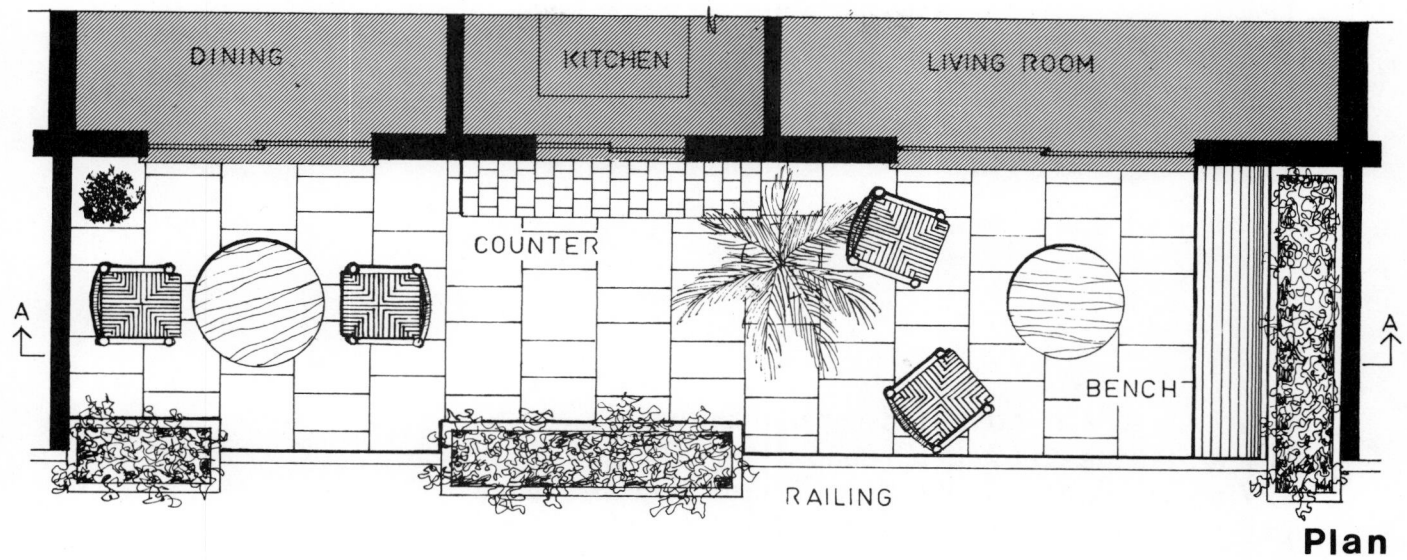

DINING KITCHEN LIVING ROOM

COUNTER

BENCH

RAILING

A

A

Plan

Section A-A

Elevation

DESIGN: ADRIÁN MARTÍNEZ

Balcony Garden

they look so attractive and cover a multitude of sins without taking up too much space.

Window boxes are fine if they are sturdily constructed and securely anchored in place. Do not just suspend them from railings without adequate support. Put window boxes within the perimeter of the balcony, never hanging in midair.

During the winter, bring the potted plants indoors (except evergreens). Container plants at a bright window, or in any area where they receive some light and cooler temperatures, can then decorate the interior of your home.

PENTHOUSE GARDENS

Today's high-rise buildings often have community garden terraces on the top floor, supervised by building personnel. But a terrace off a personal penthouse apartment can be a unique garden. A terrace is bigger than a balcony or deck, made of concrete or tile, and provides room for entertaining and cooking.

Besides considering the weight of plants on the terrace structure (discussed in the next section, "Roof Gardens"), you must establish a center of interest—sometimes two areas—along with tubs, boxes, and handsome planters. A statue and a small water garden are ideal accents. However, note that the water garden requires care and patience to make it really beautiful.

Finally, a seating area is also almost mandatory to pull the space together. The selection of outdoor seating is more vital for this garden than for other types. Choose tasteful but comfortable furniture, using only what is necessary. Do not overload the terrace with furniture, and be sure the furniture does not distract from the beauty of the garden.

ROOF GARDENS

Roof gardening is one of the oldest forms of gardening; the ancient Greeks were masters at it. In Chicago, my next-door neighbors had a lush greenery on top of a garage, and the windows of their two-story home were a perfect vantage point for viewing the pretty scene.

But before you start growing plants on a roof, consider the practical requirements. Only when you have considered these basic factors should you start planning the garden.

A typical penthouse garden where roses abound. Plants are wholly container-grown and, once established, a garden such as this takes care of itself. (Photograph by Matthew Barr)

A secluded place, a place to meditate—a handsome penthouse garden area away from city worries. (Photograph by Matthew Barr)

Everything on the roof—soil and plants—is grown in planters or built-in beds, boxes, pots, or containers of some sort. Can the roof support all that *weight?* In northern climates roofs are built to endure heavy snow loads, but in winter soil-filled, rain-and-snow-soaked boxes are particularly heavy. Check with the building owner or an architect or someone else familiar with roof structures before you start your garden. Most roofs can take the extra weight, but it is always wise to be sure.

The roof must also be perfectly *watertight,* or excess water draining from plants will create a batch of problems. Most roofs are built watertight, but through the years small leaks or cracks may develop, so a coat of asphalt may be in order. Also consider *drainage:* excess water must freely drain off the structure. No water should accumulate on the roof; if it does, there will be eventual ceiling problems. Connect drain tiles to outlets

if necessary. Be sure that all plant boxes are constructed so that soil, leaves, and twigs do not wash into roof gutters. If they do, the gutters will become clogged and damage the building.

Roof gardens must have *railings* or other obstructions to prevent accidents; you must consider people's safety. Also, railings or fencing act as windbreaks from blustery gales. Fencing can be made of glass, plastic, or wood. You can build the fences yourself (see Chapter 6), but remember to create a visually pleasing scene.

Consider the type of *flooring* necessary for the garden;

Here is a merging of planter plants, container plants, and a statue to provide beauty on this small rooftop terrace. The effect is totally handsome. (Photograph by Matthew Barr)

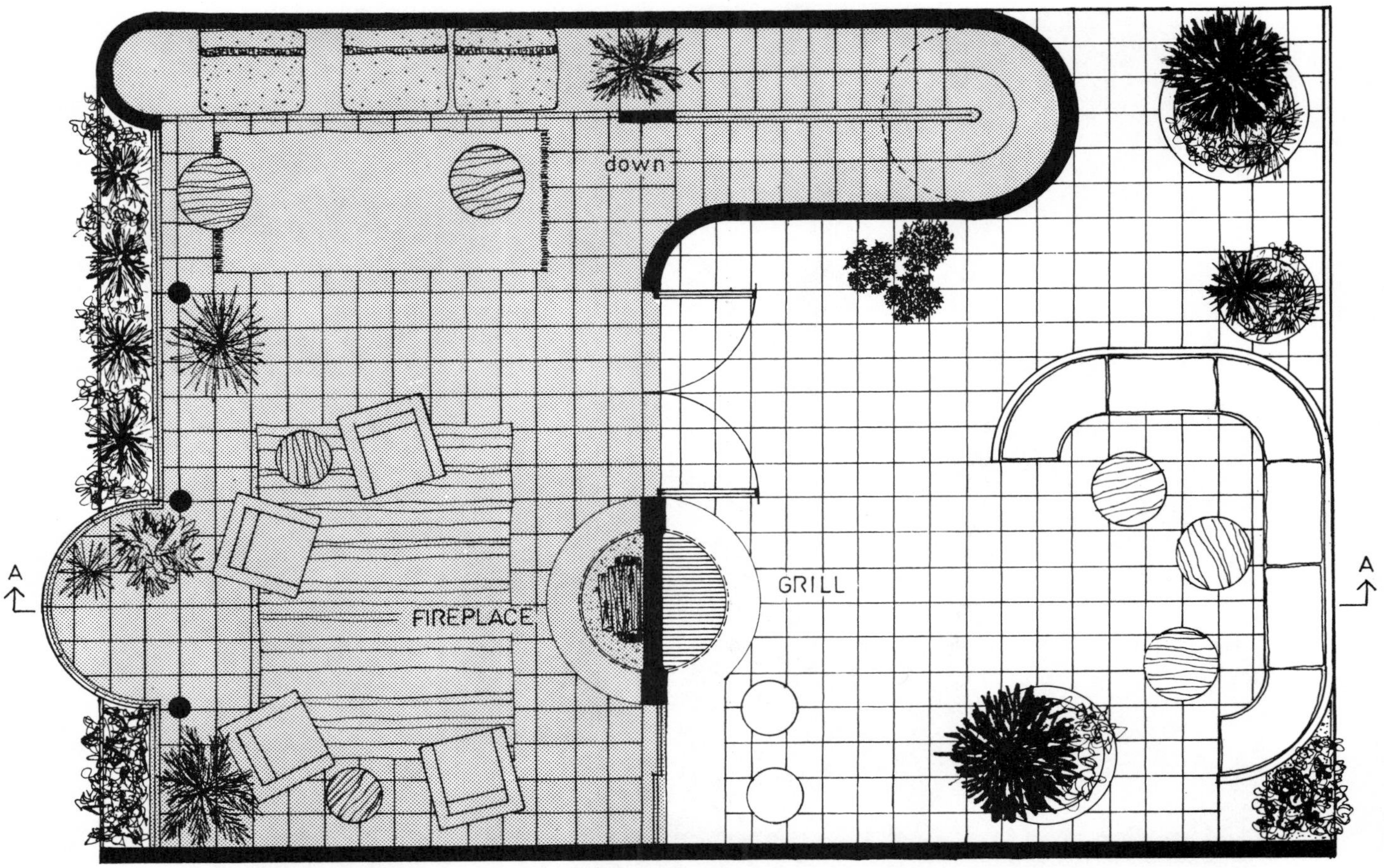

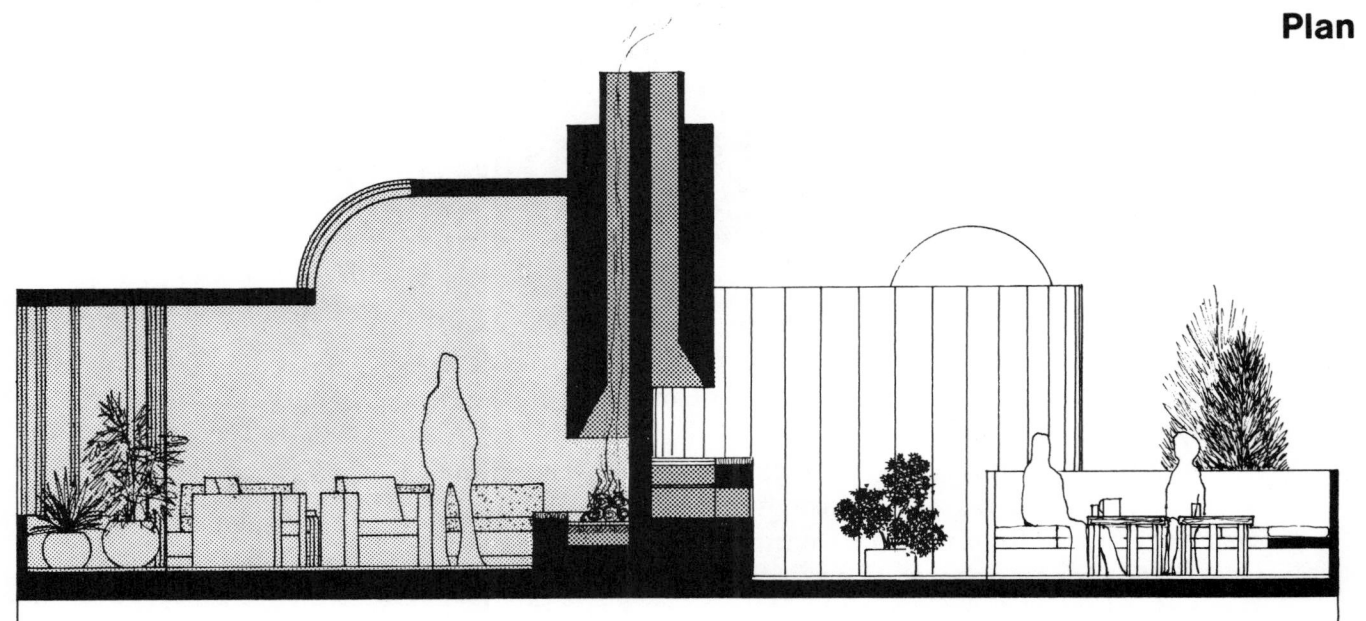

Plan

down

FIREPLACE

GRILL

Roof Garden

Section A-A

DESIGN: ADRIÁN MARTÍNEZ

the in-place asphalt is not attractive. Brick and tile are extremely heavy, so the roof may not hold the weight, but pea gravel and similar, inexpensive materials (for example, fir bark) are good substitutes. You can easily put these materials in place and mold them into patterns with your hands. Their disadvantage is that they must be renewed periodically.

This in-the-air garden has only a few container plants and a large planting of pittosporum. It is still a quiet place in the city. (Photograph by Matthew Barr)

Wind and Sun Protection

Wind can quickly desiccate certain plants (some varieties can withstand wind). A careful selection of plants and proper wind protection is essential if you want a thriving rooftop greenery.

Wind increases evaporation in plants, which rapidly injures soft young leaves. Do not enclose all sides of the roof with a fence or screen, or you will close off views and and create an overheated boxed-in space. Determine the windiest side and use buffers there. If you need still more protection, install louvered boards with spaces between them; a louvered fence lessens wind without blocking air circulation. Covered wind fences with climbing plants add a decorative note to the garden.

On a roof, direct sun can bake plants. To avoid this uncomfortable situation, place arbors and trellises so that they can distribute shade where it will be most needed.

Planting

Many kinds of plants can be used in the rooftop garden, but you want an assemblage of interesting shrubs and trees with varied shapes and leaf patterns, accented with flowering beauties. Remember that in winter (unless you use evergreens) you must take the tender plants inside.

On a roof, plants have no help from surrounding greenery because around them is either empty space or concrete and glass buildings. It is important to use bold and dramatic contrasting plants to create an intimate space.

Trees and shrubs, annuals and perennials, herbs and vines—almost any plant can be grown in roof gardens (see Chapter 8).

Instead of large trees, which are out of scale in roof

gardens, grow small trees with picturesque growth habits, like weeping willow or crab apple. Multiple-stem trees are sculptural and break harsh lines; magnolia and gray birch are two outstanding types. These trees grow in an upright pattern and take little space.

As we mentioned earlier, vines are excellent for covering an unsightly wall, making a tapestry of green on a trellis, or softening the edge of a planter. There are many wonderful flowering vines, and most adapt well to rooftop conditions.

Plantings in the rooftop garden have to withstand severe wind and sun at various times of the year. Avoid tall-growing, weak-limbed trees because wind can rock trees mercilessly and loosen roots. Even with wind-breaks, supplemental wire support may be necessary during extreme exposures. Use guy wires anchored in deep containers, and be sure to sheathe the portion that goes around the tree in a piece of rubber.

Spread a peat moss or fir bark mulch over the soil in the containers to prevent the soil from rapidly drying out and to help keep roots cool and moist. Soil on the roof, in containers, dries out more rapidly than it does on the ground, so water slowly and deeply. Do not skimp on the water if you want lush plants. Prune trees and shrubs carefully. In early spring, remove all dead wood, including small twigs and large branches—limbs rubbing against each other produce wounds in the bark through which diseases may enter. Trim away all wood broken by high winds.

Use planting boxes for vegetables. Buy the best soil you can get. Know the planting depths of the vegetables you plan to grow. For instance, radishes and lettuce need only three to four inches of soil. Carrots need deep beds. To succeed with vegetables on roof gardens you must water them copiously and frequently.

PART II
CONSTRUCTION

The city garden requires more construction than the country scene. Fences and walls are generally needed and wooden planters of all kinds are necessary in many places because in-the-ground gardening may be impossible.

You can of course buy ready-made planters (but they are expensive) and with only a little know-how you can make your own containers for plants.

The idea of building a fence or wall may scare you, but don't let it. There are many simple barriers you yourself can make, and in the following pages we show you how to make them—and without spending exorbitant amounts of money.

Construction is part of any city garden. Learn how to do it yourself—it can be enjoyable and very rewarding.

City container garden in
Phoenix, Arizona.

Pavings

In city gardens the addition of a paved surface adds dimension and texture and defines an area, no matter how small it is. And too, a brick or concrete floor is handsome and decorative. Putting in a terrace or patio floor scares many people but it should not—it is not difficult and with today's new materials can be done in a weekend.

CONCRETE

Concrete may not be as handsome as some other pavings, but it is a durable, low-cost, and permanent surface. It is easy to clean and can be completely installed by a paving contractor in a few hours. If you object to the cold feeling of concrete, it can be mixed with color or painted. Or the top layer can be dyed with liquid that seeps deeply into the pores of the concrete. It can also be rough or textured.

An aggregate floor is another idea. It is made of concrete that has small stones on the surface. The textured finish is handsome and blends with plantings and lawns. The uneven texture breaks the monotony of a large area of paving, especially when it is framed with wood grids. The pebbly surface of aggregate concrete also eliminates glare and guarantees sure traction in wet weather. And when this paving collects dirt—as it will—it is easy to wash clean with a strong hosing.

While you can install a small area of concrete yourself, it is best to hire a professional for the large job. However, you can save part of the cost of the floor by having the area ready for him. Outline the patio by

Concrete aggregate in wood grids is the patio floor in this city backyard; it is a durable surface for the outdoor area. (Photograph by C. D. Luckhart)

setting out 2×2-inch stakes with string stretched between them. Dig out and remove all trash from the soil. Set either permanent or temporary header boards in place. Be sure to set headers so the top surface is flush with the grade you want for the concrete. Drive additional stakes at 2-foot intervals along each side of the patio, lined up carefully with the guide string. Nail 10-inch strips of ¼-inch plywood to the insides of the stakes to act as forms for the concrete. Forms can be brushed with oil to make it easier to remove them after the concrete is poured and set.

Wet the soil a few times the day before the concrete is to be poured. The night before, wet it again so it will be damp when the concrete is poured. Soil that is dry takes moisture from the concrete and weakens it.

To build a small patio, rent a portable mixer—ask for a half-bag machine—revolved by a gasoline motor. Put 1 cubic foot of sand and half a sack of cement into the revolving drum. Allow the materials to mix. Then add 1 cubic foot of gravel, and let the drum revolve for a few minutes or until the pebbles are uniformly coated. Now

The owners of this city garden needed an ample area for walking and playing space for children; the concrete aggregate floor was the answer.
(Photograph by C. D. Luckhart)

An attractive concrete aggregate terrace; small shiny black stones are used in the concrete. (Photograph courtesy Portland Cement Assoc.)

Texture is the beauty of a concrete aggregate floor. (Photograph courtesy Portland Cement Assoc.)

Slabs of concrete aggregate create this garden area. (Photograph courtesy Portland Cement Assoc.)

Leveling the ground for a terrace; note the wood grids between the concrete. (Photograph courtesy Portland Cement Assoc.)

Smoothing the concrete for a plain finish. (Photograph courtesy Portland Cement Assoc.)

Putting down a concrete aggregate patio floor; note the 2 × 4-inch boards laid on end. (Photograph by author)

The patio partially finished. (Photograph by author)

add to the drum about 2 gallons of water, and let the mixture tumble for about four minutes. Pour it into a wheelbarrow (rented from a hardware store) and dump the mixture into the forms. Make pavings 3 to 4 inches thick. Smooth out the wet concrete with a wood-float tool. Different finishes can be applied for variation.

The slick, or hard, finish is made by moving a steel trowel over the surface when it is partially hardened. Do the first troweling lightly, just enough to smooth the float texture. Then trowel again with more pressure. This floor is slick and somewhat uninteresting.

The wood-float method leaves the floor smooth but not shiny. It is done with the mason's wood trowel (float).

The broom finish gives an interesting texture. It is made by brushing the slightly hardened concrete with a push broom.

CONCRETE BLOCKS

There are several types of concrete rectangles for patios. Some have a smooth texture; others are covered with small pebbles or chips. Some are the color of concrete; others are pastel. Sizes range up to 16 inches square and 1½ inches in thickness.

These blocks, easy to install, can be laid in sand. It is simple to lift out a few blocks for planting pockets. Water penetrates rapidly between the blocks and into the soil. All in all, they make an inexpensive, durable surface.

SLATE

In rectangles, squares, or irregular pieces, and in numerous colors, slate makes a striking floor. It has a slightly textured finish, is resistant to stain, and comes in 1-inch or ½-inch thicknesses. One should set thick slates in a sand base, thinner ones in mortar.

TILE

Tile makes a handsome paving; the brown or red color is especially pleasing with green plants, and tile is smoother than brick, easier to clean. It is virtually impossible to stain it, and if the patio floor extends into the house, tile is always the decorator's choice. It has a lovely finished look when properly installed.

There are many sizes, shapes, and colors to choose from, but outdoor tile is almost always rough-surfaced and usually ¾-inch or ⅞-inch thick. Of all the tiles, the quarry type makes the best patio floor. It is a heavy-duty ceramic material that comes in square or rectangles or in many special sizes and shapes. Standard sizes are 3×3 inches to 9×9 inches. Some have lightly textured surfaces; others have fired-in designs. Colors run from off-white to blue-green, with the red hues the most popular.

While large patio tiles can be laid on sand or earth, most tiles need a mortar bed to be safe from cracking.

If the soil is flat and stable and you want to lay a tile floor, by all means do so. Simply set the tiles on a sand base. At a later date they can be taken up and reset in a bed of mortar.

To lay a small area of tile (or large space if you are ambitious), dig out the soil to about 1 inch below the desired grade. Tamp down or roll the earth smooth. Set the outer border in place—rows of tiles or header boards—and allow a drainage slope of ⅛-inch per foot.

Pour in sand, and level it with a board. Do not use more than a ½-inch bed of sand or the tiles will tilt when you step on them. Start in a corner, and set the tiles in place; butt them tightly against each other. Tap each one with a wooden block to bed it tightly into the sand.

For tile set in mortar, let a professional do the floor. In the long run it saves money.

FLAGSTONE

A flagstone floor gives a rich finish and lasts a lifetime. It is solid and durable, and the colors—buff, brownish red, gray—add warmth to the patio. The irregularity of flagstone is part of its charm; as is the sculptured surface that brings texture and pattern to the floor. Flagstone is hard, stratified stone (sandstone, shale, slate, or marble) split into flat pieces. It may be laid dry or in mortar. For masonry use 1-inch-thick stone; for dry laying, 1½-inch-thick stone.

If the soil is well drained and level, flagstone can be put directly on ground. The flags may shift or settle in very cold weather, but they will remain in place. In the desired area remove the soil to a depth slightly less than the thickness of the flags; then fit them in place. Pack the joints with soil, or put in low, creeping plants.

For a sturdier and better floor, set the flagstones in sand. A 2-inch bed is fine. Firmly place flags over the entire surface. Make sure they are really in place so no listing will occur. Fill in the joints with soil that is flush with the surface of the stones, and wet it down thoroughly.

For a permanent paving, set flags on a 3-inch bed of concrete.

FIELDSTONE

Fieldstone makes a casual floor because of its natural variations in shape, texture, and color. Select flat stones for the upper side with bottom irregularities sunk into the bedding. They can be laid dry on 4 inches of sand on compacted earth or about 8 inches of crushed gravel or stone. Success of the pattern depends upon your patience to fit and align the stones properly.

This fieldstone terrace walk has an attractive pattern and adds charm to the garden area. (Photograph courtesy Portland Cement Assoc.)

BRICK

Brick is the most popular paving material. It is difficult to commit a serious error when paving with it. If the first attempt is not pleasing or accurate (when using the simple method of brick on sand), it is easy enough to take up the section and re-lay it.

Brick is a handsome paving material; it is decorative and colorful—and makes this garden a charming place. (Photograph by C. D. Luckhart)

When there are masses of plants, brick paving harmonizes with the overall green—the combination of plants and red brick is always handsome. (Photograph by C. D. Luckhart)

Brick comes in a variety of earthy colors which look good outdoors and impart a pleasant contrast in texture. There are rough- and smooth-surfaced bricks, which may be glazed or unglazed. Other shapes are available, too—hexagon, octagon, fleur-de-lis. Because the units are small, they never steal the show, and they stay in scale with even the smallest foliage display.

While there are many kinds of brick, the best ones for patios are smooth-surfaced or rough-textured common bricks. Face brick, including Roman and paving brick, is easier to work with and less expensive than slick brick. Common brick is usually available with pit marks on the surface. Sand-mold brick is smooth-textured and is slightly larger on one face than on the other, and clinker brick has irregularities on the surface. If you can, select hard-burned rather than green brick. It should be dark red in color rather than salmon, which indicates an underburned process and less durability. Used bricks or colored ones are fine, too. When you select the brick flooring, be sure the dealer has a sufficient quantity to complete the area. There is usually some dimensional variation and color difference in later orders of brick.

In the city, a lovely patio such as this affords great privacy and pleasure. The floor is brick laid on sand— an easy installation. (Photograph by C. D. Luckhart)

If you are in a climate where winters are severe, specify SW (severe weathering) brick.

It is simple to install a brick-on-sand paving, but it is not a job to do in haste. It takes time. Do it in sections— a small piece at a time—rather than trying to finish an entire floor in a day. Grading and leveling must be done first, and care taken to have a perfectly level sand base of 2 to 3 inches. Otherwise the floor will be wavy and visually distracting.

Bricks can be laid in a great variety of patterns— herringbone, basket weave, running bond, and so on—or combined with squares of grass or cinders in endless designs. For large areas choose the herringbone pattern; smaller patios look best with running bond or basket-weave designs. Or break the large area by fitting bricks into redwood or cedar grid patterns.

Do not let the job of installing the floor defeat you because some bricks have to be cut. This is an easy trick. Use a cold chisel or a brick hammer for making irregular cuts and for trimming. Cut a groove along one side of the brick with the chisel or hammer, and then give it a final severing blow. Cut the brick on a solid level surface; a piece of wood is good. Smooth uneven edges of the brick by rubbing it with another brick.

To lay brick in sand, grade the soil with a board, and tamp it down thoroughly. Put in a 2- to 3-inch cushion of sand. Level the sand with a 2 × 4-inch board of convenient length. Set the bricks as close together as possible, and check each row with a level. Then dust sand into the cracks.

Brick patios need handsome edgings. I prefer wooden header strips, 2 × 4 inches, held firmly in place by stakes or other reinforcement. Or use a border of bricks set in concrete and installed lower than the patio floor. And always, for all patios, allow for drainage. Slope the floor away from the house at an incline of 1 inch to each 6 feet of paving. In normal use bricks are skidproof, but in excessive shade they acquire a coating of algae or moss that is extremely slippery. Cover bricks coated this way with a masonry sealing compound if necessary.

Bricks can also be set in mortar, but this is usually a job for the professional bricklayer.

WOOD

Wooden floors are maintenance-free floors. And there is no reason why they should be restricted to mountain living. A deck, while most logical for a hillside home, can also be advantageous on a level city site.

Wood has a warm feeling, is easy to clean, dries quickly after rain, and is easier on the feet than concrete or brick. Decorative tubs and terra-cotta pots look good filled with flowering plants against a wood background, and the deck that is raised above grade has dimensional quality. It becomes an island of greenery.

Use lumber of good quality; redwood or spruce is fine. Redwood does not need a preservative and stands up well against weather, but the deck does not have to be made of it. Several woods, if coated with preservatives, will last for many years. Ask the lumber dealer in your area to recommend the best quality wood for the deck.

There are many ways to build a deck and many styles to choose from. The raised deck is handsome, and the platform is visually pleasing. A deck at the floor level of the house gives a spacious feeling, and an L-shaped deck provides a view from two sides of the home.

The basic steps in building a deck are generally given

here. Lumber and construction details will vary depending on how big the area is and how it will be used.

Outline the area with stakes and strings to locate posts. Dig holes 18 inches deep. You can use concrete footings (from lumberyards) and set them into the holes, or you can put 6 inches of gravel into the holes and then cut 4 × 4-inch posts to length and set them in place with poured concrete. Set posts in rows 4 feet apart (with posts spaced not more than 6 feet in each row). Bolt 2 × 8-inch beams to the posts.

Planking can be 2 × 3's, 2 × 4's, or even 2 × 6's if you want a very sturdy deck. Lay the planks about ½-inch apart for drainage, and arrange them at right angles to each other, or vary the size and placement across the area. Nail planking in place with 16-penny nails.

PATIO BLOCKS

Thick patio blocks or pavers are new; they are made of concrete that has been vibrated under pressure. They are uniform in thickness and have straight edges. And, best of all, they are made in several pleasing shapes: hexagonal, round, random, and so on, in several colors. With these pavers, concrete forms are not necessary and no mortar is required, so it is possible to lay a floor in a few hours. Because they are laid directly on a sand base, they are free to move and are not rigidly in place. This almost eliminates the cracking that can result in a poured concrete floor.

To install patio blocks, mark the boundaries with string and stakes. Take out about 2 inches of soil to accommodate the sand base. Dampen and tamp down the sand. It is important that the sand base be solid.

Level the sand, and establish the slope away from the house for drainage. Place a sheet of polyethylene over the sand to prevent weeds or grass from growing between the blocks. Start in a corner, and be sure that each block is level when it is put into place.

These paving blocks are fast becoming the easiest way to lay a patio or terrace floor.

WOOD BLOCKS AND ROUNDS

Blocks and rounds of wood look natural outdoors and have soft textures and warm colors that are suitable in a woodland setting. The rounds, about 4 inches thick, are cut from trunks of redwood, cedar, or cypress and can be applied in random fashion on a sand base for a patio floor. The square blocks are usually strips of lumber or cut-up railroad ties. Wood paving is attractive, but it will never produce a permanent floor. Even when coated with preservatives (a messy job), it will last only about five years. It cracks in intense sun, and it splits in severe frosts. Still, wood rounds and pieces of railroad ties are different, handsome, and can be removed and replaced with other paving material when necessary.

The redwood rounds come in sizes from 6 to 36 inches. They are easily set in place. Grade the soil, and put in a 2-inch sand base. Place the rounds in a random pattern, and fill in between them with soil or crushed gravel.

Wood blocks, usually 1×4 inches, are desirable, too. To install them, dig out the soil to a depth of 1 inch greater than the thickness of the blocks. Tamp down the earth and fill with a 1-inch sand base. Place blocks flush with the edging and space them in the desired pattern. Fill spaces between them with sand.

LOOSE-FILL MATERIALS

Flooring of loose-fill materials is generally temporary, but it can be attractive, too. Wood chips are most often bought as fir bark and come in small-, medium-, or large-grade sizes. The large-grade fir bark is the most durable. Installed in a grid system, it is handsome, and the brownish-red color gives warmth to an area.

Lava rock may be available in your area under several different names. Basically it is chunks of porous stone. It is difficult to walk on and in time wears away. However, it is a simple job to cover it eventually with a more durable surface. It is inexpensive and easy to install.

Dolomite or pieces of clean limestone are bright white. In small squares combined with other materials, this surfacing is dramatic. But with time, dolomite discolors and must be replaced periodically.

Crushed brick is easy to put down, has a bright red color that gives a striking accent to plants, and is handsome if not too much of it is used. The brick eventually breaks down and wears away. Yet, it is perhaps the best of the loose-fill materials for durability.

Gravel, marble, or granite chips make an attractive floor. These are easy to install and conform to the contour of the land. Loose gravel, pebbles, or granite washes out of place, so use a high border edge to keep it confined. Wooden strips or bricks are fine.

To install a gravel, pebble, or granite-chip floor, dig out 6 to 8 inches on the site. Cover the area with heavy polyethylene plastic to keep out weeds. Over this pour a subbase of fine gravel. Then add the patio floor of gravel or pebbles. Loose fills like these wash out of place and pack down, and you may have to replenish spots from time to time.

5

Wood Containers

Since many city gardens are in containers, making and choosing wood planters is important in the scheme of things. Many people opt to buy ready-made planters and this is fine although costly. But you can make your own wooden boxes and planters, too. It is not difficult nor is it expensive.

The advantage of the homemade container is that you can fit it to a specific area and the installation looks custom-made. Many times if you buy boxes you must take the only sizes available.

Planters and boxes may be movable or can be built into an area for permanent use; what you use depends on your garden and your own tastes.

WOOD

Wood is so easy to work with that you do not have to be a carpenter or even very handy with tools. If you do not

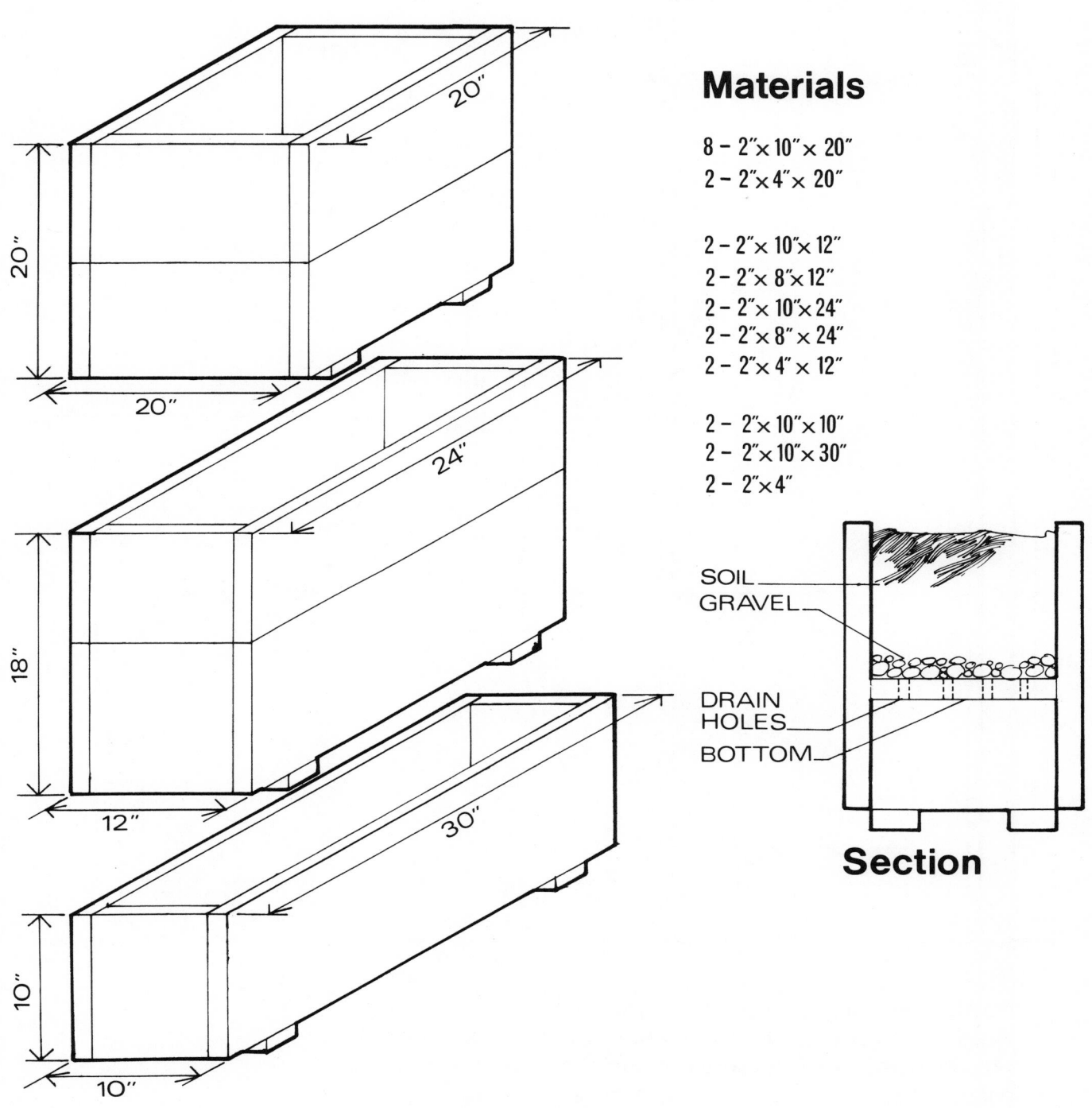

Materials

8 – 2"× 10"× 20"
2 – 2"× 4"× 20"

2 – 2"× 10"× 12"
2 – 2"× 8"× 12"
2 – 2"× 10"× 24"
2 – 2"× 8"× 24"
2 – 2"× 4"× 12"

2 – 2"× 10"× 10"
2 – 2"× 10"× 30"
2 – 2"× 4"

20"

20"

20"

24"

18"

12"

30"

10"

10"

SOIL
GRAVEL

DRAIN
HOLES
BOTTOM

Section

WOODEN PLANTER BOXES

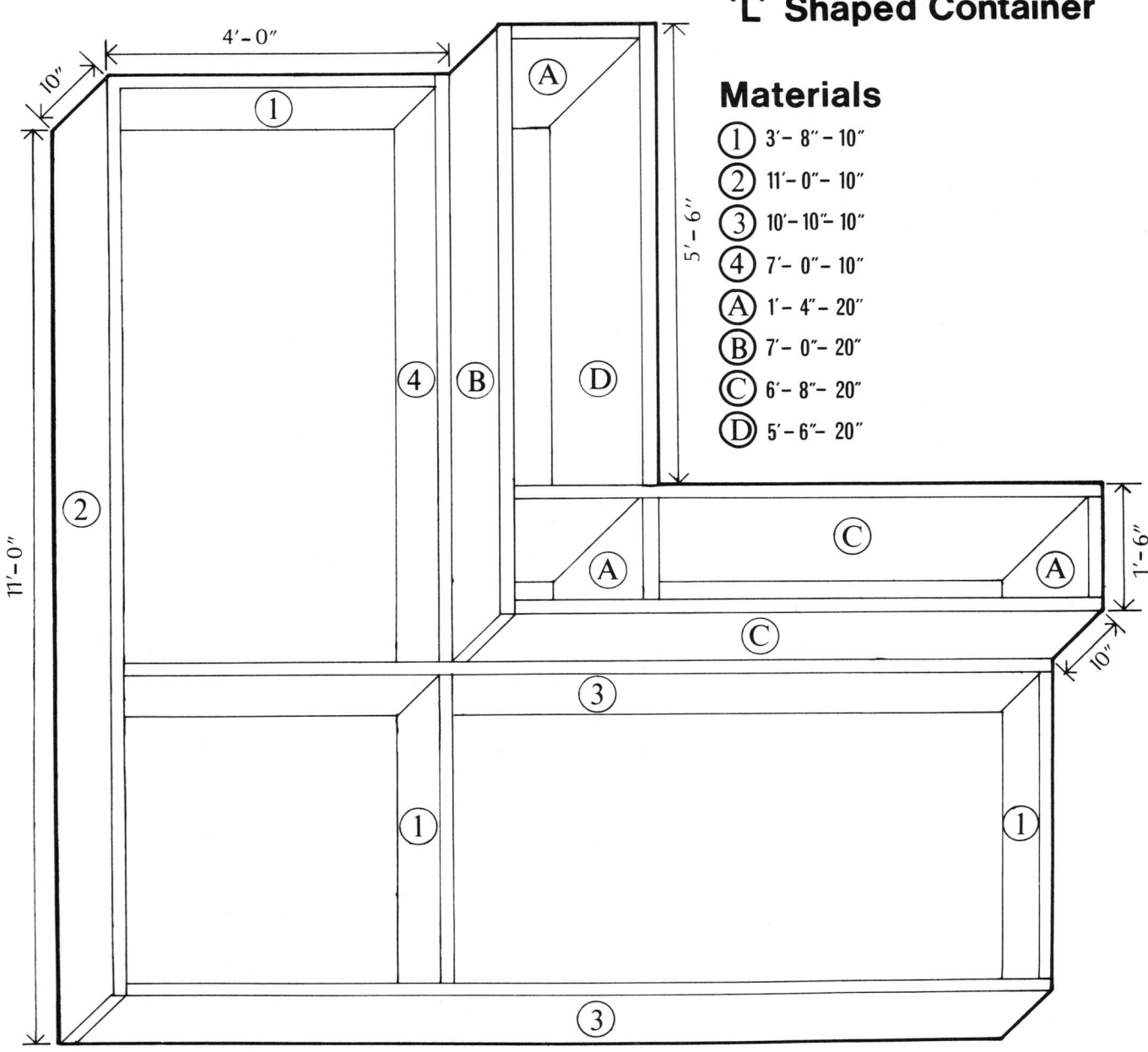

`L´ Shaped Container

Materials

1. 3´– 8´´– 10´´
2. 11´– 0´´– 10´´
3. 10´– 10´´– 10´´
4. 7´– 0´´– 10´´
A. 1´– 4´´– 20´´
B. 7´– 0´´– 20´´
C. 6´– 8´´– 20´´
D. 5´– 6´´– 20´´

want to do any cutting or sawing at home, order your wood pieces cut to size; then just nail, screw, or glue the pieces together to make your boxes and planters. And because you will be using rather small pieces of wood for your plant containers, not lumber ("lumber" denotes large boards), you really have nothing to fear. Just make sure you have the proper tools and follow the information about adhesives and wood epoxies in this chapter.

PLANTER BOXES

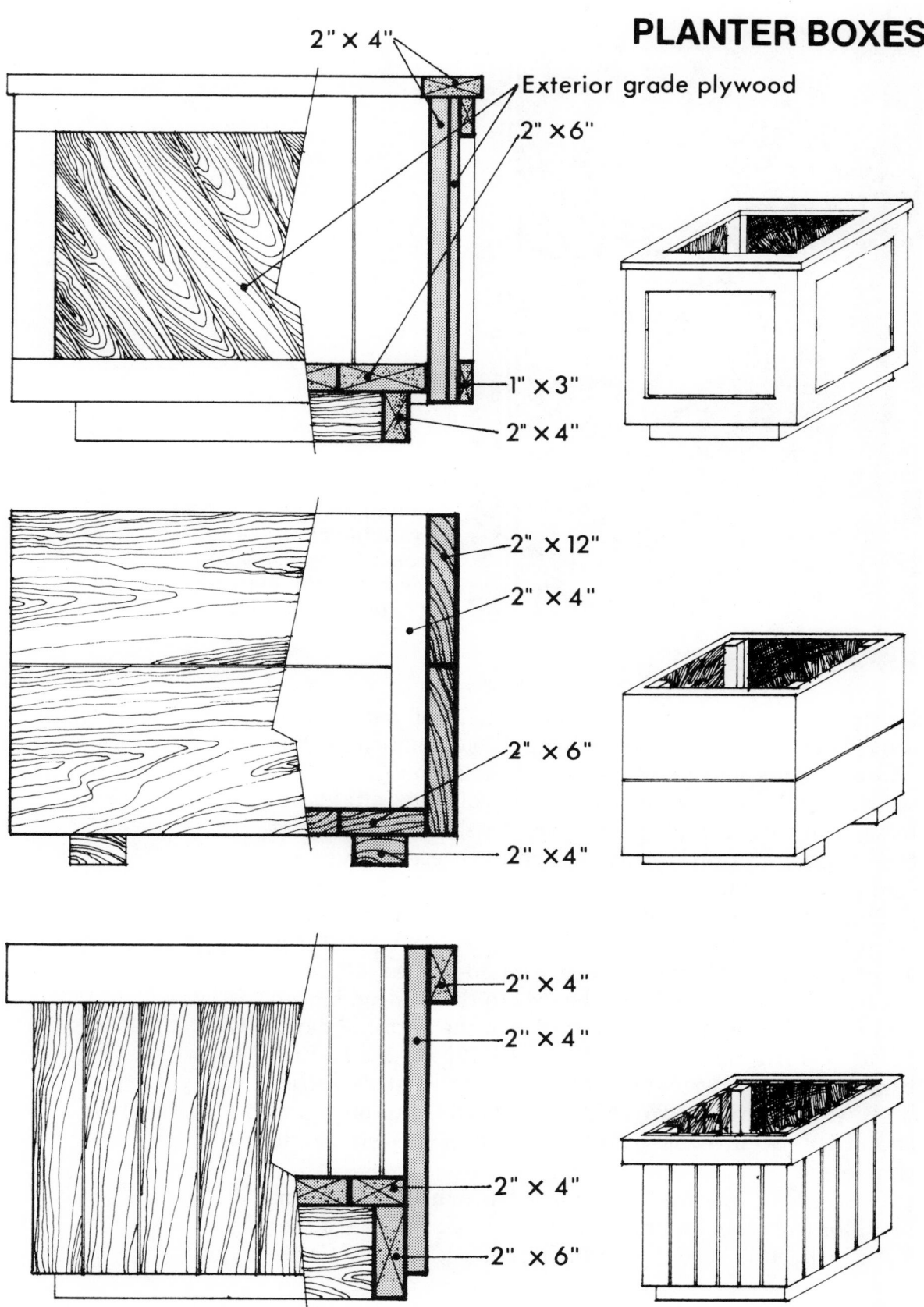

2" × 4"

Exterior grade plywood

2" ×6"

1" × 3"

2" ×4"

2" × 12"

2" × 4"

2" × 6"

2" ×4"

2" × 4"

2" × 4"

2" × 4"

2" × 6"

Lumber: pine, redwood, cedar; box dimensions: personal specs.

All types of wooden containers are available at nurseries, from planter types to soy kegs. (Photograph by Joyce R. Wilson)

ESSENTIALS

Containers for plants are ideally made of redwood or cedar because these woods resist outdoor conditions. For outdoor boxes and planters use construction-grade redwood, which is redwood with relatively few slight defects. You can also use pine or Douglas fir if you protect the woods with preservatives or paint (preservatives are sold at paint stores).

There are many kinds of planters you can make and several methods of construction. A good basic planter is 12 inches wide, 10 inches deep, and 36 inches long. Cut construction-grade redwood boards to the desired length and nail and screw all corners. Space the bottom boards ¼ to ½-inch apart. Use 2×4, 1×12, or 2×12-inch lumber. A good permanent planter is at least 24 inches high; this requires two 2×8-inch boards, one on top of the other. Secure the boards to 4×4-inch posts set in concrete.

I use 2×12-inch redwood for a 24-inch box; it seems ideal for the size of plants necessary in a small yard. For a 12-inch cube, use 1×12-inch redwood strips. Screw and glue together the four sides and the bottom. Add 2 × 2-inch wood moldings vertically to define the character of the box.

To give the box a finished appearance, stain the wood a dark color. Rather than spacing bottom boards for drainage of water in smaller boxes, install ½-inch holes in the bottom of the box so excess water can escape.

A wood tub with flared or tapered sides is attractive and good for annuals or bulbs. An 18-inch top tapering to a 10-inch base is a good size. Use 1-inch-thick redwood or cedar, and miter the corners if possible. Use

A lovely ceramic pot in a wood cradle is the accent piece for this city porch garden. (Photograph courtesy Western Wood Products)

a small, 1-inch molding as a pedestal to give the tub a finished look.

To make your own window box, use redwood or cedar, at least 1-inch thick, for the sides, and ¾-inch plywood base. Make the box at least 10 inches wide and 12 inches deep, to give plants enough root room. Drill drainage holes in the bottom of the box every 8 inches.

If you are having a lumber dealer cut your wood, order the boards first by thickness, then by width, and finally by length; for example, 2 inches × 6 inches × 8 feet. Next, specify what type of wood you want, such as redwood, and then indicate the grade, such as construction-grade, kiln-dried, rough, and so on. Remember that if you order, say, standard 2×4-inch boards, the actual dimensions of the boards are only 1½×3½ or just slightly larger. In other words, the boards will never be exactly 2×4. And remember that pieces of wood smaller than 2×4 inches are called "strips." These strips are called 2×3's, 1×2's, and so forth. Finally, posts for corners are either 2 or 4 inches square.

Boxes

A wood box for a plant can be large or small, elaborate or simple, with outside detailing or perfectly plain, with overlapped corners or crossed timbers, round or octagonal in shape, and so on. Plant boxes are cheap to make; the simplest form has four plain sides, and a bottom with drainage holes. You can merely nail a box together, but a combination of good-quality glue or epoxy and brass screws makes a box last longer.

The 12-inch cube is neat, simple to make, and quickly becoming a classic. The proportions of a modular box are generally in increments of 8 inches: 8×8, 8×16, 8×24, and so on.

These permanent planters were designed especially for the city garden: the sawtooth design adds dimension to the area. (Photograph by Lee)

Terra-cotta pots are always handsome in city gardens because their color complements green and paving areas; terra-cotta containers come in various sizes and designs. (Photograph by author)

You can create an attractive modular garden of uniformly sized boxes that can be moved about easily to create various designs. The boxes can be shallow or deep; you make them as you would a standard planter, except that the modular units fit together for a concentrated box garden or can be used separately. Modular boxes are especially effective for demarking property lines or on roof areas.

On boxes you can make such refinements as spacing the slats ½-inch apart, tracking trelliswork onto the face of the box, scoring the box with a simple design to give it dimension, tapering the box and beveling (angle cutting) the corners and using a plywood base for a more finished appearance. As you will see from our drawings and instructions, there are innumerable ways to make a plant box more than just a box.

Movable Planters

Movable planters are longer, deeper, and narrower containers than boxes.

Planters are usually just four sides and a bottom. For finishing touches use moldings or caps. Square (modular) planters can be stacked or lined up in various ways for a dramatic effect. A practical size is $20 \times 20 \times 20$ inches. A 16×20-inch redwood planter 5 inches deep is perfect for annuals, bulbs, and almost any small tree or shrub. Nail 2-inch chunks of wood supports under each bottom corner to slightly elevate the planter, to eliminate hiding places for insects (more about insects in Chapter 10); and to permit air circulation under the box for better plant growth and drainage.

Designing the planters involves some thought because they have to coordinate in scale with the plants, that is,

You can make your own planter boxes; here 2 × 12-inch boards are used. Note that planters are raised on wooden cleats to allow air to circulate beneath plants. (Photograph by author)

Some simple wooden planter boxes aglow with daffodils. Use planter boxes to direct traffic and edge walks for a handsome effect. (Photograph courtesy California Redwood Assoc.)

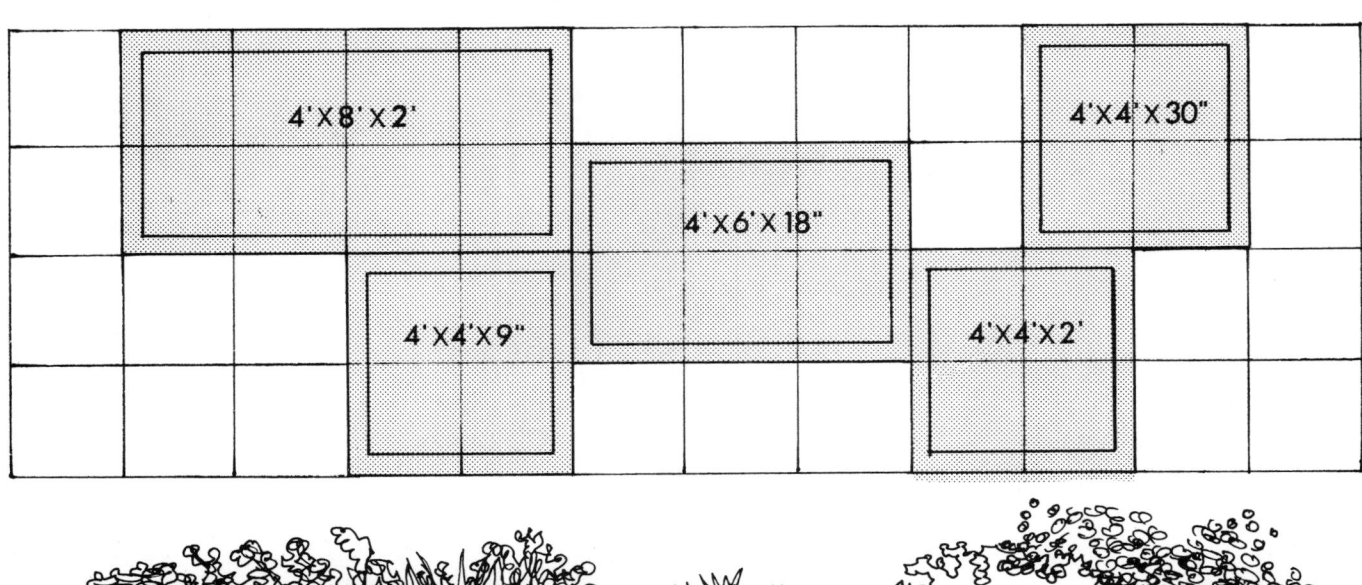

RECTANGULAR PLANTERS

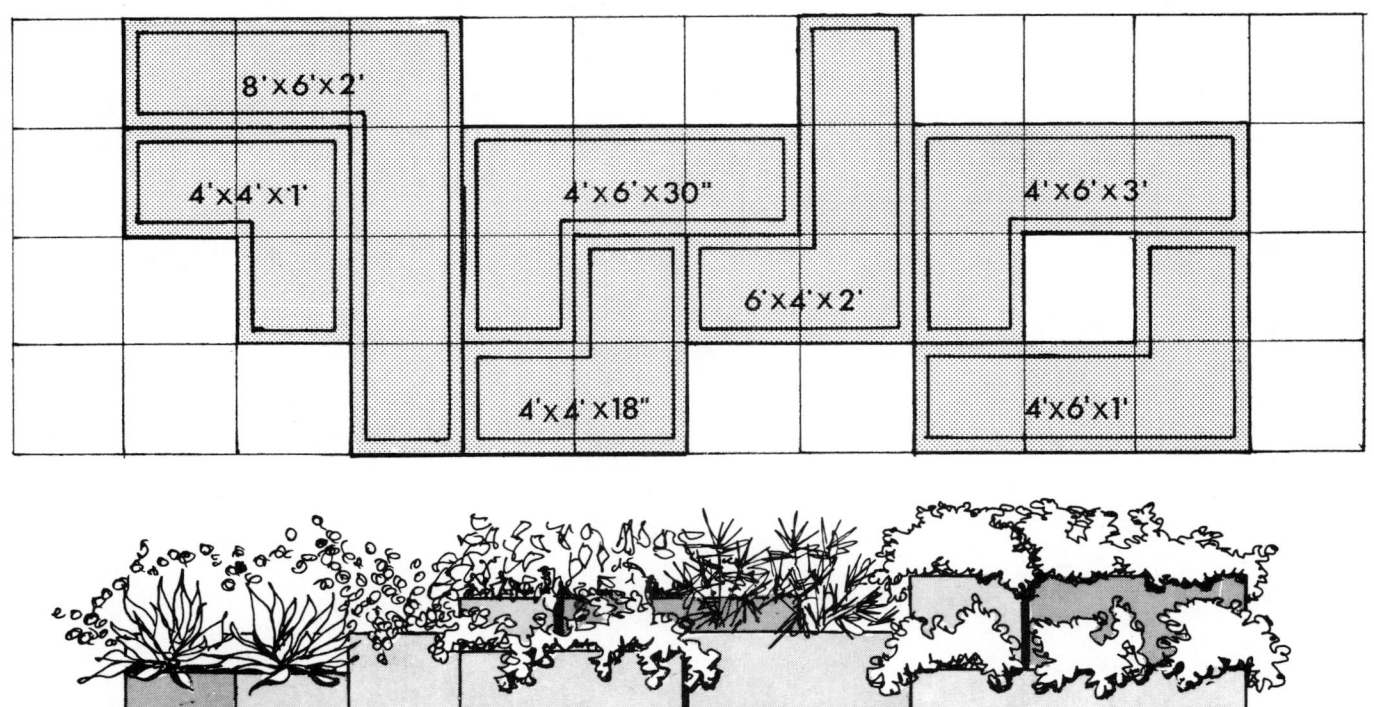

Modular Planters

L-SHAPED PLANTERS

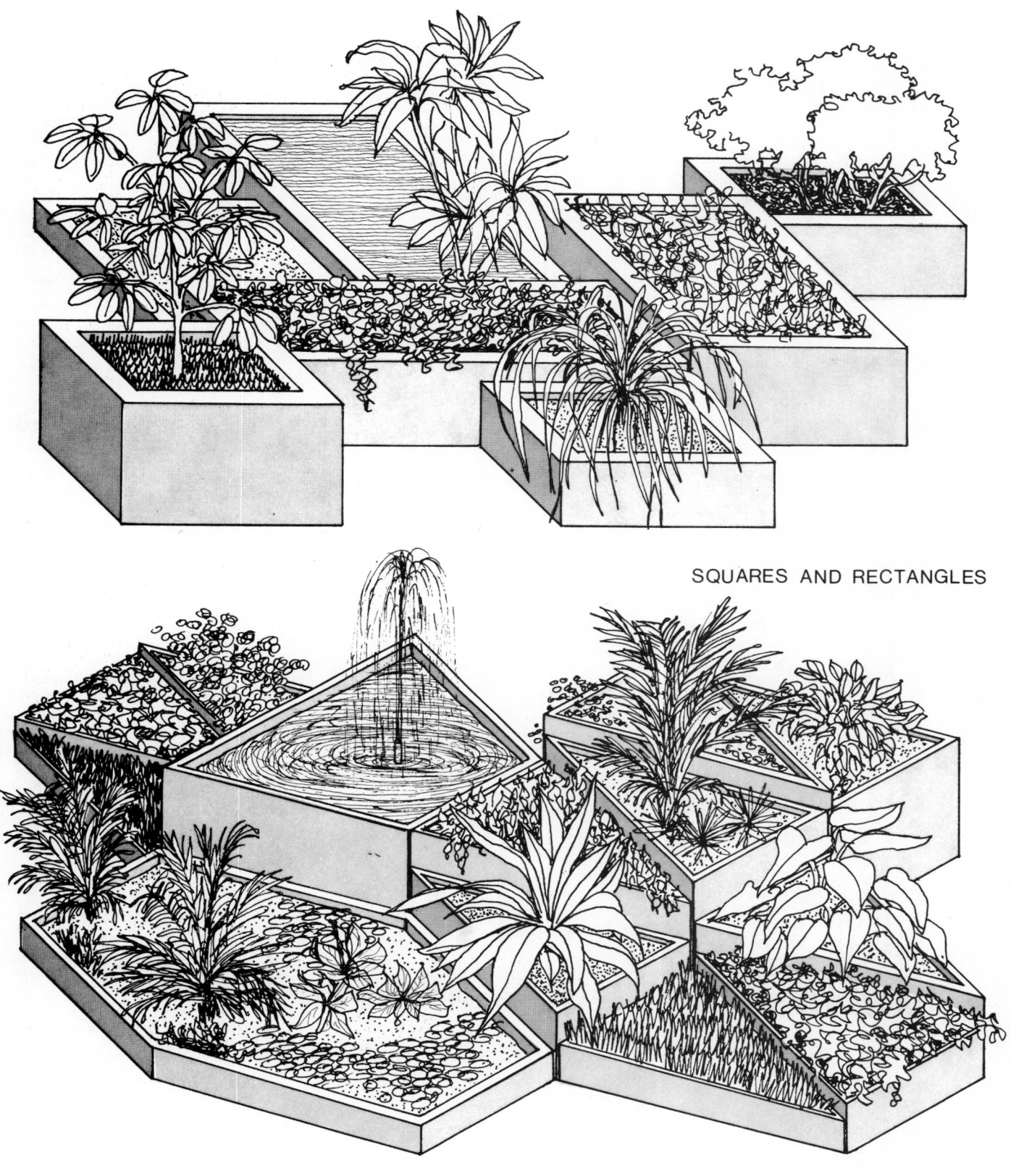

SQUARES AND RECTANGLES

TRIANGLES AND HEXAGONS

Terraced Planters

DESIGN: ADRIÁN MARTÍNEZ

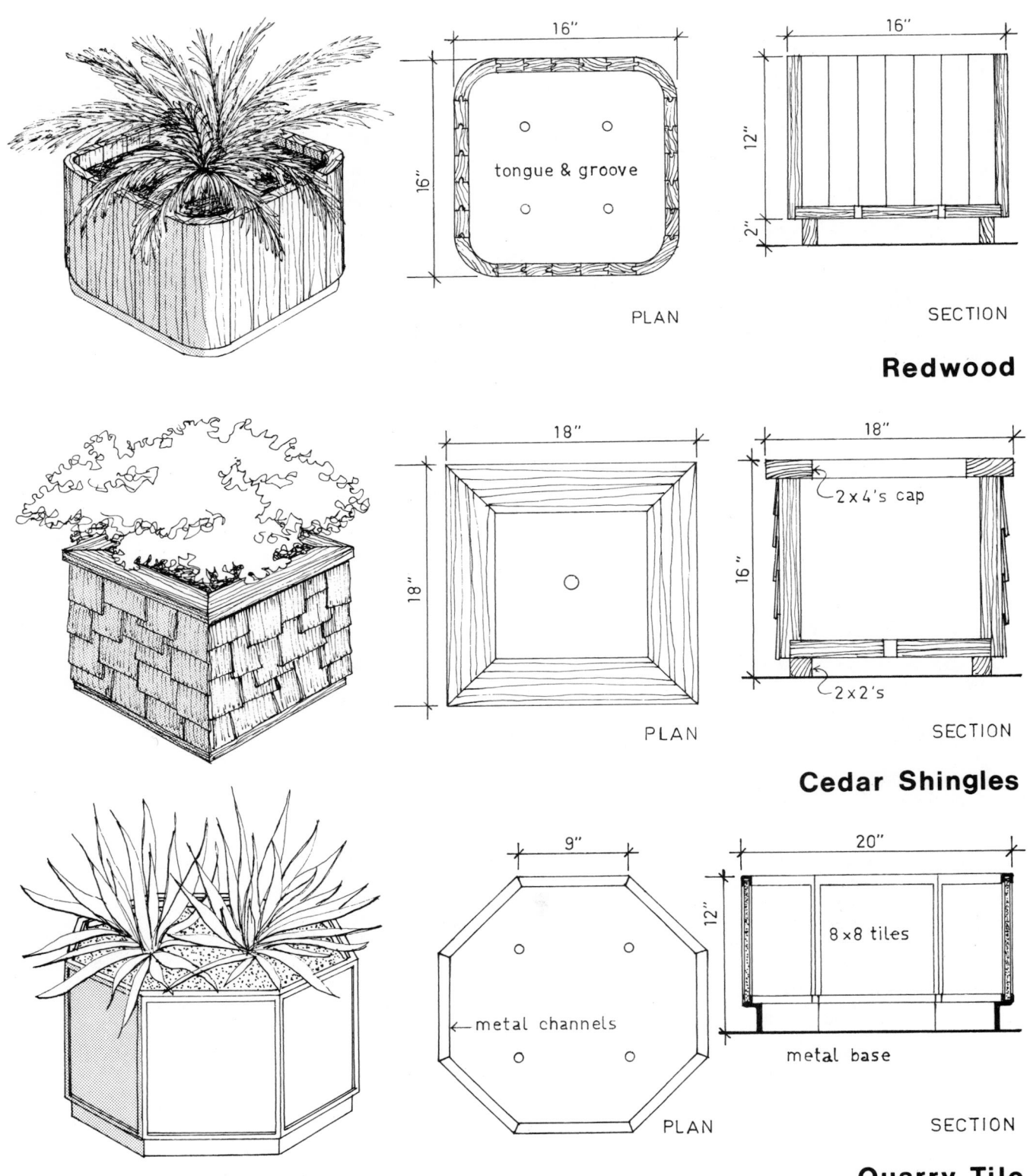

16"

16"

tongue & groove

PLAN

16"

12"

2"

SECTION

Redwood

18"

18"

PLAN

18"

16"

2 x 4's cap

2 x 2's

SECTION

Cedar Shingles

9"

metal channels

PLAN

20"

12"

8 × 8 tiles

metal base

SECTION

Quarry Tile

PORTABLE PLANTERS

DESIGNS: ADRIÁN MARTÍNEZ

small plants with small planters, large plants with large planters. Planters look equally attractive at ground level or elevated. Raised planters also make bending easier and provide growing areas with excellent drainage. The walls of the planters keep out greedy roots from nearby trees and invasive weeds. Furthermore, raised planters make the flowers and foliage appear more decorative and bring plants closer to eye level.

Window Boxes

Window boxes are very effective for growing flowers or tiny vegetables if you live in an apartment. Plants thrive in window boxes because the container is exposed to air circulation on all sides, gets the benefit of rain, and receives good light. The drawbacks are that in the winter the box must be covered and then looks bleak. Also, a window box may not be permitted in your apartment building. But window-box greenery does a lot to make some gardening possible in the city, so check with your manager. Excellent plants for window boxes include geraniums, lantanas, lobelias, petunias, impatiens, fuchsias, and nasturtiums.

The plastic or wood window boxes nurseries sell are not particularly handsome or suitably sized. It is better to build your own, as detailed earlier in the chapter. The most satisfactory sizes are 28 to 36 inches long, 10 inches wide, and 12 inches deep.

The window box can be a simple rectangle with straight sides or, if you live in an area with severe winters, build a box with outwardly sloping edges. This type of window box lets soil expand when it is frozen, without damaging the box. Very long window boxes are

Decorative stoneware and clay pots provide the accent for this tiny backyard garden in the city. (Photograph by Matthew Barr)

extremely heavy when filled with soil, and hanging them can be a problem. On a large window, use two small boxes rather than one large one.

Attaching the box to the window is more difficult than actually making the box. Use sturdy metal L-shaped brackets for support under the box; to really secure the box to the building wall, use screws, lag bolts or toggle bolts in the wall studs. Plant directly in the window box, or place potted plants (camouflage the tops with moss) into the box.

PERMANENT PLANTERS

Permanent planters of various shapes—rectangular, narrow and long, triangular or stairstep—require more construction knowledge than do the portable ones. The permanent planter must be anchored to the ground, but

Permanent planter beds such as one at right designed into a garden create harmony and beauty. (Photograph by Lee)

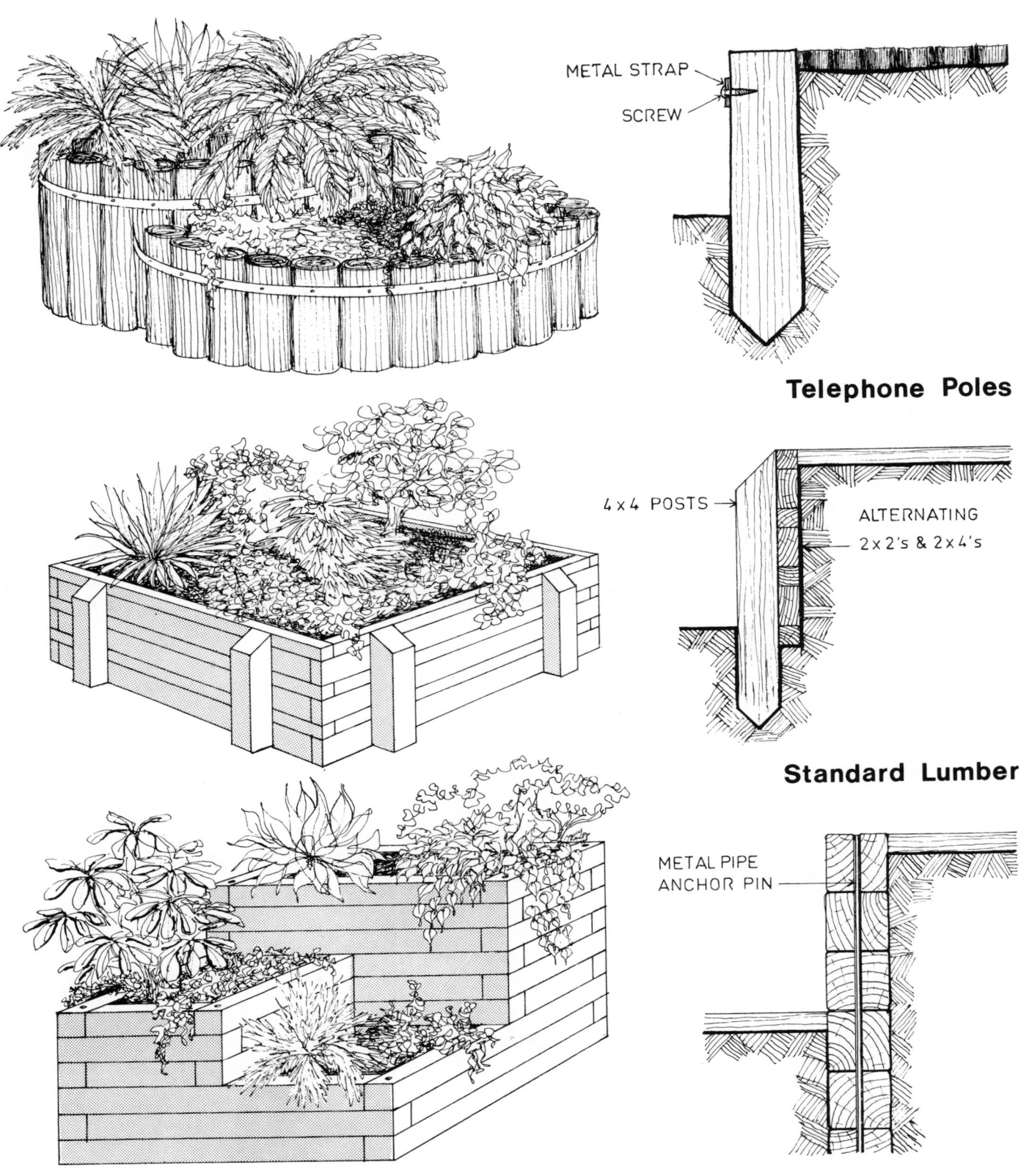

METAL STRAP

SCREW

Telephone Poles

4 x 4 POSTS

ALTERNATING
2 x 2's & 2 x 4's

Standard Lumber

METAL PIPE
ANCHOR PIN

Railroad Ties

DESIGNS: ADRIÁN MARTÍNEZ

PERMANENT WOODEN PLANTERS

no bottom boards are required. Most permanent planters are set into corners or against fences or house walls. However, always first lay out the plan on paper, sketching various shapes until you find a pleasing design.

Brick or stone planter beds (terracing) look attractive in the garden and enable you to tend plants easily. Also, spreading plants can be contained so they do not invade the garden. Use such planters against a fence, as entrance-way accents, or as retaining walls around patio perimeters or walks.

A concrete and brick planter area in the author's yard, brimming with nasturtiums. This becomes a colorful summer display. (Photograph by author)

TOOLS

You do not need many tools to make wood containers: The basics are a good hammer, screwdrivers, a saw, chisels, a miter box, nails, glues, epoxies, screws, sandpaper, paints, and finishes. I prefer a claw hammer of forged, high-quality steel. Hammer faces (heads) are flat or slightly convex; the convex hammer, which lets you drive a nail flush without marring the wood surface, is the best one for your purposes. Long-handled hammers provide more leverage than short ones; the average-sized handle gives you plenty of leverage for the standard planter or box. It is also a good idea to use a short-handled hammer for the finishing work; the head of this hammer should weigh about 16 ounces.

The screwdriver is an important tool because containers last longer if they are screwed together. You need three basic screwdrivers: one with a square shank; a long screwdriver, which gives you more leverage than a short one; and a small screwdriver for working in tight places like corners. An ill-fitting screwdriver is always a headache; for example, if the tip is too large for the screws' heads, the screwdriver mars the surface of the wood. Magnetized screwdrivers greatly reduce the possibility of the screwdriver's tip slipping from the screw head, so you may want to invest in one.

You certainly need a handsaw of some sort; a power saw is not absolutely necessary (although it is easier to work with). The shape, number of teeth, and blade size determine the type of cutting a saw will do. The crosscut saw is probably the most popular; this saw cuts across the wood grain, and it can cut both plywood and hardwoods. A 20-inch saw and a smaller saw for detail work are basically all you need for making containers. If you are cutting patterns, use a coping saw.

You need chisels for outside detailing. Chisels make small grooves and cuts and are driven with a hammer. A set of four chisels in blade widths of ½, ¼, ¾, and 1 inch is fine. When you do chisel work, use light taps with the hammer and remove the wood in small stages, a step at a time.

Miter Box

Moldings cover many mistakes, and most boxes look best when capped with a molding. The best tool for making moldings is an inexpensive miter box, which enables you to cut the precise 45° angles needed for joining moldings. The miter box comes with a 45° angle saw slot; apply the wood molding against the framing edge, and make your cuts with a backsaw. This is an easy and effective way of cutting precisely and accurately.

Nails

The right nail for the right job is important. Nails come in bright and galvanized finishes and are designated as box, casing, common, or scaffold. For your purposes the common nail is satisfactory, although the box nail is somewhat better because it is less likely to split the wood. For finishing work use the finishing, or casing, nail.

Standard box and casing nails come in sizes from 2- to 16-penny. Once the term "penny" meant the cost of 100 nails—a hundred of the smallest nails cost 2 pennies. Today the term indicates the length of the nail.

Glues and Epoxies

Glue applied at the corners of planters and boxes strengthens the containers, and epoxy holds the joints almost forever. For a very strong waterproof joint, use a resorcin resin, which is one of the most durable glues. Mix the powdered catalyst with liquid resin; you then have about 10 minutes to form the joint after mixing the glue. Ask your hardware dealer for particulars.

Epoxies for wood are generally easy to use. The drying

times for these adhesives vary, and you may have to clamp the wood pieces together until the epoxy sets. Again, ask your hardware dealer for advice on the best one for the job.

Sanders and Sandpapers

Sand your container with the grain of the wood. Once sanded, coat the container with a clear finish or paint. You can rent small belt sanders, or make a sander: Wrap a piece of sandpaper around a block of wood.

There are basically three grades of sanding papers: garnet paper, which is reddish black; aluminum oxide paper, which is black; and silicon carbide paper, which is rust-colored and the one most widely used. The three grades of paper come in various grits, the grit being the density of the coating of the paper. Usually three densities are necessary to achieve a smooth finish on wood; you start with the denser grit, working up to the finer. You can even do finer sanding if you like, but generally this is not necessary. The idea is to remove any flaws or defects in the wood to get a smooth, even finish.

The amount of sanding you have to do depends upon the type of wood and your personal preference. If you want the container to have a clear finish, more sanding is necessary than if it is to be painted because paint covers any mistakes or uneven surfaces.

Finishes and Paints

You can use any number of clear sealants and paints to finish and protect boxes and planters. There are numerous types of finishes, sold under different trade names, so it is difficult to recommend a specific brand. A clear, tough finish is what you want; ask your paint dealer for a wood finish that dries quickly.

A finish protects the wood container and gives it a lustrous appearance. With any finish, the trick is to brush it on evenly and smoothly, using one or two coats. You can also get a clear finish by using waxes on unfinished wood; the buildup of wax creates a protective finish that is handsome and lustrous. Various types of waxes are available at paint and hardware stores; consult the dealer about what to use to achieve the type finish you want.

An infinite number of types of paint can be used on wood containers, and just what you select depends on your personal tastes. In any case, wood containers and wood housings should be sanded smooth before you apply the paint. Also, use outdoor-type paints, that is, oil-based paints.

DETAILING WOOD CONTAINERS

Wood planters and boxes can be handsomely detailed on the outside with wood strips, sandblasting, or tools. This detailing puts the finishing touches on the containers and adds a note of elegance.

A simple but effective outside-the-container motif is a raised rectangle outlining the container; this creates a shadowbox effect. For the average container, this design requires 16 pieces of 1×2-inch strips of wood. Another method is to place strips of 1×1-inch wood vertically or horizontally $\frac{1}{2}$-inch apart. This adds flair and covers any construction mistakes.

When you detail a planter or box with wood strips, always add a molding (or cap) at the tops of the corners to give the container finish and dimension. Nail the caps into place, letting the outer edge overhang the container by ½ to 1 inch.

If you are handy with tools, you might want to score a container with a beautiful bas-relief design. Use a wood chisel to create various patterns. A basic scoring pattern is a simple knife edge ¼-inch deep, spaced ½ to 1 inch apart, vertically or horizontally. Sandblasting adds a textured, handsome look to a container. You can rent a sanding machine, or, if you are making a small container, sand the wood by hand to a lustrous, smooth finish.

Because the detailing of the outside of the container mainly depends upon the box or planter's size, always consider proportion and symmetry. For example, large containers can be detailed with big strips of wood, whereas smaller containers need more meticulous detail and smaller strips.

Fences & Walls
(wood & masonry)

TYPES OF FENCES

Today's fences are both beautiful and functional and can be fashioned in many different designs. Basically the wood fence is the most popular one. Fences are classified as picket, slat, louver, board, basket weave, trellis or lattice, panel, grape stake, rail, split rail, post and rail, post and board, and lapped joint. The picket and grape-stake fences are not recommended for city gardens because they are more decorative than functional.

Slat

Slat fences are simple to build and look handsome, somewhat formal, but neat. The wood used is usually rough-finished redwood sawed into 1×1 or 1×2-inch strips. These fences can provide complete privacy and very effective wind control (tests indicate that closely

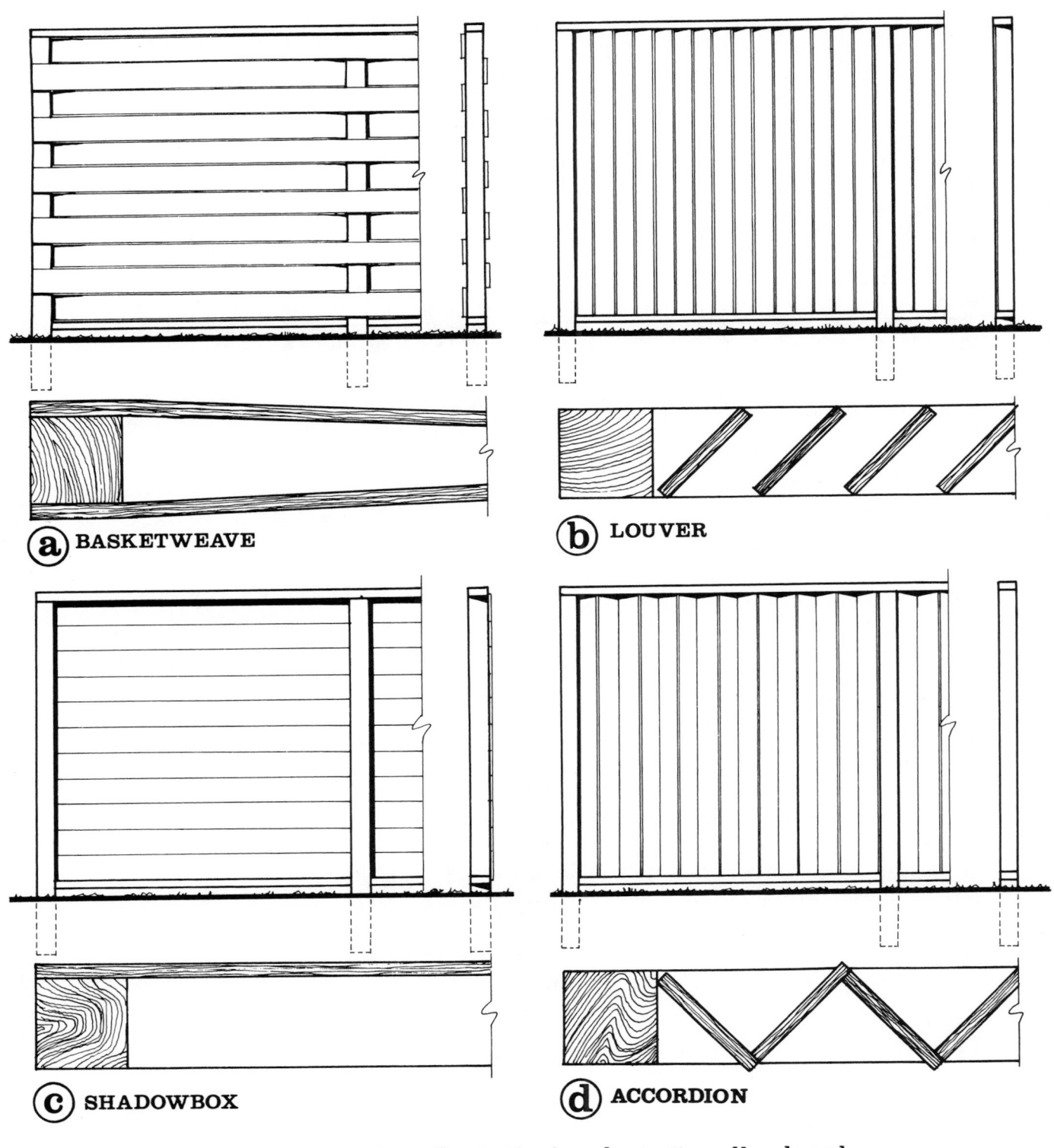

a BASKETWEAVE

b LOUVER

c SHADOWBOX

d ACCORDION

note: posts - 4x4's rails - 2x4's boards - 1x6's all redwood

ADRIAN MARTINEZ

Types of Fences

A simple wood fence does much to contain a small city space—it gives it privacy and defines the property, as well as adding design beauty. (Photograph courtesy California Redwood Assoc.)

This wood fence adds decorative beauty to the garden and is simple to install. (Photograph courtesy California Redwood Assoc.)

spaced slats break up and disperse the wind). Slats can be run vertically, close together or spaced apart; they can also be used horizontally for a different look or in combination with vertical slats for a dramatic effect.

Fences need not be barriers; here openings are left in the fence to afford see-through and create a dimensional feeling. (Photograph courtesy California Redwood Assoc.)

Louver

If you need a windbreak but want it to be good-looking, consider the louver fence. By adjusting the louvers you can have either maximum light or almost total shade. And, when faced across the path of prevailing winds, a louver fence tempers the wind but still allows air circulation.

Vertical-spaced louvers give some privacy, but part of the garden will always be visible through the fence as a person moves along it. For complete privacy, use the horizontal design.

For louver fences you need a larger amount of material than with any other wooden fence. Also, because the louvers are supported only at the ends, warping and twisting might occur, so expensive kiln-dried lumber is recommended. This is a heavy fence whose structure requires substantial posts and foundations.

Board

A board fence is simple to build—a sturdy post and rail frame. The solid design provides maximum privacy but

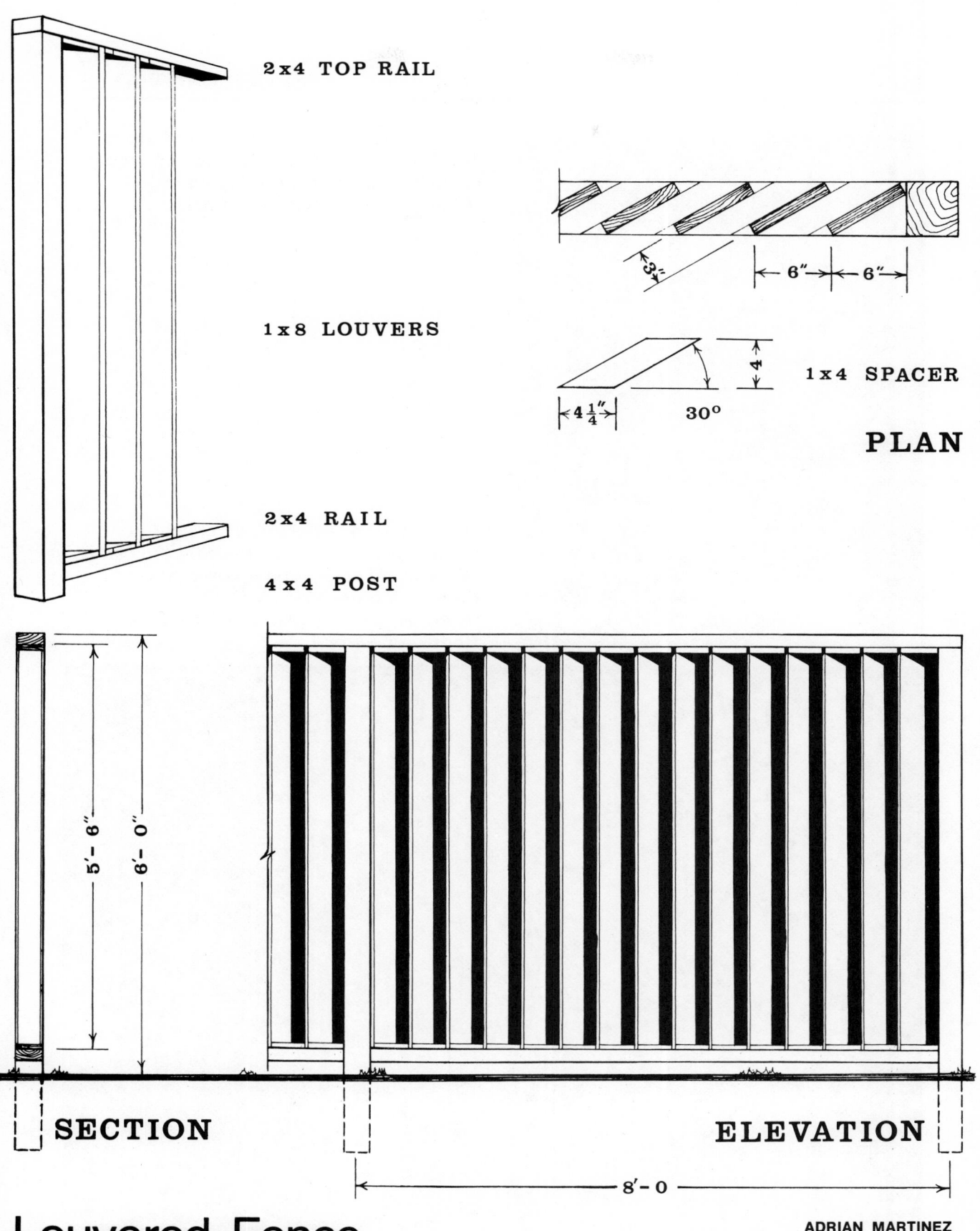

2x4 TOP RAIL

1x8 LOUVERS

6" 6"

3"

4

1x4 SPACER

4 1/4" 30°

PLAN

2x4 RAIL

4x4 POST

5'-6" 6'-0"

SECTION

ELEVATION

8'-0"

Louvered Fence

ADRIAN MARTINEZ

Common rough redwood is used for fencing in this city garden; the effect is rustic and provides total privacy. (Photograph by Matthew Barr)

Here a board fence (used vertically) creates privacy in a city scene; the beauty of redwood cannot be ignored and a fence is handsome to look at. (Photograph courtesy California Redwood Assoc.)

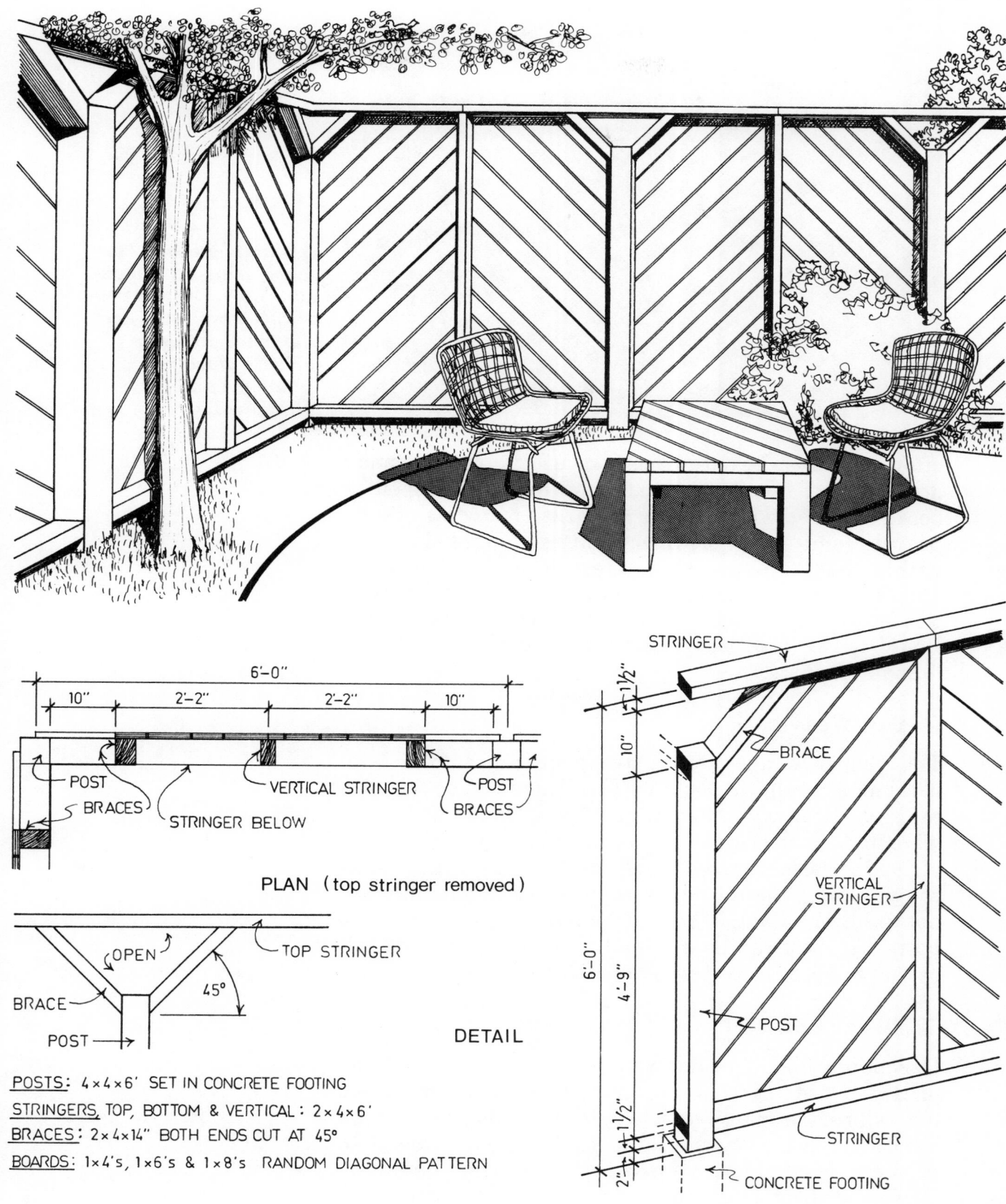

PLAN (top stringer removed)

10"   2'-2"   2'-2"   10"   6'-0"

POST
BRACES
STRINGER BELOW
VERTICAL STRINGER
POST
BRACES

OPEN
BRACE
POST
TOP STRINGER
45°

DETAIL

STRINGER
BRACE
VERTICAL STRINGER
POST
STRINGER
CONCRETE FOOTING

1-1/2"   10"   6'-0"   4'-9"   1-1/2"   2"

POSTS: 4×4×6' SET IN CONCRETE FOOTING

STRINGERS, TOP, BOTTOM & VERTICAL: 2×4×6'

BRACES: 2×4×14" BOTH ENDS CUT AT 45°

BOARDS: 1×4's, 1×6's & 1×8's RANDOM DIAGONAL PATTERN

design/drawing: Adrian Martinez

Diagonal Board Fence

A handmade wooden fence using 2 × 2-inch slats on 4 × 4-inch posts is very handsome and the fence creates a private place. (Photograph by Matthew Barr)

often creates a boxed-in look, so use it only in small areas. Spaced boards, say, ½ to 1 inch apart, left open, or boards covered with 1 × 1-inch boards to create a design, provide semi- or total privacy. Boards placed slantwise within the frame are an interesting design variation. Thin batten designs, placed either horizontally or vertically in somewhat of a trellis effect, are appealing. Board fences are heavy, so be sure to use substantial foundations.

Basket Weave

The basket weave's attractive appearance from both sides makes it quite popular. The design can be horizontal or vertical, with the weave varying from flat to very wide and open. Triangular designs made of thin wooden strips can also be used. The basket-weave fence looks complicated to build but is not because often rails are not used, so all you have to do is nail strips or panels to posts. The cost can be minimal if you can buy prefabricated panels of basket-weave fencing.

Trellis or Lattice

Depending upon the lumber—heavy or light—and the grilles—close together or far apart—trellis or lattice fences provide many versatile designs and always look handsome. A tightly woven lattice fence offers complete privacy; a slightly open design lets air circulate. However, the trellis fence is not easy to construct; it requires painstaking attention to detail.

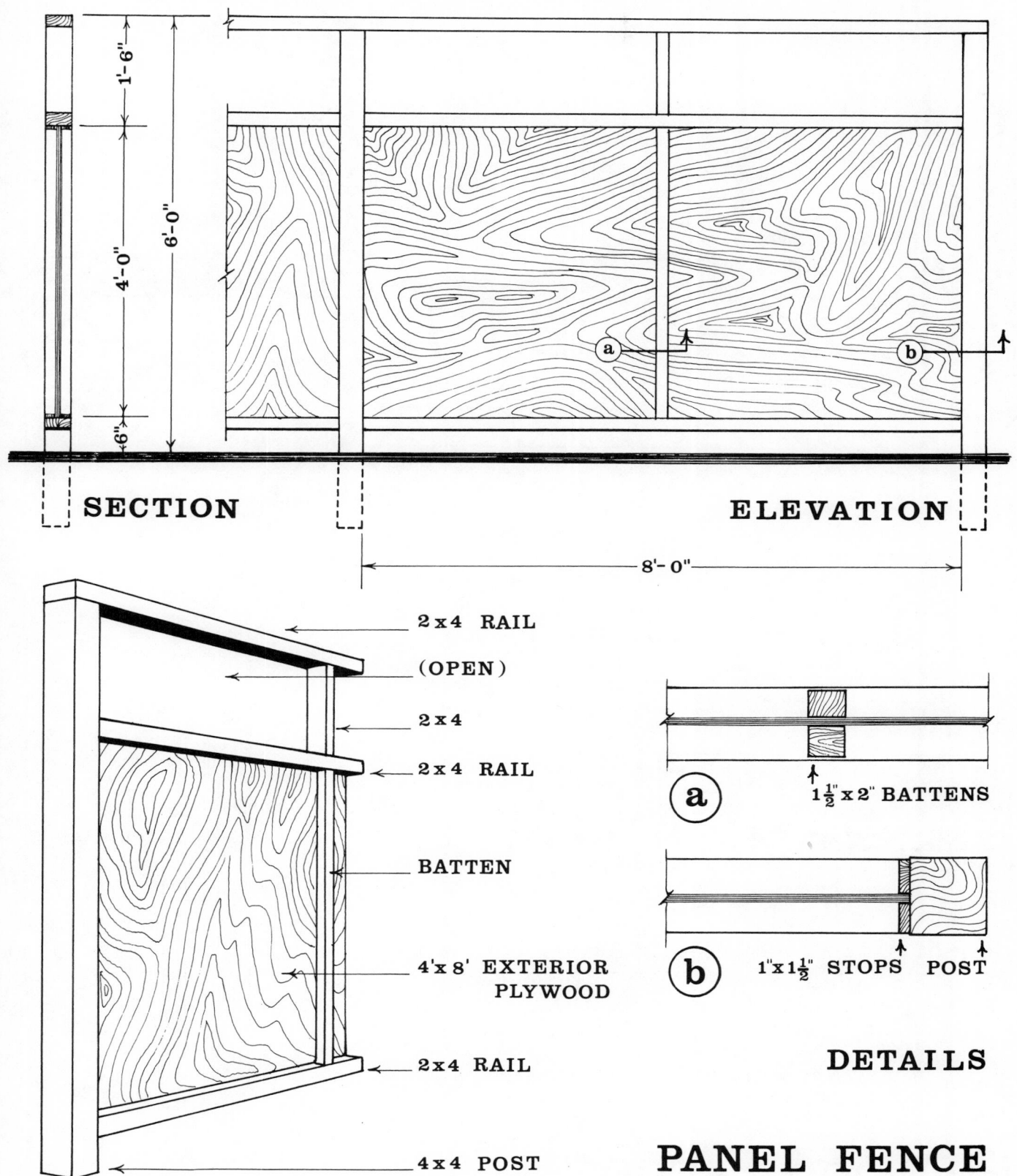

SECTION

ELEVATION

1'-6"

6'-0"

4'-0"

6"

8'-0"

2 x 4 RAIL

(OPEN)

2 x 4

2 x 4 RAIL

BATTEN

4'x 8' EXTERIOR PLYWOOD

2 x 4 RAIL

4 x 4 POST

a $1\frac{1}{2}$" x 2" BATTENS

b 1"x $1\frac{1}{2}$" STOPS POST

DETAILS

PANEL FENCE

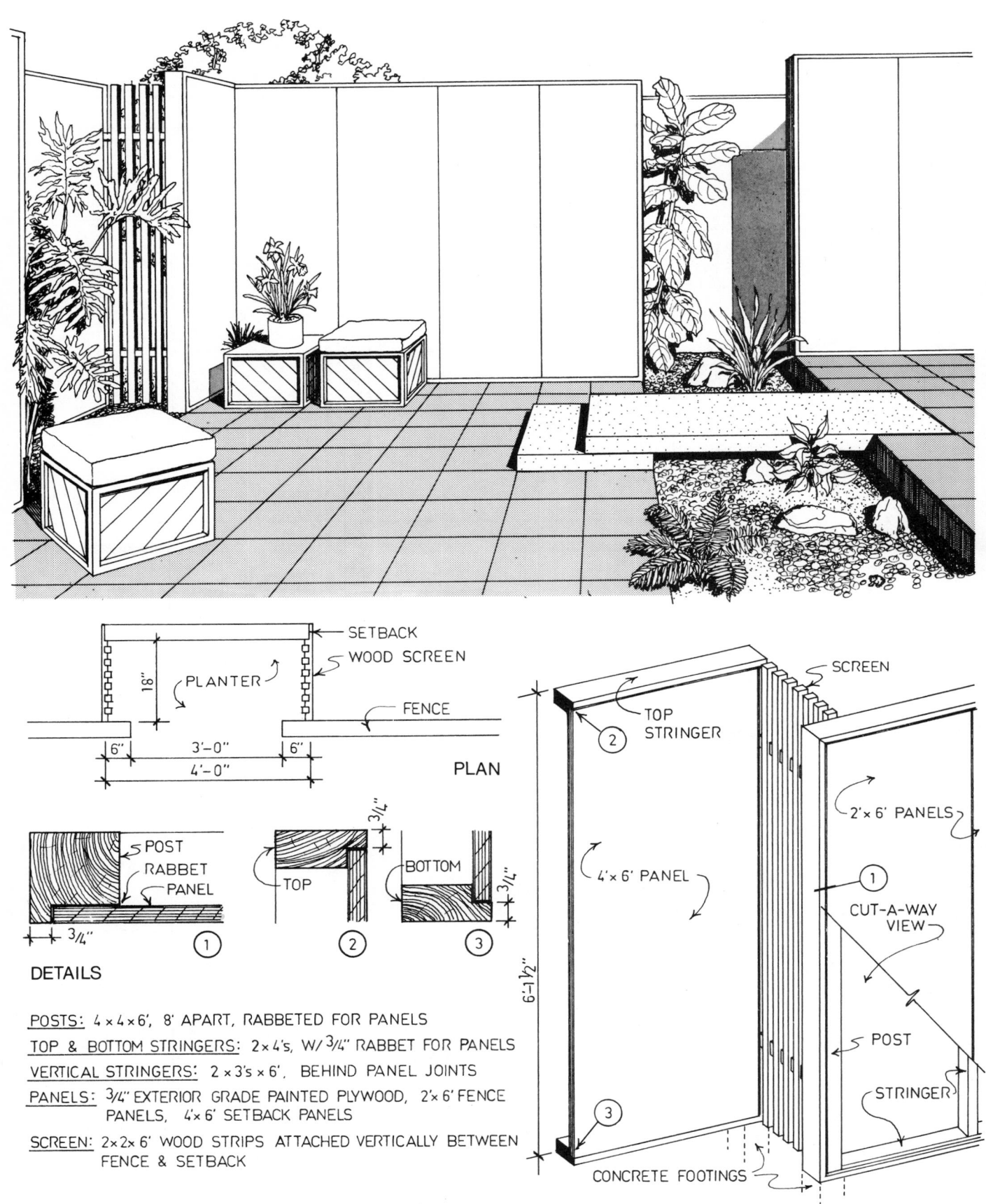

SETBACK
WOOD SCREEN
18"
PLANTER
FENCE

6" 3'-0" 6"
4'-0"

PLAN

POST
RABBET
PANEL
3/4"
①

3/4"
TOP
②

BOTTOM
3/4"
③

DETAILS

POSTS: 4 × 4 × 6', 8' APART, RABBETED FOR PANELS
TOP & BOTTOM STRINGERS: 2 × 4's, W/ 3/4" RABBET FOR PANELS
VERTICAL STRINGERS: 2 × 3's × 6', BEHIND PANEL JOINTS
PANELS: 3/4" EXTERIOR GRADE PAINTED PLYWOOD, 2' × 6' FENCE
          PANELS, 4' × 6' SETBACK PANELS
SCREEN: 2 × 2 × 6' WOOD STRIPS ATTACHED VERTICALLY BETWEEN
          FENCE & SETBACK

SCREEN
TOP STRINGER
②
2' × 6' PANELS
①
CUT-A-WAY VIEW
4' × 6' PANEL
6'-1½"
POST
STRINGER
③
CONCRETE FOOTINGS

Plywood Fence

design/drawing: Adrian Martinez

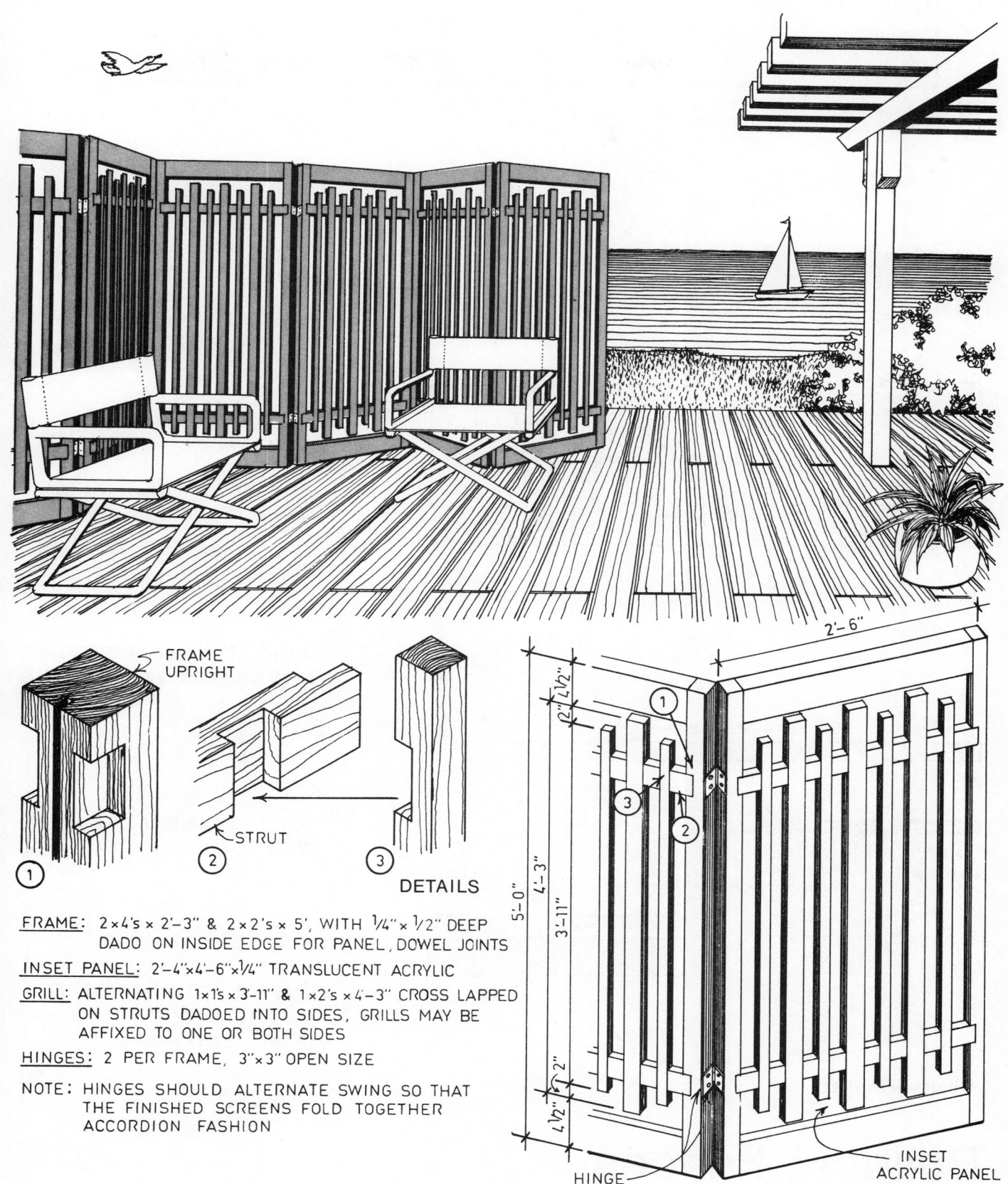

FRAME UPRIGHT

① ② **STRUT** ③

DETAILS

FRAME: 2×4's × 2'–3" & 2×2's × 5', WITH ¼" × ½" DEEP
  DADO ON INSIDE EDGE FOR PANEL, DOWEL JOINTS

INSET PANEL: 2'–4"×4'–6"×¼" TRANSLUCENT ACRYLIC

GRILL: ALTERNATING 1×1's × 3'–11" & 1×2's × 4'–3" CROSS LAPPED
  ON STRUTS DADOED INTO SIDES, GRILLS MAY BE
  AFFIXED TO ONE OR BOTH SIDES

HINGES: 2 PER FRAME, 3"×3" OPEN SIZE

NOTE: HINGES SHOULD ALTERNATE SWING SO THAT
  THE FINISHED SCREENS FOLD TOGETHER
  ACCORDION FASHION

2'–6"

2" 4½"

5'–0"

4'–3"

3'–11"

2"

4½"

① ③ ②

HINGE

INSET
ACRYLIC PANEL

Moveable Fence

design/drawing: Adrian Martinez

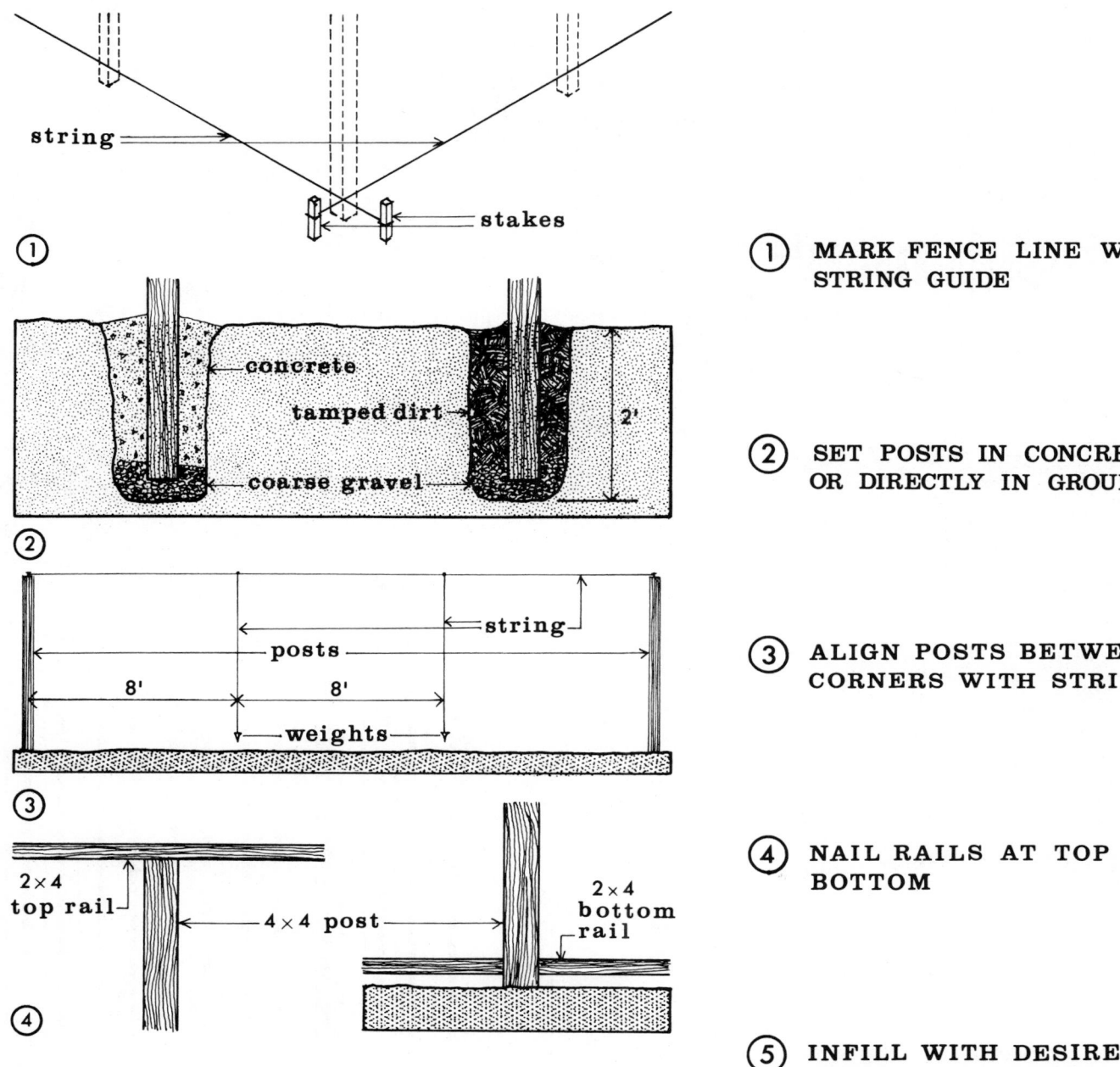

string

stakes

① **MARK FENCE LINE WITH STRING GUIDE**

concrete

tamped dirt

coarse gravel

2'

② **SET POSTS IN CONCRETE OR DIRECTLY IN GROUND**

posts

string

8'   8'

weights

③ **ALIGN POSTS BETWEEN CORNERS WITH STRING**

2×4 top rail

4×4 post

2×4 bottom rail

④ **NAIL RAILS AT TOP & BOTTOM**

⑤ **INFILL WITH DESIRED DESIGN & MATERIALS - MISC. SHOWN**

ADRIAN MARTINEZ

Building Fences

Panel

Panel fences made of either hardwood pressed board or plywood are easy to build, and the panels give complete privacy. This fence needs strong structural support. Do not use the fence in very long expanses because it is confining.

Prefabricated

"Prefabricated" means that you buy most of the components of a fence and assemble them. There are several designs available, such as basket weave and post or rail. If you do not want to make your own designs, this is a fine way of selecting fencing. Remember that a prefabricated fence kit generally does not include the posts; you buy them separately.

NONWOOD FENCING

Materials such as glass, plastic, aluminum, and wire have their uses in fencing. Glass or plastic in combination with wood offers a wide design latitude, and glass especially is desirable because it shuts out wind while maintaining a view. Also, glass or plastic enables light to enter a garden. However, glass is expensive, hard to handle, and must be very carefully installed; plastic is cheaper than glass or wood, easy to work with, and lightweight, but it does eventually fade.

Aluminum looks good in small areas. Wire fences, although not decorative by themselves, are excellent security barriers and ideal for confining pets and children. In combination with wood, wire fences can be decorative. Years ago wire fences cost less than wood, but today wire fencing is more expensive.

Glass

The glass fence keeps wind from the property, maintains a view, lets sunshine in, provides a boundary, and in most cases lends a sophisticated look to a property, blending well with wood or brick for a very ornamental design. Some glass offers complete privacy; frosted glass allows only shadows to be seen on the other side.

Wood can be combined with other materials to make fences; here glass and wire are used to create an unusual design. (Photograph by C. D. Luckhart)

Always use tempered (safety) glass. Because regular glass is hazardous, many states do not allow its use for fencing. But even when using tempered glass, avoid large expanses of clear glass that can be mistaken for an opening. Put furniture or shrubbery in front of it, stick some brightly colored decals on it, or install a handsome wood railing to prevent people from walking into the glass areas.

Construction of glass fences requires professional help because the wooden members must carry the weight of the glass (¼-inch glass in large sheets is heavy). It is best to use a design with a small sheet of glass (perhaps framed in wood) rather than large expanses.

Plastic

Plastic is a versatile material for fencing because it comes in many colors and is flat or corrugated, but generally it is not attractive unless handled very wisely. In combination with wood framing, plastic can be pleasing, but design is most important.

Plastic sheets are lightweight, easy to handle, can be sawed or cut even by the novice; thus, plastic is the cheapest fencing material you can buy, and a fence goes up rapidly, generally in one afternoon. The ugly corrugated sheets were first on the market; the flat sheets are more pleasing to the eye, and in combination with wood they can be handsome. For example, white plastic panels contrast handsomely with dark wood framing.

Plastic screening is common window screening sealed in a plastic sandwich. It is available in many combinations and colors, and the material has a variable range of light transmission. Plastic is an excellent choice when used to reduce wind velocity and light transmission, and it is cheaper than glass or wood and very easy to work with. The average person can easily put a plastic fence together (installed with molding strips or battens) for a minimal cost. However, plastic screening can be troublesome because after a year or so the panels usually crack or craze and need replacement.

Plastic panels (fiberglass) are available in flat or corrugated sheets in many colors and patterns. This fencing material is cheap, easy to install, an effective windbreak, lets diffused light enter the garden, and is impervious to weather conditions, but after some time it looks grimy and fades if in sunlight. Also, the plastic never really looks at home in a garden and does not blend well with plants; there is something artificial about it.

Aluminum Panels

Aluminum-panel fencing is relatively new. The designs vary, from basket weave to simple solid panels enclosed in wood. As a fencing material it is certainly satisfactory because it is permanent, strong, and requires only low maintenance. Its problem is that it is not indigenous to a large garden setting. It is available in many colors and finishes but is not easy to work with because it is somewhat heavy and difficult to put together. (It should be installed by a professional).

The panels are installed with either aluminum or wood posts. Fencing is available in different heights: 3 to 4 feet or 5 to 6 feet.

Wire

Wire is the best fencing material for security. The secret is to combine wire with other materials, such as wood;

wire can be an attractive fencing with proper framing and wood grids. A common application of wire is wire mesh attached to wooden posts; sometimes rails are added for appearance. The wire mesh comes in many patterns—hexagonal, triangular, square—and many weights. What you choose depends upon the design and degree of security you need.

The all-wire fence generally comes as a complete unit with posts, rails, mesh, and gates. There are several patterns, usually designated as chain-link or metal-picket. The latter is usually made of plain or plastic-coated galvanized steel. The chain-link fence is galvanized steel, aluminum-coated, or plastic-coated in a wide range of colors. Green is the most acceptable and blends in more readily with plants than other colors.

The wire fence requires an expert to install, so do not tackle it yourself. It is a difficult job—the bracing and anchoring of corner posts, the stretching of wire, and general handling of the large rolls of wire are hard to manage.

SETTING POSTS

For most fences you have to dig postholes at least 24 to 30 inches deep. The deeper the post is set in place the stronger your fence will be. A good rule of thumb is to set posts into the ground at least one-third their length. To dig the holes use a posthole digger (a clawlike tool with handles) available from rental supply stores. Make the bottom of the posthole wider than the top so there is a good solid base for the post (the width of the posthole should be twice the diameter of the post), and insert 2 to 4 inches of gravel at the bottom of the hole. The gravel will eliminate any water that accumulates at the bottom, which can cause the wood to rot. The basic post for fencing is a 4 × 4-inch size.

To set the post in place (this is called plumbing the post), shovel some gravel into the hole and put the post on top of it. Add several shovelsful of concrete, jiggle the post slightly, and then check the two sides with a carpenter's level to be sure the post is absolutely straight up and down and side to side. Now add concrete to the hole so the concrete is flush with the ground, and then again check the two sides with a carpenter's level. If the post is not correct, move it slightly and correct the alignment. Use a lean concrete mix: 1 part cement, 3 parts sand, and 6 parts gravel. The mix should be dry, never runny. Once it is aligned, hold the post by hand a few minutes. It takes a few hours for concrete to harden so do not nail any other boards in place till the next day.

(See end of this chapter for details on mixing concrete.)

WOOD RETAINING WALLS

Redwood or cedar boards are frequently used for low retaining walls, and they function well if built properly. However, do use a fungicide preservative on any wooden member that comes in contact with the soil. Generally 2 × 12-inch boards are run horizontally, with 3 × 4-inch posts supporting them. Dig deep postholes (about 28 inches), and use a gravel base as for regular fence work. Place posts every 4 feet for support; you may also want to brace the wall with wooden members.

WALLS (MASONRY)

Walls can define a garden area, such as a low wall at the edge of a flower border, define a property boundary, and deaden sound or protect the garden from hot sun. Finally, walls—especially those of brick and stone—have an old-time charming quality.

You can tackle small decorative walls (up to 3 feet) by yourself. Higher walls require foundations, which involve digging and pouring concrete. Such work is not

Concrete block serves many purposes—for walls and retaining walls—and can be used effectively with suitable plantings as shown here. (Photograph courtesy National Concrete Masonry Assoc.)

A designer's concrete fence; note the handsome pattern and dimensional qualities. (Photograph courtesy National Concrete Masonry Assoc.)

beyond the average person, but high solid-concrete walls should be done by professionals because making wood forms and pouring great amounts of concrete can be tricky.

Check local building codes about building permits, heights, and frost lines (how deeply you have to dig to install a solid foundation so freezing will not crack the wall).

Brick is the most popular material for walls, but concrete and decorative blocks, cement, and stone are other good materials. Designs vary with the material, and each type of wall gives the property a different look. The brick wall is perennially charming and well suited

All photos by Matthew Bark unless otherwise noted.

Container roof garden in New York City. (Preceding page) (Photograph by Max Eckert)

Deck garden in San Francisco, California. (Photograph by author)

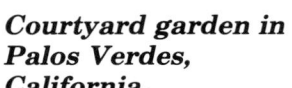

Courtyard garden in Palos Verdes, California.

Walled city garden. (Photograph by Max Eckert)

Deck garden in San Francisco, California.

Terrace garden in Louisiana.

Courtyard garden with impatiens in California. (Lower left)

An entrance garden in Chicago, Illinois. (Lower right)

Acres of flowers in a Georgia city garden.

Courtyard garden in Louisiana.

Rooftop sanctuary in New York City. (Below)

Rock garden in Chicago, Illinois. (Inset)

Terrace city garden in Savannah, Georgia.

Rooftop garden in New York City.

Terrace garden in Virginia.

Rooftop garden New York City. (Photograph by Max Eckert)

Terrace garden in San Francisco, California. (Above)

Flower garden on rooftop in New York City.

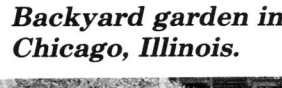

Backyard garden in Chicago, Illinois.

Evergreen garden rooftop area in New York City.

City container garden in Phoenix, Arizona. (Right)

Rooftop retreat in San Francisco, California. (Lower right)

Courtyard garden in Palos Verdes, California.

Entrance to garden in Jackson, Mississippi.

Herb garden in Jackson, Mississippi.

Rooftop garden in San Francisco, California. (Photograph by Max Eckert)

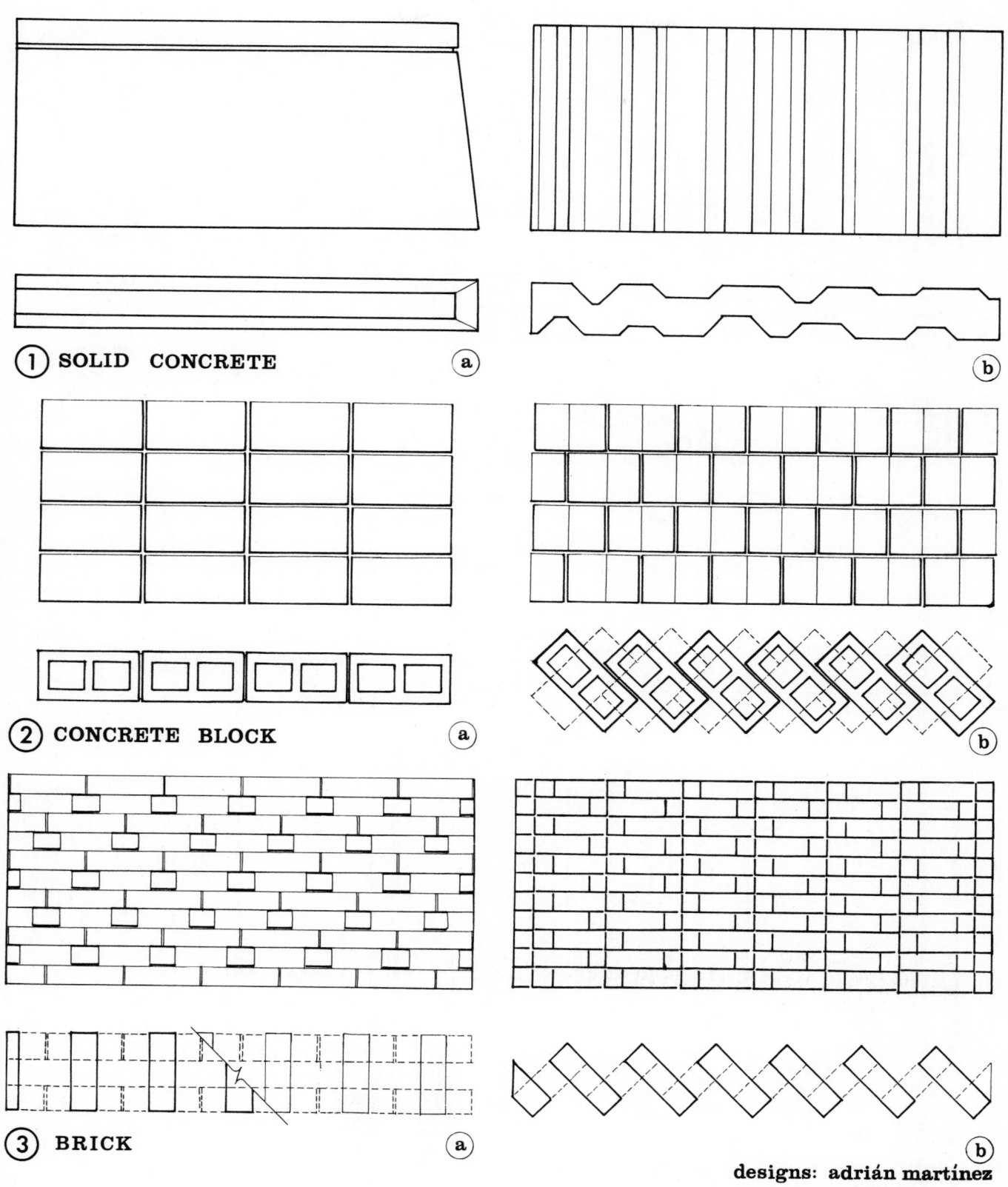

① SOLID CONCRETE ⓐ   ⓑ

② CONCRETE BLOCK ⓐ   ⓑ

③ BRICK ⓐ   ⓑ

designs: adrián martínez

Patio & Garden Walls

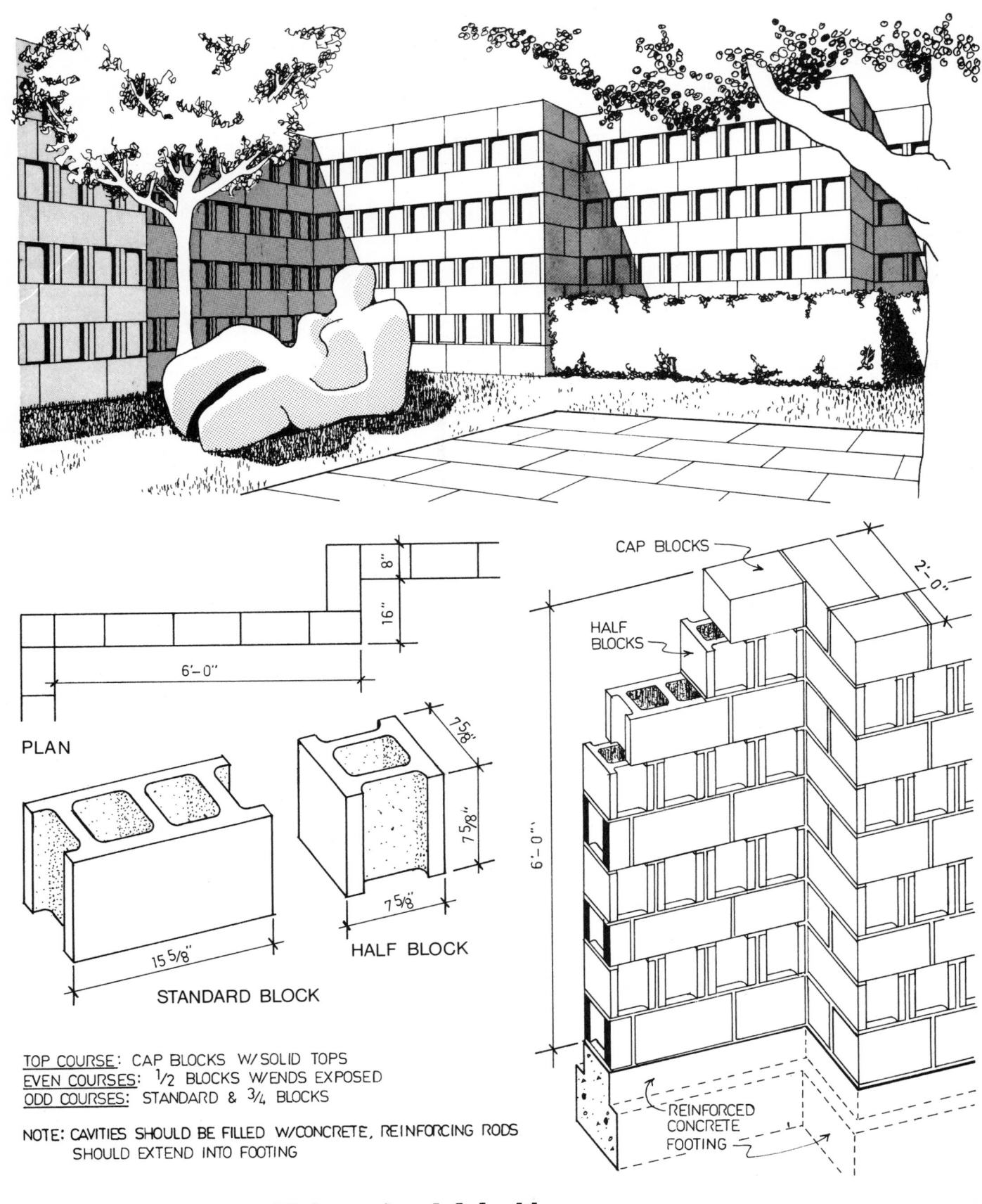

PLAN

8"

16"

6'-0"

7 5/8"

7 5/8"

7 5/8"

15 5/8"

STANDARD BLOCK

HALF BLOCK

CAP BLOCKS

HALF BLOCKS

2'-0"

6'-0"

REINFORCED CONCRETE FOOTING

<u>TOP COURSE</u>: CAP BLOCKS W/SOLID TOPS
<u>EVEN COURSES</u>: 1/2 BLOCKS W/ENDS EXPOSED
<u>ODD COURSES</u>: STANDARD & 3/4 BLOCKS

NOTE: CAVITIES SHOULD BE FILLED W/CONCRETE, REINFORCING RODS
SHOULD EXTEND INTO FOOTING

Concrete Block Wall

design/drawing : Adrian Martinez

to large property, but too heavy for small sites. The concrete-block wall (in the right design) fits almost any situation, as do decorative blocks. Stone walls are eminently handsome and look rustic; they are fine for most but not all properties.

Block

The easiest walls to build are those made of concrete or decorative blocks. This is a comparatively rapid procedure, and the average handy person can do it. Block is also the most exciting and versatile building material. Some blocks have a green or tan color cast into them. You can paint blocks with rubber-based masonry paints or keep them their natural gray color by waterproofing them with a silicone liquid. Patterned and textured

Concrete walls of two designs provide beauty and privacy for the patio setting. (Photograph courtesy National Concrete Masonry Assoc.)

An unusual side of concrete for a city garden wall; it is highly decorative and allows air and light through into the garden. (Photograph courtesy National Concrete Masonry Assoc.)

blocks can be stacked, staggered, running bond, or on edge. For walls, use the lightweight blocks because they provide better insulation, more effectively deaden sound, and are easy to lift. The most common size is 16 inches long, 8 inches high, and 8 inches wide. Foot-square and 4-inch blocks are on the market, and blocks are also available in solid brick shapes. Other shapes include half, corner, double-corner, bullnose, and channel.

For a textured wall, use textured split block and slump block. The split form has a rough face; slump block has sags or slumps, lending itself to interesting dimensional effects. You can also use two types of blocks in one wall for an interesting pattern; for example, alternate a row of 8-inch blocks with 4-inch ones.

Decorative block (grille) is also very popular because each unit has a frame surrounding a grille, fretwork, or contoured design. Depending upon the pattern, the decorative screen-block wall can be very open or very closed. The design is invariably pleasing compared with a solid wall and provides air circulation and a modicum of privacy. The blocks are lightweight; inexpensive; easy to clean by hosing; impervious to fire, termites, or rust; and can be laid by the average person with little difficulty. The handsome patterns range from Mediterranean motifs to Moorish designs.

Laying the Block Wall

A block wall needs substantial footing (foundation) of concrete; the foundation can be 18 or 24 inches (check local frost lines). Pour the foundation in forms; when it is completely dry, start the wall work. Use a mortar mix or 2 shovelsful of masonry cement to about 5 shovelsful of mortar and sand. (More information about mortar and the tools for working with it is in the "Brick Wall" section.) Use just enough water to make the mix plastic enough so that it clings to the trowel and block without running or squeezing down when you lay the block. As you work you will learn the right consistency for the mortar.

Lay out the blocks on the foundation without mortar, and shift them around until they fit; the idea is to save you from having to cut blocks. Keep spaces between the blocks no wider than ½-inch, no narrower than ¼-inch. Clean the foundation and wet it down. Now mix mortar, or use a plastic cement or a premixed mortar (you add only water). Now trowel on a 2-inch bed of mortar, and seat the first block. Tap it into place with the trowel handle. Repeat the process, putting mortar on the inside end of each succeeding block.

For a sturdier wall, lay the block on a footing that is still in a plastic state (consistency of mortar). The first course of blocks is then solidly attached to the foundation. When the consistency of the concrete foundation becomes like mortar, position the blocks on the ground along the foundation so you have enough blocks and little cutting. Then seat the block about 2 inches deep into the mortar. You want the foundation concrete still to be pliable so you can level blocks. Start at the corner with a level and square-shaped corner block, and trowel mortar in strips on the outside edges of the first course. Do one block at a time and tap it into position. Always be sure it is level and flush with the block underneath. Keep courses even with a mason's line. Put down just enough mortar for one block at a time.

There are different ways to treat the mortared joints. A tooled joint is sort of a half-round cove or squeezed joint, where the mortar is allowed to show between the joints. A raked joint produces a sharp relief; this is done by cleaning the mortar from the joint to a depth of ½-inch or less.

If you place a wall where there is a drainage problem, you will have to install drain tiles along the outer edge. Slope the wall about 1 inch for each 15 feet. Be sure to cover the joints with roofing paper and backfill with gravel.

For tall walls (over 5 feet), set reinforcing rods vertically and solidly into the concrete foundation. Space them according to local building codes. Lay the first course of the wall in wet concrete, and then drive the rods through the cores. The holes for the rods must match the holes in the blocks, so alignment is vital.

A screen-block wall (one with designs) is laid on a foundation, and then the block is installed with epoxy mortars; these mortars are extremely strong, and thus generally no reinforcing rods are necessary. Cover the tops and side of the blocks with epoxy (from a caulking gun), and set the blocks in place. All materials are sold at local building-supply houses.

Brick Wall

Brick is a natural material that harmonizes with most garden situations, whether in a straight, L-shaped, or serpentine pattern. Brick offers a multitude of patterns: thin, thick, colored, rectangular.

The average brick wall is 8 or more inches thick (2 bricks wide) and requires steel reinforcing rods in mortar joints at frequent intervals.

Very large walls have to be reinforced about every 12 feet with a brick pier or pilaster; this type of construction requires the help of a professional mason. You can dictate the pattern to suit your tastes, but the actual building of the wall (unless you are very handy with tools) generally must be farmed out. However, for those who want to try constructing their own brick wall, read on.

If you want to try to build your own brick wall, you will need a pointed trowel for buttering the mortar, a broad-bladed cold chisel, a hammer, a level, and a carpenter's square.

Common brick must be damp to be laid; to hold the mortar you need a mortar board, which is a piece of wood, like the top of an orange crate. Scoop the mortar (enough for only a few bricks) from the board with the trowel, and spread it over the top course of bricks. Put each brick in place, trim away the mortar to butter the end of the next brick, and continue until more mortar is needed. Set bricks in perfect alignment; *gently* tap them into place. Build the ends or corners first in steps because this makes it easier to set the next bricks in line. Be sure to use a strong nylon guideline when laying the bricks. Anchor the ends of the line into mortar joints. Before the mortar sets, trim away loose bits and smooth off all joints.

Mortar for bricklaying is a mixture of cement, fine sand, and water, with some lime added for plasticity: 2 parts portland cement, 1 part fireclay or lime, and 9 parts garden sand. Supplies are sold at hardware and lumber stores.

Stone and Poured Concrete

Stone walls are like a jigsaw puzzle in that each piece must fit perfectly. A skilled stoneworker can create a wall that looks as if each stone was precut before being assembled. As an amateur you will have to be content with less than perfection because stone walls are difficult to build (but not impossible).

Round stones are used to make a wall in this area; the effect is natural and appealing in a garden. (Photograph by Matthew Barr)

The beauty of stone as a wall cannot be ignored; it is natural and very suitable for gardens. (Photograph by Matthew Barr)

The beauty of stone walls is their natural look and their countrified character. And there are many beautiful stones to use: Stratified rock such as limestone, shale, and sandstone is very pleasing, and granite and basalt rock are equally handsome.

Stone walls can be made of either uncut stones, known as rubble, or with cut stones, known as ashlars. Unstratified stones are difficult to cut and thus are generally laid in rubble form. I think the rubble wall is more difficult to perfect than the ashlar type because with rubble you have to fit and juggle, whereas ashlars are relatively simple to put in place.

When you are working with stone be sure of your design from the start; the wall should appear natural, just as you would see the stones on the ground, never upended or in an awkward position. You will have to work as you go along with the design, so an eye for esthetics is necessary. There is no set pattern for a stone wall; it depends upon the stones used and your personal judgment. Like most walls, stone walls require a good foundation of concrete to avoid cracking and splitting.

Start the actual stone structure a little below the surface of the ground and lay it directly with mortar on a good concrete foundation.

If you decide to tackle your own stone wall (and let me warn you, it is not easy), follow these hints:

1. Keep plenty of stones ready. It is much easier to fit a stone in place when you have a choice rather than to force one in place.

2. Use plenty of mortar to fill in all joints. Where there are spaces, fill in with chunks of stone and mortar over them.

3. String guidelines and keep the face of the structure flush.

A poured concrete wall can be almost any shape, is extremely strong, and its surface can be textured in several finishes, including smooth or embossed. But cast concrete is hardly a job for the do-it-yourselfer. Precise forms are necessary, and careful pouring of concrete is essential to create a handsome wall. This particular kind of wall building is best left for professionals.

Stone Retaining Walls

Retaining walls do more than hold a hill; they can and should be decorative. A dry stone wall installation with plants in earth "pockets" is quite effective in the garden, as are cascading plants covering the sharp edges of masonry or wooden retaining walls.

An easy dry wall can be installed by placing stones against a slope; between the stones leave earth pockets. The stones should pitch the wall back toward the thrust of the slope. Dry stone walls are not difficult to build. Keep dry walls to a maximum of 4 feet; higher walls will tumble with time if there are severe rains.

A retaining wall of over 4 feet is not easy to construct, so it is best to seek professional help. Remember that if the wall is not properly engineered and built, it might collapse after the first few rainstorms.

Any retaining wall should have ample provision for water drainage. Soil absorbs much water during a rainy season; it flows downhill below the surface. Where the water hits the wall it accumulates and collects, building up pressure, and it may burst through the wall.

The simplest way of getting rid of excess water is to install weep holes in the wall. Tile and gravel backfill also prevent a wall from becoming undermined. If you use weep holes, construct a special gutter to carry off water so it does not ruin the patio or lawn. Standard drain tiles or rounded concrete gutters can be used. All gutters should be wide enough to fit a shovel so you can remove leaves and twigs.

OTHER RETAINING WALLS

A masonry retaining wall can be brick, concrete block, or cast concrete. It is better to have a series of low walls than one high one that is likely to lean or break under pressure. Concrete foundations and reinforcing rods are necessary for any masonry wall.

Brick retaining walls are lovely but difficult to build, and even when securely mortared they do not have the holding power of a concrete wall. Reinforcing rods are necessary in brick, as are weep holes, so this is a job best left to the professional.

MIXING CONCRETE

Concrete is a versatile plastic material of sand, fine aggregate (stones), coarse aggregate (larger stones), portland cement, and water. Fine aggregate is stone less than ¼-inch in diameter; coarse aggregate is well-ground gravel or crushed rock. Portland cement is sold in 1-cubic-foot sacks. You can buy these ingredients and make your own concrete, buy concrete already mixed and delivered to your site, or buy dry mix concrete (sold in sacks) and add water. The amount of water used per sack of cement determines the strength of concrete. Usually, less water used per sack of cement gives a better concrete.

For foundation work and solid walls of concrete, your

best bet is to buy ready mix delivered to the site. For laying stone, brick, or block, you will have to mix your own concrete or buy it in sacks.

To estimate the amount of concrete you will need for a job, measure the length and breadth of the wall in feet and the thickness in a fraction of a foot. Multiply the three figures to determine just how many cubic feet of concrete you need. For example, if a foundation is 3 feet by 20 feet with a 4-inch thickness, you need about 20 cubic feet, or about 4/5 cubic yards of concrete.

To mix concrete by hand you can use a wheelbarrow, or rent a power or hand-operated concrete mixer.

Generally, for wall footings and foundations, you should use 6 gallons of water for each sack of cement. To mix the concrete, put 2 shovelsful of sand into the wheelbarrow and add 1 shovelful of cement. Mix thoroughly, add 3 shovelsful of gravel, and mix again. Add water from a garden hose, a little at a time, mixing as you go. Continue mixing all ingredients until they are well combined and of the desired stiffness. If you have added too much water, add some more sand, gravel, and cement. If the mixture is too thick, add more water. When using a hand or power mixer, follow the same procedure.

PART III

GROWING

We have discussed the planning of your city garden and making the necessary fences, walls, and planters. Now it is time to look at the many ways of cultivating plants so they grow and prosper. In the following sections we look at soils and watering, mulches and insect prevention, and other odds and ends that make a garden glow and grow.

Included are lists of hundreds of plants and how to use them—trees, shrubs, perennials, annuals, vines, bulbs—all the attractive things that make a garden. The choice is vast, so dig in and get your garden growing and enjoy it day after day for years to come.

Rooftop hideaway resplendent with flowers in San Francisco, California.

7
Plant Culture

The amount of work necessary to maintain your city garden depends upon the garden's size and design. A simple plan—a few trees and shrubs—requires only minimal care. If your garden is somewhat elaborate, you will need more time and energy. However, the rewards are many.

In the country you can do some experimenting with plants, putting them here and there and moving them if they do not succeed in a particular spot. But in the city, proper selection of plant material and where it goes is necessary because the urban gardener does not have the time to test or the money to spend on additional soil.

No matter what the size of your garden or what you are growing, good soil is essential. Containers like planters and raised beds are other prime requirements for successful city gardens. If you start right, later care will be reduced. And, finally, a careful selection of plants that can tolerate some neglect if necessary and still survive is wisest. Feeding and watering are important too, along with pruning and transplanting, fertilizing, keeping insects out of the garden, sun orientation, and watering.

SOIL FOR GROUND-LEVEL GARDENS

To support plant life adequately, soil should be fertile and of the proper consistency. It must be porous in texture so water and air can enter, and it must be rich in nutrients so plants can grow.

Natural soil in city yards is rarely adequate to support plant life. Usually, it has not been worked for years and is drained of nutrients. But too often the comment that nothing will grow in city soil is completely wrong; if the soil is good, plants will grow.

In new properties conditions may be even worse. Builders often strip the essential topsoil from the site, and the ground is compacted by heavy machinery. Little if anything will grow in a subsoil base.

No matter what the condition of the soil in the city ground-level site, there will be evidence of a distinctly darker upper layer that was once rich and friable. This is the topsoil. Under this is the subsoil; this layer of earth must be reworked before you can do anything else. Dig down about 12 inches and work the soil with a spade and hoe until it is friable. Now condition the soil. Add humus, maintaining the right proportions if you want good plant growth. Humus—animal manure, compost, leafmold—is decayed organic matter, that is, rotted, once-living organisms. Humus gives soil its body and serves as food for plants and microorganisms, so it must be replaced.

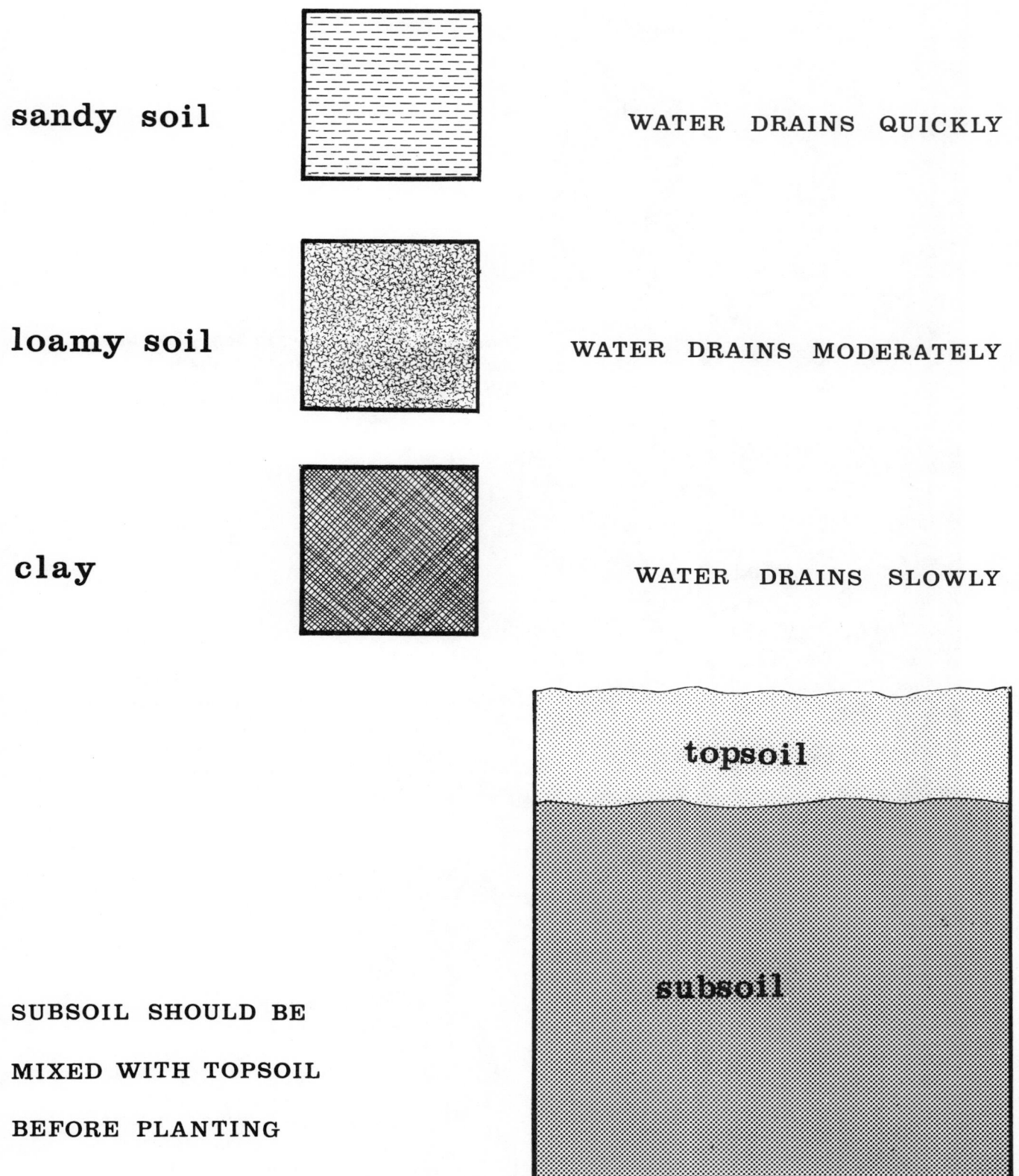

sandy soil

WATER DRAINS QUICKLY

loamy soil

WATER DRAINS MODERATELY

clay

WATER DRAINS SLOWLY

topsoil

subsoil

SUBSOIL SHOULD BE

MIXED WITH TOPSOIL

BEFORE PLANTING

Soil Structure Chart

Note the fresh soil used to help plant this tree. Old soil would hinder growth. (USDA photograph)

It is essential to spade old soil; mix it up and crumble it and add fresh soil to get a garden going well. (USDA photograph)

Sample of soil: clay (left), sandy (center), and good tilth (right). Note that good soil is granular and porous. (USDA photograph)

You must decide yourself how much humus to add, based upon what plants you want to grow and the amount of humus now present in the soil. I have found a mixture of about 1 inch of compost to about 6 inches of soil very satisfactory.

You must also use fertilizers in the soil because they contain nitrogen, phosphorus, and potassium (potash), all essential to healthy plant growth. (We discuss fertilizers later in this chapter.)

A good soil lets moisture pass quickly through its pores (which carry away excess water) to reach a plant's roots; there it is stored for future use. Soil must never be allowed to become waterlogged; if it does, air will not circulate freely, and the plant's growth will be affected. Good drainage of soil is absolutely necessary; otherwise, the roots of plants get shallow and die because they cannot reach down for the stored water. Poor drainage is common to most soils and is usually caused by a layer of hard earth.

Soil must be porous so plant roots can get oxygen. The soil should be crumbly and of an open texture for perfect air and water circulation. (Air enters with the water that drains through the soil.) You can improve the soil's physical structure by turning it, keeping it porous, and using composts and mulches year-round. Remember that porosity is the key to good soil.

Buy new soil by the truckload from building-supply yards or garden centers, generally in a 6- or 8-cubic-foot load. Soil is available in various grades; the best (the most expensive) is screened and already has fertilizer. Lower-grade soils are not screened and cost a little less, and there are some soils (which are actually "fills" and nothing more than subsoils) that can be purchased for as little as $2.85 per yard. Buy the best soil you can possibly afford because it will pay off in a bountiful harvest of flowers rather than a scanty yield. Soil delivered in trucks is dumped at your property; you must do the hauling and spreading, which is not as easy as it sounds.

Soil is available by the bushel from local nurseries. This is excellent all-purpose soil ready for the garden and can be used if you do not need too much. Soils packaged in 50- and 100-pound bags are also satisfactory but generally more expensive than those bought by the truckload.

pH Scale

The pH scale measures the acidity or alkalinity of soil. Soil with a pH of 7 is neutral; below 7 the soil is acid, and above 7 it is alkaline. You should know the pH of your soil so that you can get the maximum use from all fertilizers supplied to it. To determine the pH, have it tested by state agricultural authorities or do your own test, using one of the commercial kits.

Most trees and shrubs prefer a more or less neutral soil (between 6 and 7), although there are a few exceptions. In alkaline soils, potash becomes less effective and eventually is locked in. In very acid soils, the aluminum becomes so active that it is toxic to plants. Acidity in soil controls many functions: It determines the availability of the food in the soil, governs which bacteria will thrive in it, and somewhat affects the rate at which roots can take up moisture and leaves manufacture food.

To lower the pH of soil (increase the acidity), apply ground sulfur: 1 pound per 100 square feet. This lowers the pH of loam soil about one point. Spread the sulfur on top of the soil and then apply water.

To raise (sweeten) the pH of soil, add ground limestone: 10 pounds per 150 square feet. Scatter it on the soil, or mix it well with the top few inches of soil and water. Add ground limestone or hydrated lime in several applications at six- or eight-week intervals rather than using a lot at one time.

SOIL CONDITIONERS

Peat moss is a soil conditioner, not a fertilizer. It holds moisture like a sponge and is useful when added to claylike soil because it aerates it and allows oxygen to reach plant roots. In large quantities it has a slightly acid tendency. Add one-third quantity of peat moss to one-third new soil for your ground-level site; dig and fork it into the soil.

Leafmold is high in fertilizer value and an excellent soil conditioner; it furnishes nutrients in their most natural form. You can collect leafmold from woods, or buy it in bales from nurseries. It lightens any heavy soil and can be used in equal parts with topsoil.

Compost is a real tonic for plants. This decayed vegetable matter—grass cuttings, vegetable tops, rakings—is what good soil is made of. It is enriched with manure and fertilizers and is an essential soil additive.

SOIL FOR CONTAINERS

Small bags of packaged soil are fine for a few small containers, but it takes a lot of packaged soil to fill just a 30-inch square box. Packaged soil is sold under many trade names, in different mixes. It is difficult to know just what kind of soil you are getting when you buy packaged soil. As of this writing soil packagers still are not required to list the ingredients on the sack, so often you are buying 20 percent filler and 80 percent soil. Also, there are soil-conditioning mixtures that are frequently mistaken for complete soil mixes. So, shop carefully when buying packaged soil, and remember that packaged soil costs more than bulk soil.

Finally, in some cases you will have to add humus and seasoned manure to packaged soil. Small sacks of humus are expensive. Just how much you add depends upon the size of the container, but for a box, say, 24 × 24 inches, you will need 1 part humus to 5 parts soil and 1 small package of manure.

If at all possible buy bulk soil, which is screened and has the necessary humus and added nutrients. Feel the soil and smell it: it should be crumbly to the touch and smell woodsy. Remember that in a confined container plants are dependent upon the soil you give them; they cannot reach out with their roots for other soil as ground plants do.

If you are going to plant several large boxes, buy soil by the truckload. Six cubic yards, the standard delivery, is enough for several boxes. When you order bulk soil, ask for screened topsoil; there are various grades and it pays to get the best. The screened soil has no foreign matter such as stones or debris and is enriched with humus. Bulk soil is delivered tailgate to your site; that is, it is dumped at a specific spot. Then you must haul the soil to the containers. Always have the soil dropped at the most convenient place so long-distance hauling is not involved. A 6-cubic-yard truck of soil occupies a space of about 5 × 5 feet. Move it with a shovel and wheelbarrow.

WATERING PLANTS IN THE GROUND

During the summer months it is difficult to water plants too much because there are few plants that really enjoy being dry. Even cacti and some succulents that can withstand drought if necessary still need good moisture to thrive. Most garden plants need a steady supply of moisture in the ground; without it they quickly succumb.

Because city plants are not growing in optimum conditions, watering is quite important. In cities, plants must exist between walls and fences, walks and concrete, and often in shallow soil; moisture that would descend in the form of dew in the country is absorbed in the atmosphere before it reaches city ground. Reflected heat from concrete buildings further intensifies arid conditions.

When to water depends upon variable factors, but just how much to water is easy to decide: water thoroughly and deeply. It takes water almost one hour to penetrate about 40 inches of soil. Thus, if you are watering for ten minutes, hardly any of the plant roots are getting moisture. If you keep only the top of the soil wet with scanty waterings, roots have to reach up instead of down; the result is a shallow-rooted plant that rarely fares well. To ensure a healthy plant, roots must work deeply into the soil to seek out moisture.

Although it is important to water thoroughly and deeply, you do not want to cause an overwatered condition—a flooding of the soil—or the supply of oxygen to the roots is blocked and plants start to drown. Allow enough time between waterings for complete moisture absorption by soil and plants. This is the tricky part of watering: not how much, but how much when. This

When watering newly planted plants, water thoroughly; it takes a great amount of moisture to get plants growing. (Photograph by author)

depends upon such variables as wind, temperature, light intensity, soil, and rainfall.

Watering is important for all plants, but it is vital to newly transplanted ones and seedlings, which really need copious amounts of water to get them growing. If you let them become dry for even a day, you may harm the plants seriously, particularly in hot weather. After the first few critical weeks, you can develop a regular watering schedule.

Air pollution, soot, oil, and dust clog plant leaves. Plants breathe through their minute pores, so you must wash and hose the foliage of city plants. In fact, many plants that do not ordinarily succeed in city gardens can be given longer life with frequent washings. Not only does washing keep plants healthy, but it keeps them looking better. A strong but fine mist from the hose early in the morning a few times a week does wonders for city plants.

Washing not only applies to perennials and deciduous plants but to conifers and evergreens. In spring, these plants really need a good washing to rid them of city soot accumulations. Use a mild soap-and-water solution and take a soft brush (or even a sponge) to the leaves. Rinse plants thoroughly so they are shiny clean.

DEPTH	COARSE SAND	SANDY LOAM	CLAY w. LOAM
0			
6"			
12"	15 MINUTES	30 MINUTES	60 MINUTES
18"			
24"		60 MINUTES	
30"	40 MINUTES		
36"			
42"			
48"	60 MINUTES		

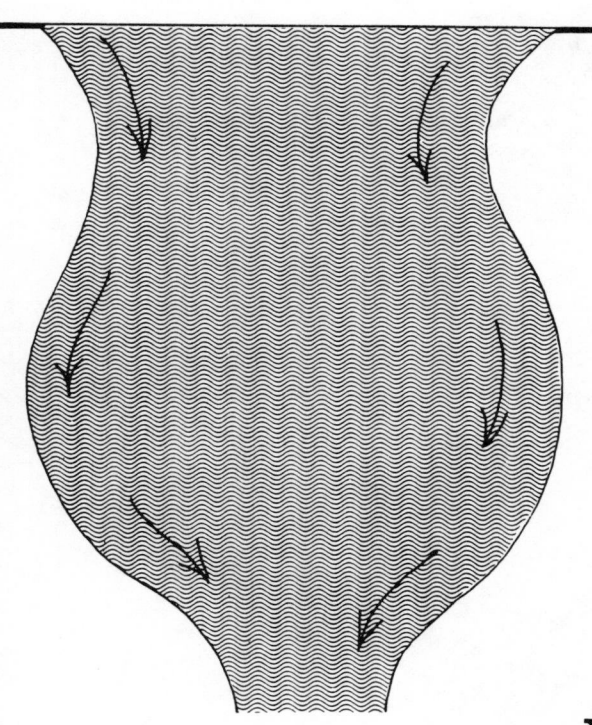

WATER MOVES LATERALLY
DOES NOT FAN OUT TO ANY DEGREE

Water Absorption Chart

DRIP WATERING SYSTEMS

The new drip watering systems have been a boon to home gardeners in both city and country areas. This watering technique releases small amounts of water to plants at frequent intervals. Drip watering saves water, of course, and saves you time (you can water an entire

Drip watering systems conserve water and help put moisture at roots of plants where it is needed. Here the outlet is shown. (Drip Mist System Irrigation Co.)

Soaker hose watering systems also conserve some water and are now being used. Here water oozes from hose to provide moisture for plants. (Photograph by Michael Jay)

Close-up of drip watering system unit.

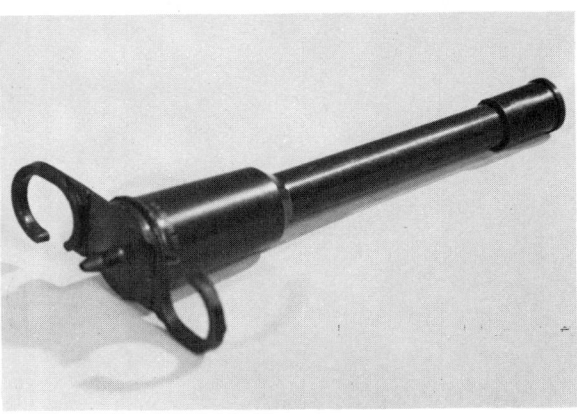

garden in about ten minutes). More important, by putting water where it is needed (at plant roots), your plants grow faster and more uniformly than with conventional sprinkler watering.

In drip irrigation, water is given to plant roots through tiny emitters located at selected points along water delivery lines. There are also misting and sprinkler emitters. The basic drip system is a network of flexible plastic pipes and tubes of graduated sizes. A large pipe (usually ½-inch in diameter) brings the water to the site; a series of smaller main lines connects to the large pipe. The lateral lines are connected parallel to the plants on or just below the surface of the ground. The water is discharged from the lateral lines through the emitters, which allow a slow trickle of water to moisten the immediate root zone.

The main concern of the average gardener when using drip watering is to be sure not to overload the setup—too many emitters in a given system. If the lines have too many emitters the steady flow of water is interrupted.

The water is filtered at the starting point so it does not clog emitters. Most drip systems have a filter unit that removes particles that might clog the working of the hoses. Pressure regulators or hoses (valves) to control the flow of water are also used. Systems can be manual or automatic. The equipment for drip systems comes in a variety of shapes, sizes, and costs.

You can install your own drip watering setup or have someone do it for you. Almost any company offering sprinkler systems also installs the new watering devices. Most hardware stores carry component parts for drip units or you can buy kits with all the necessary parts. Costs are modest and much less than, say, for a standard-type sprinkling system.

There are endless advantages to the drip way of watering—it uses less water and puts the water where you want it; thus plants grow bigger and better. For more information on drip watering systems, see my book *Drip System Watering,* published by W. W. Norton.

WATERING PLANTS IN CONTAINERS

Watering plants in containers is vastly different from watering those in the ground. If properly potted and with sufficient drainage, plants in containers can take a great deal of water, but not so much that the soil becomes soggy. When you water a garden in the ground, excess water drains through the soil, so it rarely creates a stagnant soil. But in containers too much water can be a problem because there is not an unlimited supply of soil for it to drain through.

When you water makes a difference. On bright sunny days water copiously, but if there is a stretch of cloudy days, water sparingly. When the sun is not shining, plants have a difficult time assimilating foods; some plants must have a drying-out time before they can be watered again.

It is better to water in the morning than at night because at night too much moisture and humidity can cause fungus disease to start. Be sure to water early so that plants have a chance to dry out before evening comes. Be forewarned that cold water can shock plants; plants like tepid water best.

How do you water really large containers? Be prepared to wield a hose, but do it thoroughly—no scanty sprinklings, just a good steady stream of water. It takes at least forty minutes for water to penetrate 24 to 30 inches, which is the depth of most large containers. Smaller containers can be watered in five minutes. Sparse watering creates air pockets in the soil, resulting in a plant that is less robust than a properly watered plant.

If you are growing trees and shrubs in large containers, drip or trickle watering is a good idea. Attach a bubbler or other irrigation device to a hose, and set the bubbler on the soil in the container. Water will be released slowly over a long period of time, furnishing sufficiently even moisture throughout the soil.

FERTILIZERS FOR PLANTS IN THE GROUND

Because the nutrients in soils are absorbed rapidly by plants, you must use fertilizers. Annuals and other flowering plants especially need feeding to make them yield a harvest of blooms. From early June to September, fertilize new plants every two weeks. Use fertilizers more frequently but in smaller quantities on shrubs and woody plants; infrequent feeding with large doses of fertilizers can injure plants. Do not feed shrubs and woody plants after August or you will encourage soft growth, which is susceptible to cold weather.

The three most important elements necessary for plant growth are nitrogen, phosphorus, and potash. These are most likely to be deficient in cultivated soils.

Nitrogen stimulates vegetative development and is necessary for healthy stem and leaf growth. Phosphorus is needed in all phases of plant growth, and potash promotes the general vigor of a plant by making it resistant to certain diseases. It also has a balancing influence on other plant nutrients. Various trace elements, such as copper, iron, sulfur, zinc, and manganese, are also important.

To feed shrubs, vines, flowers, and vegetables, spread fertilizer on the ground around the plant and then water thoroughly to dissolve the fertilizer.

Today there are many plant foods, but basically most have nitrogen, phosphorus, potash, and some trace elements. Contents are on the package or the bottle, marked in numbers. The first numeral is the percentage of nitrogen; the second, of phosphorus, and the third, of potash.

Fertilizers are offered in the following five forms:

1. *Powdered*   Good, but blows away on a windy day.
2. *Concentrated liquids*   Used for all fertilizers.
3. *Concentrated powders*   Diluted in water and applied to foliage or roots.
4. *Concentrated tablets*   Used mainly for houseplants.
5. *Pelleted or granular*   Most popular; easy to spread. Add water after spreading.

In addition to these synthetic fertilizers, there are nitrogen materials that help plants grow. These include organic matter such as animal and vegetable tankage, manures, and cottonseed and other meals and ureaform compounds, which are synthetic materials made by a chemical union of urea and formaldehyde. Do not confuse urea (quickly available nitrogen) with ureaform.

There are also fertilizers for specific plants. Because there are so many plant foods, know which ones will do what for your garden. For flower beds and plant blooms, select a food with a high phosphorous content, like 12-12-12. If you need something to improve soil structure and release nutrients slowly, choose an organic food like blood meal or bone meal (available in packages at nurseries).

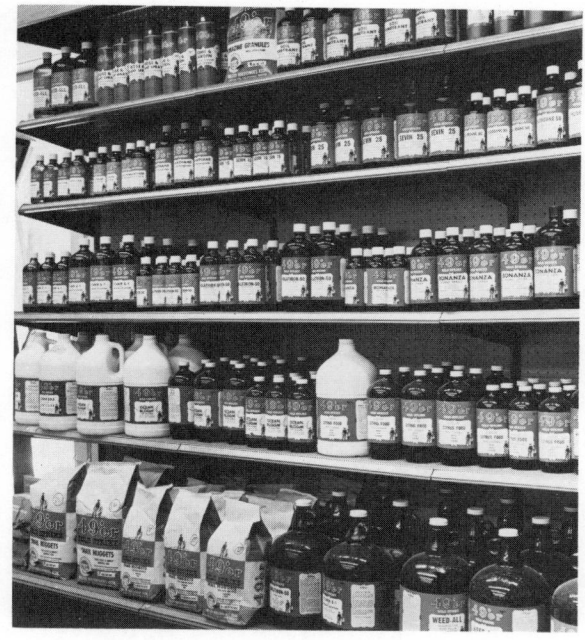

Dozens of fertilizers are available for gardens; next-to-bottom shelf shows some of the many used. (Photograph by Matthew Barr)

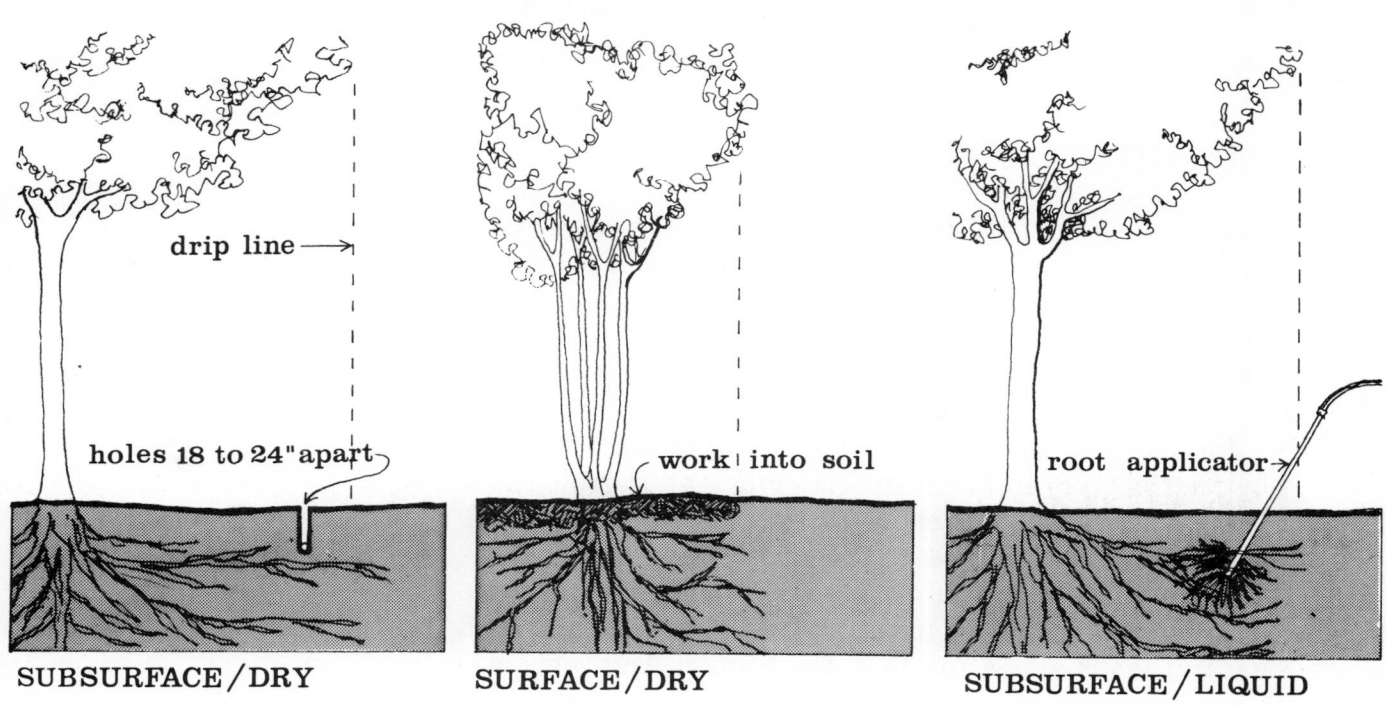

SUBSURFACE/DRY SURFACE/DRY SUBSURFACE/LIQUID

Fertilizing Trees

FEEDING CONTAINER PLANTS

Do not get mired in the muddy waters of endless plant food products. Basically all you need for most container plants is a good all-purpose plant food, such as 10-10-5. The easiest form of plant food to use is granular: just sprinkle the granules on top of the soil and then water in. Liquid plant foods are also easy because all you do is mix them with water and then apply the mixture to your plants. Tablets, stakes, and other sophisticated paraphernalia are available but not necessary. As a general rule it is not necessary to buy special plant foods for special plants, such as citrus, cactus, and so forth. They will only make the manufacturer richer, not your plants.

SUN ORIENTATION

It takes only a few days to determine whether your garden is sunny, half-shaded, or fully shaded. Indeed, just how much sunlight your property gets may be a deciding factor in purchasing a plant. Note where the sun is at a particular time of day; it is then easy to buy appropriate plants for your individual conditions.

Morning sun is preferable for such plants as vegetables, herbs, and annuals; in fact, you cannot grow these plants without sun. Afternoon sun is fine for perennials, shrubs, and certain trees. Although the sunny site is best, there are many, many plants for the shady garden. Actually, a garden of green plants has a certain lush beauty that is appealing to many people. And there are many trees and shrubs that will adjust, if not prosper, in the shady garden.

TRANSPLANTING

Generally, transplant shrubs, trees, and perennials in the early spring and late fall. When good weather is on the way, the plants have a far better chance of succeeding than they do in inclement weather. Remember to try to order trees, shrubs, and vines balled and burlaped or in cans. These plants have a better chance of surviving in the city than do bare-rooted dormant plants. In the country, bare-root stock, which is cheaper, is fine because conditions are better. However, in the city, bare-root plants are apt to be a headache and more expensive in the long run if you have to replace them.

When planting, be sure the hole is somewhat deeper and wider than the root ball; then refill the excavation with rich topsoil. A good rule of thumb when planting shrubs and trees is to leave 1 foot below the root ball and 1 foot more width on all sides. When the plant is in place, untie the burlap but do not remove it; let it decay naturally so it contributes a bit of humus to the soil. Firm the topsoil in place around the tree, but do not pack it down tightly. Eliminate air pockets in the soil; they prevent roots from making contact with soil and are detrimental to good drainage.

Prepare the ground so there is a saucer depression around the collar of the plant. Fill this depression with water, and keep it filled until the whole root ball is saturated. Remember to water the tree or shrub faithfully during its first weeks with you. This means slow, deep waterings. If necessary, punch some holes about 20 inches deep around the outside of the planted root ball so water can reach the deeper roots. A pole or crowbar is fine for making the holes.

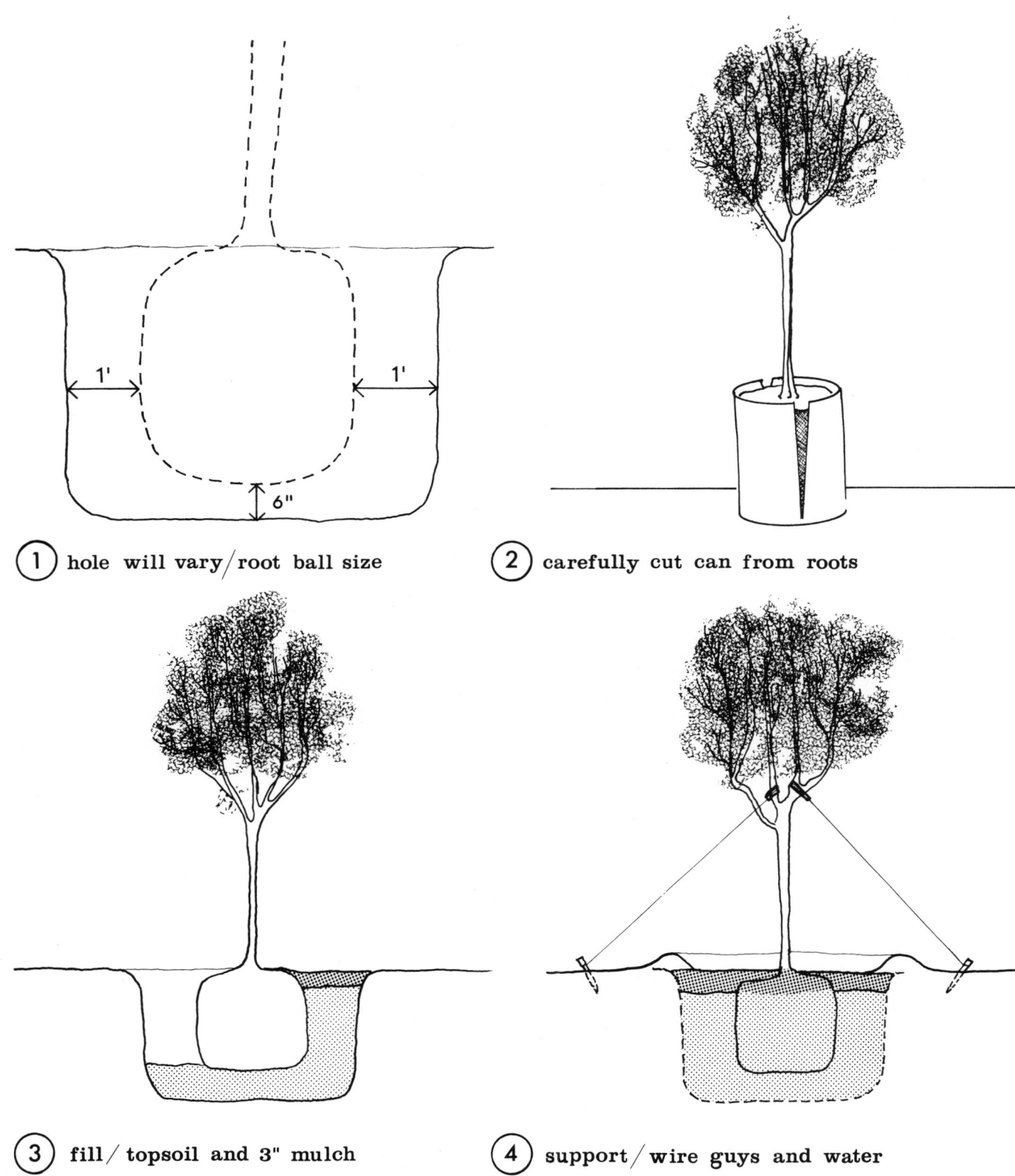

1. hole will vary / root ball size
2. carefully cut can from roots
3. fill / topsoil and 3" mulch
4. support / wire guys and water

How to Plant a Tree

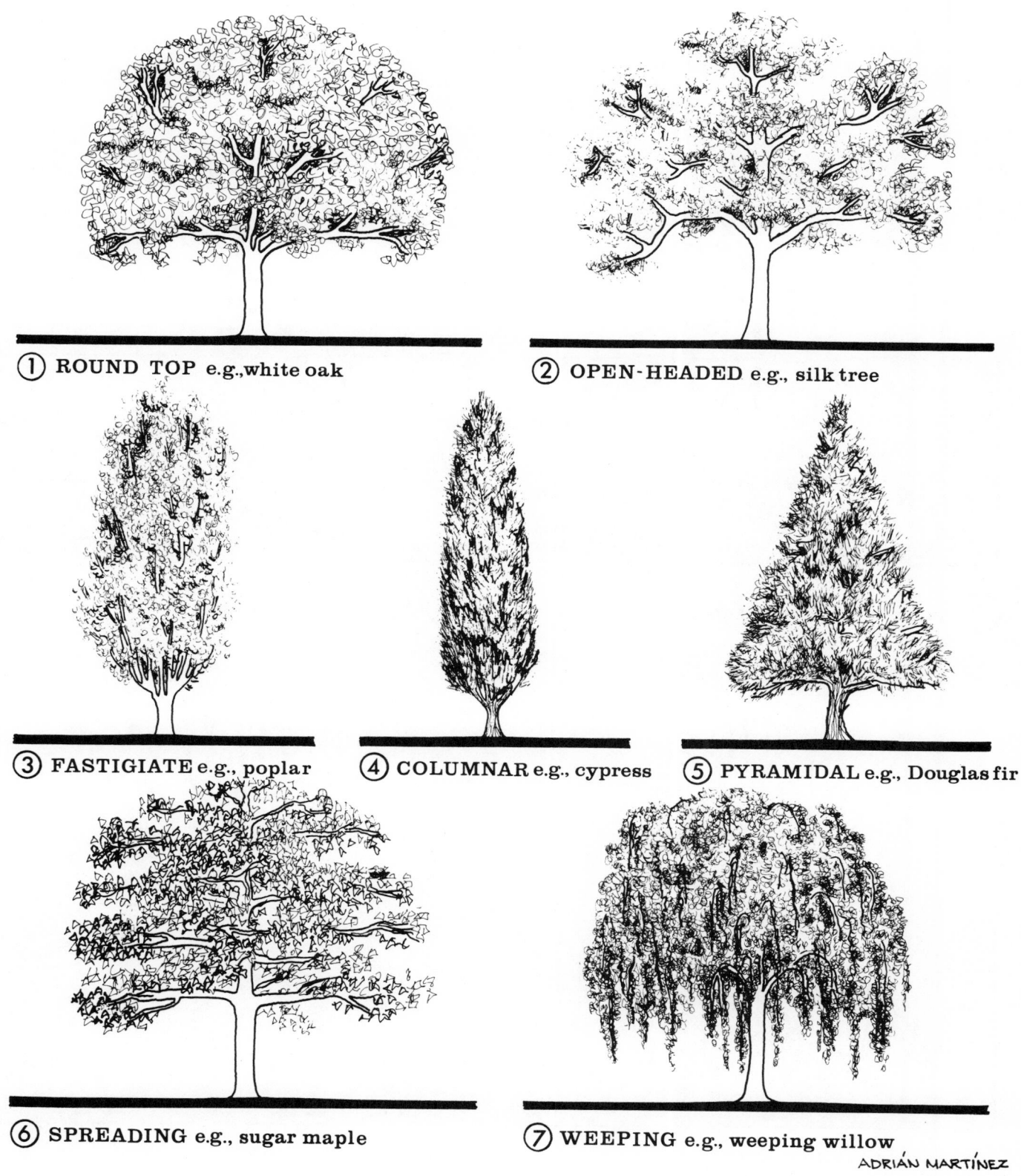

① **ROUND TOP** e.g., white oak

② **OPEN-HEADED** e.g., silk tree

③ **FASTIGIATE** e.g., poplar

④ **COLUMNAR** e.g., cypress

⑤ **PYRAMIDAL** e.g., Douglas fir

⑥ **SPREADING** e.g., sugar maple

⑦ **WEEPING** e.g., weeping willow

ADRIÁN MARTÍNEZ

Tree Forms

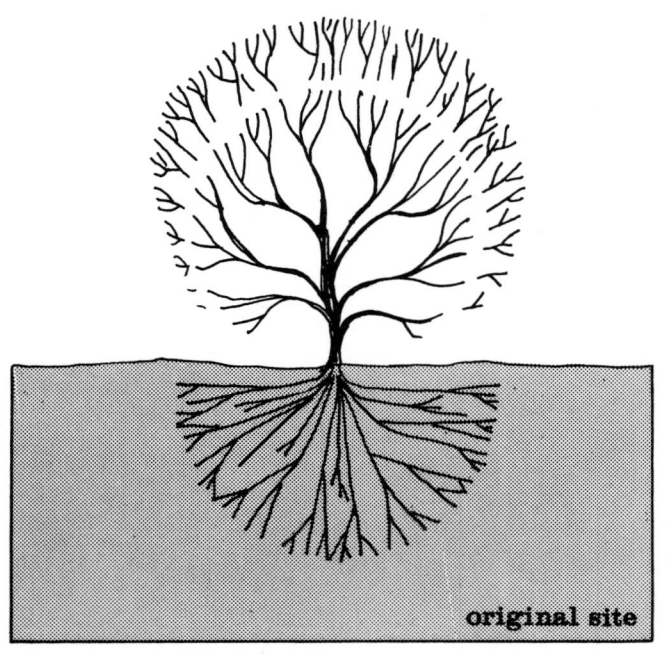

① prune ⅓ of the shrub

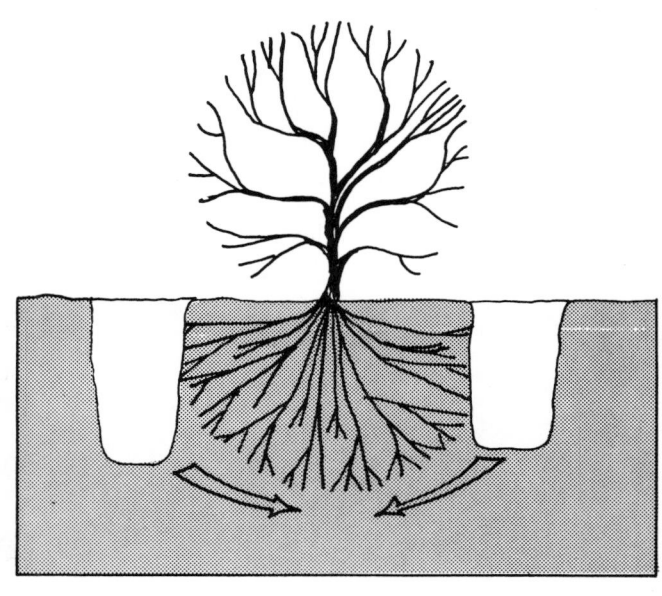

② dig trenches to remove root ball

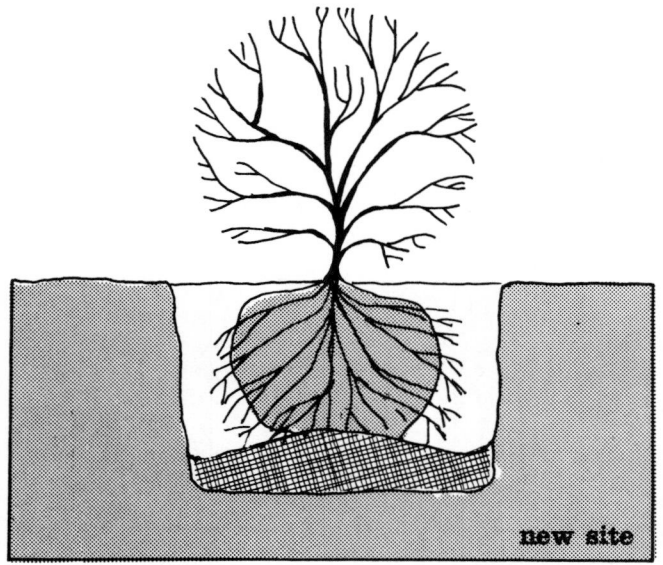

③ add 2" compost, mound soil; spread roots

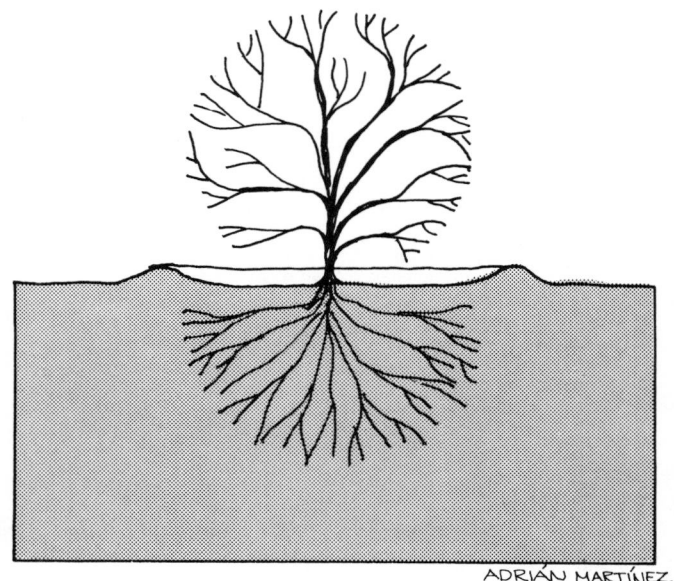

④ fill w. topsoil; ridge & water

Transplanting a Shrub

POTTING AND REPOTTING

The first potting of a new plant is easy. Put suitable drainage pieces like pot shards or large pieces of rubble into the container. Put in at least one inch of pea gravel and some charcoal granules to keep the soil sweet. Then fill the container with new soil to half the depth of the container. Now center the plant in this soil, filling in and around the plant with more new soil, tamping down to firm the soil. You want a firm but never tight potting; the idea is to eliminate any air pockets in the soil.

Do not plant most plant crowns too deeply in the soil or they may rot. The soil line for the crown should be at the same place it was when you got the tree or shrub from the nursery. With annuals or perennials there is no crown to worry about. Just put these plants into the soil, usually about 4 to 6 inches apart, and tamp the soil around the plant. Water all potted plants thoroughly.

Repotting a tubbed or boxed plant is quite a different matter, one requiring muscle and time. If you are dealing with a big box or tub, you must scoop out the soil with a shovel or trowel, remove the plant, trim away brown roots, and then proceed as you would when potting a new plant. This sounds easy but is not.

PRUNING

If the city garden is allowed to get out of control, it will look unkempt. Country gardens can to some extent be neglected and allowed to grow in a natural state, but this is not so with city gardens. Prune any tree with dead wood; if the tree is too large for you to handle, call in a tree service.

Pruning should not be neglected because it encourages bushiness instead of spindly growth; it cleans out winterkill branches, which are eyesores, and encourages flowers and sturdier wood. Although pruning is generally done in spring, remove broken and dead wood regardless of the season. However, do not prune early spring-flowering shrubs like forsythia until after they bloom.

Shrubs that bloom late should have annual pruning, according to species and variety, sometime in the spring. Rose pruning depends upon the type of rose being grown.

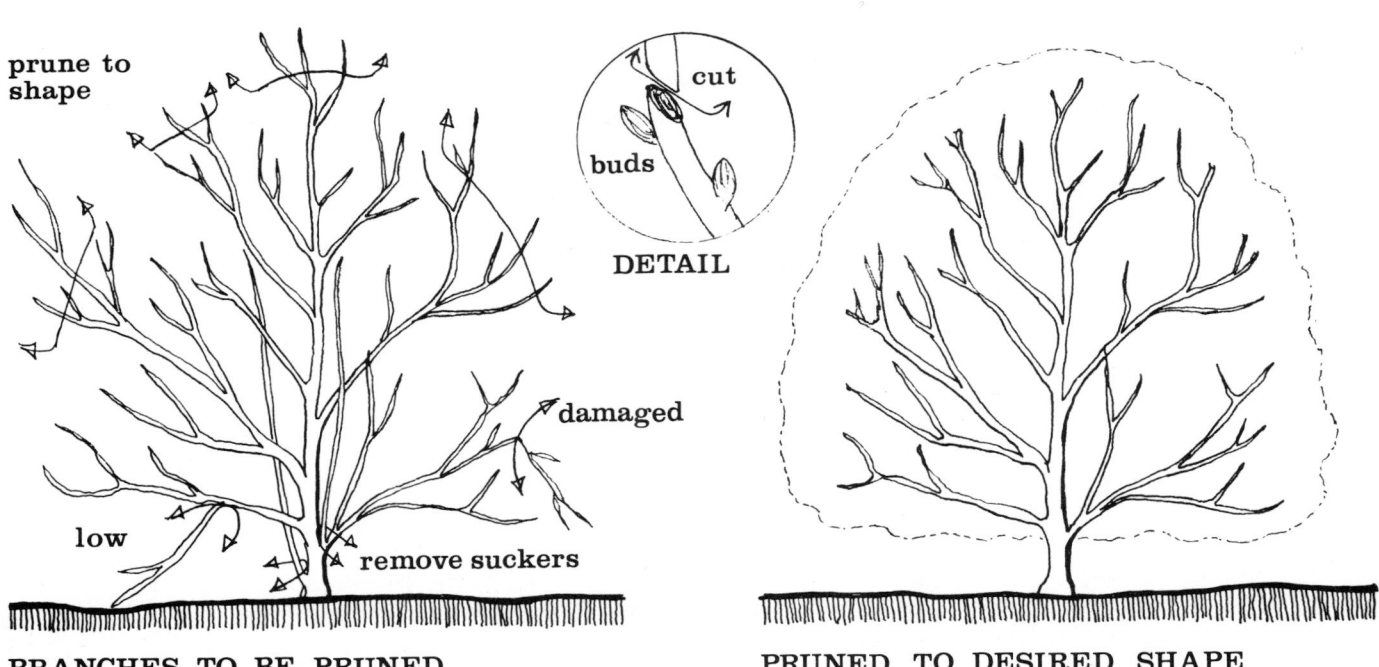

BRANCHES TO BE PRUNED   PRUNED TO DESIRED SHAPE

Pruning Shrubs

Cut hybrid teas to within 4 inches off the ground. Prune bushy roses less; cut back to about one-third of the natural growth. With rambling roses, clean out dead wood and treat the plants like early-blooming shrubs. Do the main pruning after bloom; then cut to the ground.

Most conifers and evergreens need little pruning; hemlock and yew, for example, require just an occasional clipping.

Pruning methods vary, but generally you prune from the inside of the plant outward and from the bottom up. "Top-lighting" fruit trees or shrubs means opening the center of the tree to let in more light and air. Take out crossing branches and branches of lesser value. Cut them cleanly at the trunk or the first strong crotch and do not leave stubs—these become infected. It is *vital* to know where to make a cut when pruning; you must avoid haphazard cutting. Make a cut only above a bud, small side branch, or main branch. Cut branches in the direction you want the new growth to take.

WEEDING AND GROOMING

Weeding is a necessary evil in the garden, but it need not be so unpleasant if you do it a few times a week rather than once a month. It is important to get rid of weeds because they rob plants of nutrition and eventually take over. May and June are prime weeding months.

When annuals start to look straggly in midsummer, cut them back to about half their height to give them a fresh start. Pinch back all annual seedlings while they are small, to encourage bushiness and side branching.

Grooming and weeding the garden is important; a good way to do it and get exercise at the same time is shown here using burlap pull-around sack. (Photograph by Matthew Barr)

Get rid of weeds quickly before they get a foothold; weeds sap plant's strength and moisture.

Petunias, zinnias, and marigolds in particular need this treatment.

After the first killing frost, discard all annuals and cut perennials to the ground. Remove all leaves, stems and garden rubbish.

TEXTURES AND PATTERNS

No garden should just be put together without considering how it will look as a whole. Select plants not only for easy growing and shade or sun placement, but for what they can do in the garden to create an interesting picture.

Study leaf size, texture, and color; some plants are feathery in appearance, whereas others are bold accents. Strive for a pleasing combination of plant materials judiciously placed to delight, not insult the eye. Try to use the gradation scale: small-leaved plants followed by medium-leaved plants and then large, bold foliage to give the garden a sense of rhythm. Or start at the other end of the scale, with large-leaved plants diminishing to small-leaved varieties.

With flowers, choose colors that go well together; for

instance, red zinnias next to white flowers are jarring, but red and orange flowers alongside each other are charming.

THE ALL-YEAR GARDEN

Gardens are meant for all seasons, and here lies the beauty of many plants. Remember that because the city garden is very much a part of the home it is constantly within view, and an attractive picture throughout the four seasons is what you want to aim for. Plan ahead for a beautiful all-year garden; it does not cost a penny more than a garden good for only one season.

In September, October, and November, lay the foundation for next year's garden. Plant evergreens for winter color, and get the wonderful perennials into the soil for next summer's flowers. Remember to get bulbs, the first harbingers of spring, into the ground—they can bring so much early color to gardens.

Place evergreens in the background, and use deciduous and flowering shrubs closer to the house; in summer they serve as foils for other plants, and in winter, when deciduous plants lose their leaves, the evergreens come forth in all their lovely dark green colors to keep the garden attractive.

March is the gardener's busy time. Repair such structures as fences, screens, canopies, and so forth. Build planters and check tools to be sure you will have equipment on hand when needed. This is the time to plant dormant trees and shrubs and to turn soil as soon as it is workable. Mulch newly planted material with peat moss or other mulches. If you have a basement or a garage where temperatures can be maintained, start slow-growing annuals to get a head start on spring.

Deciduous trees and shrubs need a light feeding now, and broad-leaved evergreens can be pruned; remove dead or damaged wood. Check trees and shrubs for broken branches from winter storms, cut them off cleanly, and apply a treewood paint. Trim back rampant vines like honeysuckle now; rake up accumulated leaves for compost. Remove all other debris that has accumulated over winter because debris breeds insects.

If your container plants have become root-bound, repot them and press down soil around the edges of boxes and other containers. Wash off soot and dust from all hardy trees and shrubs. This is especially important for evergreens because, unlike deciduous trees, they cannot shed foliage. If dirt is not removed, contamination builds up. If you are economically minded, start summer bulbs indoors for brightening your garden later.

In April, continue to plant trees and shrubs as well as container-grown or balled-and-burlaped stock. Prepare soil in boxes or beds so they will be ready for annuals; add humus or leafmold to ensure a nutritious, well-balanced soil. Divide old clumps of summer- and fall-blooming perennials and replant the divisions. Try to have all perennials in the ground by late May. Feed summer-blooming shrubs and lawns with a high-nitrogen fertilizer such as 10-10-5. Depending upon the rainfall, start moderate watering. Roof gardens need more water than backyard gardens, where only newly planted shrubs and trees need moisture.

May is the month for bedding plants; get seedlings into the ground, and put in less tender bulbs like gladiola and cannas. Now is the last chance to get trees and shrubs into the ground, unless they are balled and burlaped or container grown. But even the latter plants have a better start if they are put into the ground in May.

Increase the watering schedule, especially if you have a roof garden. Keep soil wet so plants have a chance to grow. When warm weather comes, insects become active, so keep a keen eye out for them and catch trouble before it starts. Use the home remedies described in Chapter 10 for pests. If pests are particularly bothersome, select nonpersistent poisons like rotenone and pyrethrum sprays. If mildew becomes a problem, try to water early in the day so the garden is dry by night; if mildew has already started, dust plants with sulfur. May is also the time to introduce natural predators such as lady bugs and praying mantes, which are available from suppliers.

Continue to plant annuals and summer bulbs this month, and do not forget the biennials like foxglove and sweet william, which are available this month at nurseries.

Increase watering at the end of the month, when plants are starting active growth. Keep all foliage washed clean of soot and pollution.

Planting should be over by June, and the garden should be starting its show. Roof gardens need a tremendous amount of water now, and backyard sites too need ample moisture to sustain their lush growth. Plant summer flowers and pot-grown plants like impatiens and caladiums to brighten the scene. Keep feeding plants and pruning shade trees whenever necessary.

Water plants thoroughly in July and August, and be ever alert for insects. Lightly prune conifers and feed lawns. Divide perennials, and pinch and snip tips of chrysanthemums. Remove dead flower stalks from perennials. Keep dead flowers off such annuals as marigolds, lantanas, and ageratum.

In September, pick dead flowers off annuals, and divide perennials (except late-flowering ones like chrysanthemums and asters). Start to plant some of the smaller bulbs. If rainfall is adequate, sparingly water plants in the backyard garden. Continue regular watering of plants in the roof garden, however, because wind and sun dry out plants.

Now is the best time to put in hardy perennials for summer bloom. They are available in cans or flats and will generally survive the winter without harm.

October and November are the last times to plant. Remove annuals before a killing frost sets in so that it will be easy to plant spring-flowering bulbs. October is the month to plant tulips, hyacinths, and daffodils and also trees and shrubs, unless the ground is already frozen. However, trees like birch and magnolias should be planted in spring. Plant conifers and broad-leaved evergreens now too. Mulch the evergreens at planting time, and keep them moist until frost arrives. Do clean-up chores.

November is the last chance to plant perennials and evergreens. Plant deciduous shrubs and trees as long as the soil is workable. Mulch your garden now because it is one of the best ways to protect plants from severe weather.

Plant
Material

This chapter contains a host of plants for your city garden (annuals, perennials, trees, shrubs, vines, bulbs); I have grown a great many of these plants through the years in both city and country settings. Because many city gardens use plants in containers I have made special note in remark section of those specimens that do well in pots and boxes. In Chapter 9 we discuss growing vegetables and herbs in boxes and tubs for those people with limited space. Chapter 10 covers insect and disease prevention and control. Following are my favorite annuals that, along with others equally fine, are described in handy reference charts.

FAVORITE ANNUALS

Ageratum, Floss Flower

Ageratum houstonianum. These blue, white, or pink varieties grow from 4 to 22 inches tall and bloom from early summer until fall. The plants need well-drained soil and somewhat heavy watering; they form compact mounds of pretty accent.

Alyssum

Lobularia maritima. Available in several colors, this low-growing annual generally is grown as an edging plant, although it has a multitude of uses in the garden when combined with other plants or used as fillers around perennials. Alyssum will grow in hot, dry climates.

Aster, China Aster

Callistephus chinensis. These 1- to 3-foot plants have wiry stems and beautiful white to deep red flowers. Some are early blooming, others bloom in midseason, and still others provide late color. These are some of the best annuals for cutting.

Bachelor's Button, Cornflower

Centaurea cyanus. Growing to a height of 2½ feet, these fine plants bear blue, pink, white, or wine flowers. Their gray-green foliage makes a dramatic display, and although they require pinching and pruning, they bloom profusely.

Calendula, Pot Marigold

Calendula officinalis. These bright, rounded flowers come in a variety of colors: orange, cream, gold, or yellow. Pot marigolds grow 12 to 24 inches tall and bloom all summer. They grow with almost no care.

Aster

Lobularia 'Carpet of Snow'

A handsome shrub at the right, some container impatiens, and a single specimen tree make this small city garden complete and comfortable. (Photograph by C. D. Luckhart)

Candytuft

Iberis umbellata. Masses of flowers make candytuft a good choice for the beginning gardener. Plants mound to 12 or 15 inches, and in late spring and early summer bloom their heads off in pink, salmon, or white. These are good flowers for cutting or garden display.

Cineraria

Senecio cruentus. This annual will bloom in the shade. The daisylike flowers come in light or dark shades of blue, purple, or magenta. Plants grow from 12 to 15 inches, with handsome foliage. Keep them shady and moist in a well-drained soil.

Coleus

Coleus blumei. A foliage plant that comes in a multitude of hues, coleus has toothed leaves. The plants can reach to 3 feet or more; pinch growing tips to make them compact. This is a good background plant.

Hollyhock

Althaea rosea. Neglected in recent years, hollyhocks are making a reappearance in gardens, and I recommend them because they are so colorful and survive in practically any situation. They grow to 6 feet, with large flowers in a spectrum of colors: pink, rose, yellow, red, and white. (These are generally classed as biennials, but it is best to start them fresh every year.)

Impatiens, Garden Balsam

Impatiens balsamina. Get to know these plants because they have many virtues; they are available in many

different colors and heights and bloom profusely. They like some sun but also succeed in shade.

Marigold

Tagetes erecta. These all-time favorites are the backbone of a garden. The plants grow quickly, come in all sizes, from 6 to 40 inches, and bloom constantly from summer to fall in yellow, orange, dark red, and maroon. The plants can be grown by themselves for lovely accents or with other plantings. There are many types of marigolds. The French dwarfs grow to 18 inches in a fine array of color; African dwarfs grow to 16 inches; and some of the new varieties are even smaller. Most types need an evenly moist soil in a sunny place.

Nasturtium

Tropaeoleum majus. Underrated nasturtiums can bring an immense wealth of color to the first garden, and easier plants to grow cannot be found. Nasturtiums bloom from early summer until frost and now come in single, semidouble, or double flowers in shades of yellow, orange, crimson, pink, maroon, and multicolored varieties. Dwarf plants make colorful borders, taller varieties lend spot color. Most nasturtiums will crowd out weeds and grow rapidly with little care.

Phlox

Phlox drummondii. These annuals, which grow to 16 inches, have lovely clusters of 1-inch rose, crimson, salmon, white, scarlet, or violet flowers. The blooms are abundant, and plants are seldom bothered by insects. Grow phlox in sun with plenty of water.

Tagetes

Dianthus barbatus

Pink, Sweet William

Dianthus. There are a host of varieties; all have clusters of pink to white flowers. Pinks are easy to grow and are available in many heights.

Snapdragon

Antirrhinum majus. These tall, stately, and lovely annuals have beguiling flowers of all colors but blue. Snapdragons come in many heights and are superb vertical accent in the garden. They will tolerate some shade but basically prefer sun. To increase bloom yield, cut flowers frequently and remove faded blossoms. There are many varieties in many sizes.

Zinnia

Zinnia elegans. This popular annual has great diversity as to size, form, height, and color. Zinnias have infinite uses in the garden and are fast growers that need little care but plenty of moisture. Flower colors include orange, yellow, pink, red, purple, lavender, and some bicolors.

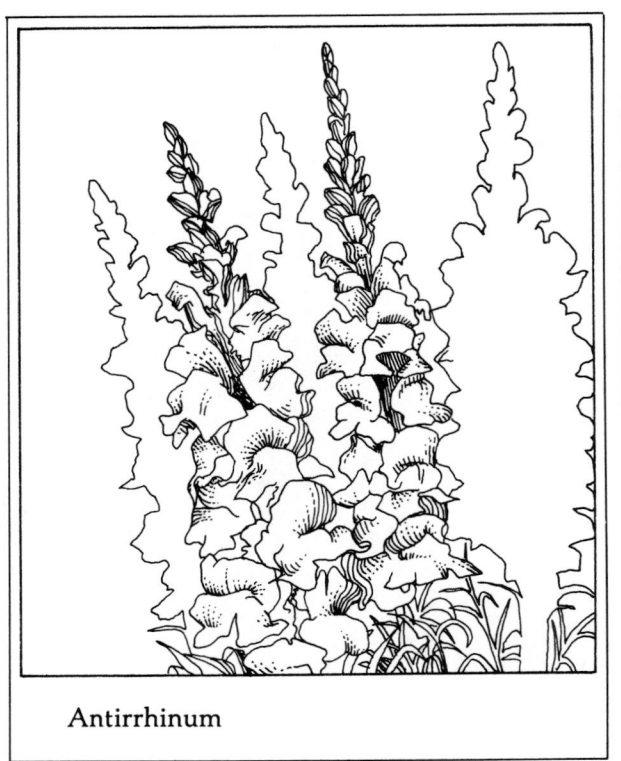

Antirrhinum

Zinnia

LIST OF ANNUALS

Botanical and Common Name	Approx. Height (Inches)	Planting Distance (Inches)	Flower Colors	Peak Bloom Season	Sun or Shade
Ageratum houstonianum (floss flower)	4–22	12	Blue, white, pink	Summer, fall	Sun or shade
Amaranthus tricolor (Joseph's coat)	12–18	18	Bronzy green brown; foliage marked cream and red	Summer	Sun
Antirrhinum majus (snapdragon)	10–48	10–18	Large choice of color and flower form	Late spring and fall; summer where cool	Sun

Botanical and Common Name	Approx. Height (Inches)	Planting Distance (Inches)	Flower Colors	Peak Bloom Season	Sun or Shade
Begonia semperflorens (wax begonia)	6–18	6–8	White, pink, deep rose	All summer; perennial in temperate climates	Sun or shade
Calendula officinalis (calendula, pot marigold)	12–24	12–15	Cream, yellow, orange, gold	Winter where mild; late spring, all summer elsewhere	Sun
Callistephus chinensis (China Aster)	12–36				
Catharanthus roseus (Vinca rosea, Madagascar periwinkle)	6–24	12	White, pink; some with contrasting eye	Summer until early fall	Sun or light shade
Centaurea cyanus (bachelor's button, cornflower)	12–30	12	Blue, pink, white, wine	Spring where mild; summer elsewhere	Sun
Coreopsis tinctoria (calliopsis)	8–30	18–24	Yellow, orange, maroon, and splashed bicolors	Late spring to summer; late summer where cool	Sun
Delphinium ajacis	18–60	9	Blue, pink, lavender, rose, salmon, carmine, white	Late spring to early summer	Sun

Botanical and Common Name	Approx. Height (Inches)	Planting Distance (Inches)	Flower Colors	Peak Bloom Season	Sun or Shade
Dianthus (pink, sweet william)	6–30	4–6	Mostly bicolors of white, pink, lavender, purple	Spring, fall; winters where mild	Sun
Helianthus annuus (common garden sunflower)	36–120	3	Yellow, orange, mahogany; or yellow with black centers	Summer	Sun
Iberis amara (rocket candytuft)	12–15	12	White	Late spring	Sun
Impatiens balsamina (garden balsam)	8–30	9	White, pink, rose, red	Summer or fall	Light shade; sun where cool
Lathyrus odoratus (sweet pea, winter flowering)	36–72	6	Mixed or separate colors, except yellow and orange	Late winter where mild; not heat resistant	Sun
Lobelia erinus (lobelia)	2–6	6–8	Blue, violet, pink, white	Summer	Sun, light shade
Lobularia maritima (alyssum)					
Lupinus hartwegi (lupine)	18–36	12–18	Blue, white	Early summer	Sun, light shade
Myosotis sylvatica (forget-me-not)	6–12	6–9	Blue with white eye	Spring, late fall	Light shade or dappled sun

Botanical and Common Name	Approx. Height (Inches)	Planting Distance (Inches)	Flower Colors	Peak Bloom Season	Sun or Shade
Petunia hybrids	12–24	6–12	All colors except true blue, yellow, orange	Summer and fall	Sun
Phlox drummondii (phlox)					
Reseda odorata (mignonette)	8–18	12	Greenish brown clusters	Late spring to fall	Sun
Senecio cruentus (Cineraria)	12–15				
Tagetes patula (French marigold)	6–18	9	Russet, mahoggany, and bicolors	Early summer	Sun
Tithonia rotundifolia (Mexican sunflower)	72–100	30	Orange	Summer	Sun
Tropaeoleum majus (nasturtium)	12–18	12–15	White, pink, crimson, orange, maroon, yellow	Spring and fall; summer where cool	Sun or shade
Viola tricolor hortensis (pansy)	6–8	9	"Faces" in white, yellow, purple, rose, mahogany, violet, apricot	Spring and fall; winter where mild	Sun, light shade
Zinnia elegans (zinnia)	8–36	9	Red, orange, yellow, purple, lavender, pink, white	Summer	Sun

Petunia

Viola

Begonia

FAVORITE PERENNIALS

Aster, New England Aster

Aster frikartii; Aster novae-angliae. Their abundant and dramatic blue and purple daisylike flowers make these two outstanding perennials bright and showy. Plants are available in several heights and make fine displays in large drifts or recurring accents of color or shape. They like lots of sun and water.

Baby's Breath

Gypsophila paniculata. These dainty, lacy plants grow rapidly to 2 feet and bear small, rounded white flowers in masses. There are also pink-and-white varieties. Blooms last more than a month; the plants make excellent garden fillers.

Basket of Gold

Alyssum saxatile. Splashes of golden flowers make this a desirable garden plant. The foliage is gray and provides an interesting contrast. Do not confuse this plant with the annual sweet alyssum, which is called Lobularia.

Bellflower

Campanula persicifolia. These perennials should be grown more often because they offer so much color. With their white or blue flowers in June and July, they form mounds of color and grow from 8 to 10 inches. Give plants full sun or light shade, and be sure they are in well-drained soil.

Native plants abound here interlaced with some perennials and sculptural evergreens; the plantings are sparse and yet the garden is complete. (Photograph by Matsumoto)

Blanketflower

Gaillardia aristata. Gaillardias produce showy flowers over a long period of time. The blooms are daisylike and generally bright yellow, although types combining the colors of bronze and scarlet also have been introduced. Undemanding, blanketflowers do best in a slightly sandy soil with adequate sun.

Bugloss

Anchusa azurea. Clusters of bright blue blossoms make this perennial an outstanding addition in the garden. They can grow to 6 feet. Some excellent new varieties are now available.

Chrysanthemum; Shasta Daisy

Chrysanthemum maximum; Chrysanthemum morifolium. These are available in numerous shapes and colors. Shapes include spoon, cushion, pompon, and button; colors vary from white to yellow, gold, and orange. Heights are variable; there are chrysanthemums for all kinds of purposes in the garden. The plants will tolerate dry soils and still flourish.

Daylily

Hemerocallis. These large, bulbous plants have fountains of grassy foliage and yellow, cream, or bronze flowers. Plants start blooming in May and continue on and off until frost. Most are tall and rangy and need lots of space and sun.

Gaillardia aristata

Chrysanthemum

Hemerocallis

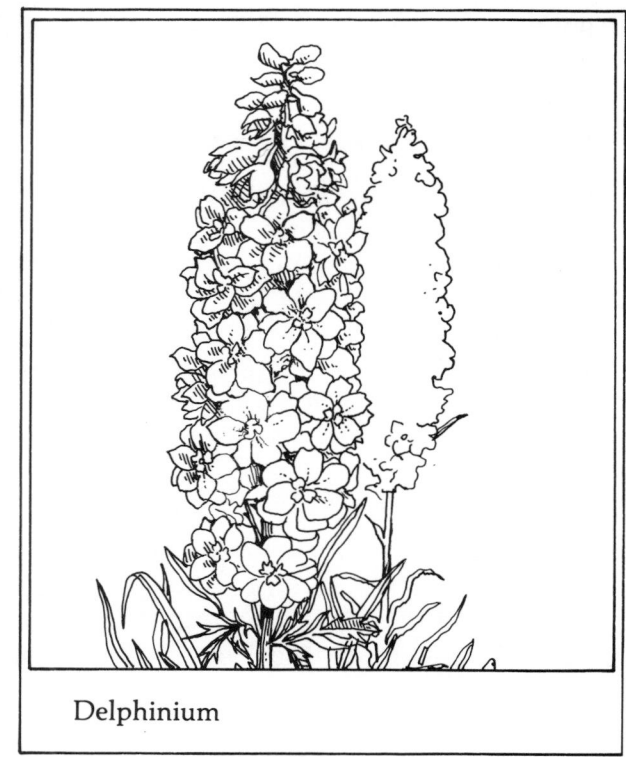

Delphinium

Delphinium, Larkspur

Delphinium elatum. These handsome, tall plants with spires of large flowers are excellent for background plantings. The flower colors range from white to pink to rich blues. Fertile, well-drained soil, and sun are essential. *D. grandiflorum,* known as Chinese delphinium, is also quite attractive.

False Spirea

Astilbe japonica. A perennial for shady places, this plant has white, pink, or red flowers on wiry stems. The bronze-green leaves are attractive; the bloom season is summer. Ideal for mixing with shrubby plants, false spirea grows to about 24 inches. Moist soil is essential.

Oriental Poppy

Papaver orientale. These perennials are coming into popularity again, and it is difficult to find more dramatic flowers than their bold orange blooms. Once established, the poppies bloom profusely. Plants are 2 to 4 feet high, with 6- to 8-inch flowers. They need well-drained soil and some sun, but not direct, intense sun.

Summer Phlox, Moss Pink

Phlox subulata. Three- to 5-foot plants bear a wealth of large pink-tone flowers. Phlox are compatible with most garden flowers and make splendid accents. They do, however, need a deep fertile soil and sun to prosper.

LIST OF PERENNIALS

Botanical and Common Name	Approx. Height (Inches)	Flower Colors	Peak Bloom Season	Sun or Shade
Alyssum saxatile (basket of gold)				
Anemone pulsatilla (prairie windflower; pasque flower)	9–15	Lavender to violet	Spring	Sun or light shade
Aquilegia alpina (dwarf columbine)	to 12	Blue	Early summer	Sun or light shade
Aster Frikartii; Aster novai-angliae (aster, New England aster)				
Bellis perennis (English daisy)	3–6	White, pink, rose	Spring; winter in mild climates	Sun
Campanula persicifolia (bellflower)	8–10	White, blue	Summer	Sun
Centaurea gymnocarpa (dusty miller)	18–24	Purple	Summer	Sun
Convallaria majalis (lily-of-the-valley)	9–12	White, pink	Spring, early summer	Light to medium shade
Coreopsis grandiflora (tickseed)	24–36	Golden yellow	Summer	Sun
Felicia amelloides (blue marguerite)	20–24	Blue	Spring, summer	Sun
Geum chiloense, aka *G. coccineum* (geum)	20–24	Yellow, red-orange	Early summer	Light shade
Gypsophila paniculata (baby's breath)				
Helenium (various) (sneezeweed)	24–48	Orange, yellow, rusty shades	Summer, fall	Sun
Heliopsis (various) (orange sunflower)	36–48	Orange, yellow	Summer, fall	Sun
Hosta plantaginea (fragrant plantain lily)	24–30	White	Late summer	Light shade

Anemone

Helenium

Botanical and Common Name	Approx. Height (Inches)	Flower Colors	Peak Bloom Season	Sun or Shade
Iberis sempervirens (evergreen candytuft)	8–12	White	Early summer	Sun or light shade
Iris cristata (crested iris)	6–8	Lavender, light blue	Spring	Light shade
I. kaempferi (Japanese iris)	40–48	Purple, violet, pink, rose, red, white	Spring, early summer	Sun or light shade
Limonium latifolium (statice; sea lavender)	24–36	Blue, white, pink	Summer, fall	Sun
Pelargonium domesticum (Lady Washington geranium)	18–48	Many bicolors; white, pink, red, purple	Summer, fall	Sun
Rudbeckia hirta (black-eyed susan)	36–48	Yellow, pink, orange, white	Summer	Sun
Solidago (various) (goldenrod)	20–36	Yellow	Summer	Sun or light shade
Viola cornuta (many varieties) (tufted viola)	6–8	Purple; newer varieties in many colors	Spring, fall	Light shade

Rudbeckia

Convallaria majalis

Geranium

TREES, SHRUBS, AND VINES

Trees, shrubs, and vines are the backbone of any garden—they are the backdrop and total canvas for flowers (annuals, perennials, bulbs). When landscaping a small yard I always start with the trees; this gives a reference point. Obviously, I try to use any existing trees but many times this may not be possible because the

A city terrace with only a few plants—some bulb, vines against the brick wall, and container begonias—provides a private place of cool greenery. (Photograph by Molly Adams)

trees may be wrong for the site (too big, too close to the house) or perhaps they are no longer healthy.

Small trees are the order of the day in most city gardens and there are numerous ones to choose from—a few deciduous trees for beauty and shade, and always some evergreens for winter color.

If the garden already has shrubs, I try to use them; they are clipped and brought into bounds to be in scale with the rest of the garden and vines. I think they are the workhorse of any garden; they hide problem areas—cracked walls, unsightly posts; provide privacy and most are beautiful; whether for foliage or flower. Most important, once established, vines grow almost by themselves.

In the following lists you will find many trees, shrubs, and vines for your garden. All are good candidates for your city retreat and the majority of them can also be grown in large containers if necessary.

LIST OF TREES

Botanical and Common Name	Minimum Night Temperature (Fahrenheit)	General Description	Remarks
Abies concolor (white fir)	−20 to −10	Stiffly pyramidal	Makes a beautiful Christmas tree
Acer palmatum (Japanese maple)	−10 to 0	Lovely lacy leaves	Handsome in soy tub or round container
A. platanoides (Norway maple)	−35 to −20	Rounded	Many varieties; adaptable; turns yellow in fall

Botanical and Common Name	Minimum Night Temperature (Fahrenheit)	General Description	Remarks
Ailanthus altissima (tree of heaven)	−20 to −10	Rounded	Grows anywhere; leaves grow to 3 feet; good shade tree
Araucaria excelsa (Norfolk pine)	Tender	Pyramid shape	Good vertical accent in Spanish flarelip pot
Betula populifolia (gray birch)	−20 to −10	Deciduous; irregular in shape	Fine patio tree or along house wall
Catalpa speciosa (Western catalpa)	−20 to −10	Pyramidal	Flowers fall in summer and seeds drop in fall
Cedrus atlantica glauca (Blue Atlas cedar)	0 to 10	Needles evergreen, with sprawling habit	Fine accent in large tubs near house corners
Citrus (orange, lemon, lime)	Tender	Dark green leaves; nicely branching	Excellent trees
Crataegus oxyacantha (English hawthorn)	−20 to −10	Round effect	Thorny branches, showy fruit, and pretty spring flowers
C. phaenopyrum (Washington hawthorn)	−20 to −10	Columnar	
Elaeagnus angustifolia (Russian olive)	−50 to −35	Wide spreading	Use as hedge or screen
Eriobotrya japonica (loquat)	20 to 30	Round-headed, with dark green leaves	Good evergreen for tubs and boxes
Euonymus europaea (spindle tree)	−35 to −20	Retains leaves late in fall	Colorful landscaping shrub
Fraxinus americana (white ash)	−35 to −20	Round; good city tree	Excellent patio shrub
Ficus benjamina (weeping fig)	Tender	Tiny dark green leaves; branching habit	Good special effect in garden or indoors in tubs

Botanical and Common Name	Minimum Night Temperature (Fahrenheit)	General Description	Remarks
Gingko biloba (gingko)	−20 to −10	Deciduous; lovely widespreading foliage	Handsome in containers; nice accent near house walls
Laburnum watereri (golden chain tree)	−10 to −5	Deciduous; columnar shape	Good patio tub plant
Lagerstroemeira indica (crape myrtle)	−20 to −10	Deciduous, sometimes with pink flowers	Showy for patio
Magnolia grandiflora (Southern magnolia)	−5 to 10	Pyramidal	Evergreen; glossy leaves make it a showcase plant
M. soulangiana (saucer magnolia)	−10 to −5	Deciduous, with round form, lovely flowers	Good plant near fence or wall
Malus sargenti (Sargent crab apple)	−30 to −20	Dwarf; round-topped form	Perimeter decoration for paved area
Philodendron amurense (Amur corktree)	−35 to −20	Deciduous, attractive branching tree	For a special garden
Phoenix loureiri (date palm)	Tender	Lovely, arching fronds	An indoor-outdoor favorite
Picea pungens (Colorado spruce)	−50 to −35	Pyramid	Can take abuse
Pinus mugo mughas (mugho pine)	−40 to −30	Irregular outline; broad and sprawling	To decorate paths, walks, and patios
P. thunbergii (Japanese black pine)	−20 to −10	Good spreading habit	Excellent container plant; another fine Christmas tree
Platanus acerifolia (London plane tree)	−10 to −5	Widespreading branches	Good city tree
Podocarpus gracilior	Tender	Graceful willowy branches	Good doorway or espalier plant
Quercus borealis (red oak)	−35 to −20	Broad when old; pyramid when young	Twiggy growth; pinch off tips of unwanted branches for vertical growth

Acer platanoides

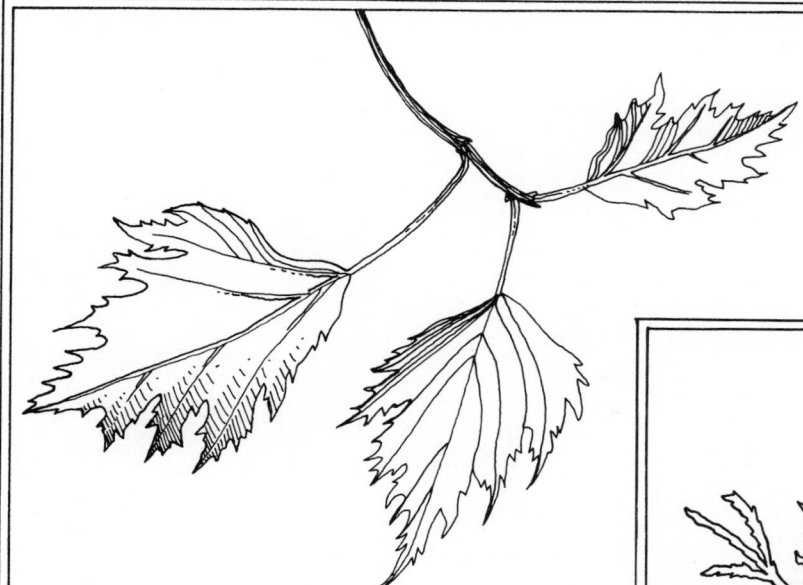

Betula pendula

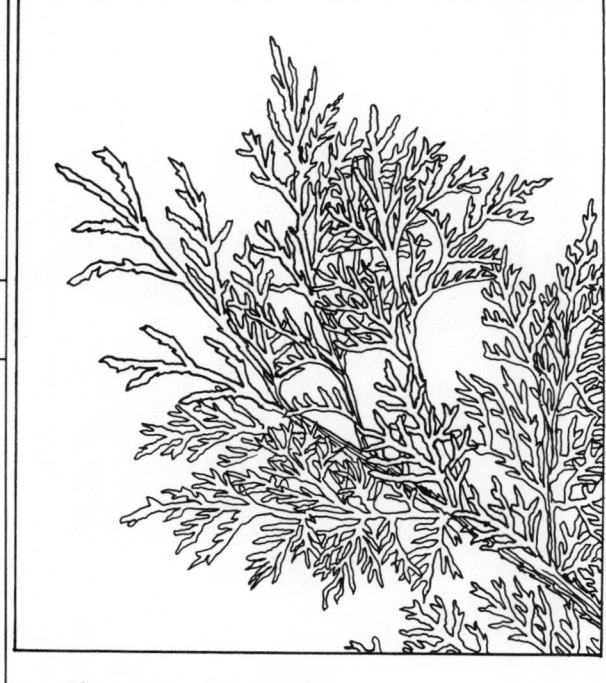

Chamaecyparis pisifera

Picea pungens

Salix

Magnolia stellata 'Dr. Merrill'

Taxus baccata

Pinus mugo

Botanical and Common Name	Minimum Night Temperature (Fahrenheit)	General Description	Remarks
Rhamnus davurica (buckthorn)	−50 to −35	Vigorous	Oblong leaves to 4 inches; flowers in dense clusters
Rhapis excelsa (lady palm)	Tender	Dark green, fan-shaped leaves	A stellar container plant
Salix matsudana tortuosa (contorted Hankow willow)	−20 to −10	Lovely sweeping branches	For a special place
Schefflera acontifolia (Australian umbrella tree)	Tender	Graceful stems tipped with fronds of leaves	Handsome in a terra-cotta Spanish pot
Taxus cuspidata (Japanese yew)	−20 to −10	Pyramid	Use as hedge or screen
Tilia cordata (small-leaved linden)	−35 to −20	Dense pyramid	Lawn, street, or patio shade tree
Tsuga caroliniana (Carolina hemlock)	−20 to −10	Compact pyramid	Graceful foliage

EXCELLENT TREES FOR SPECIAL REGIONS

Botanical and Common Name	Conspic-uous Flowers	East	North	Great Plains	West	Lower Pacific Coast	South	Lower South
Acer circinatum (maple, vine)					*			
A. ginnala (maple, Amur)		*	*					
A. negundo (box elder)		*	*	*	*			
A. platanoides (maple, Norway)		*	*					
A. rubrum (red maple)		*	*	*	*			
Aesculus hippocastanum (horse chestnut)	*	*	*		*	*		
Bauhinia	*					*	*	*
Betula papyrifera (birch, cutleaf weeping)				*	*	*		
Betula pendula (birch, paper)		*	*	*				
Caragana arborescens (pea tree)	*	*	*	*				
Catalpa speciosa (catalpa)						*	*	
Cercis canadensis (redbud, or Judas tree)	*	*		*	*	*	*	
Crataegus (hawthorn)	*	*		*	*	*	*	
Cornus (dogwood)	*	*			*	*	*	
Delonix regia (poinciana, royal)	*							*
Elaeganus angustifolia (olive, Russian)		*	*	*	*	*		
Erythrina americana (coral tree)	*						*	*

Botanical and Common Name	Conspic- uous Flowers	East	North	Great Plains	West	Lower Pacific Coast	South	Lower South
Fagus sylvatica (beech, European)		*		*	*			
Fagus sylvatica atropunicea (beech, purple)		*				*		
Frangipani	*							*
Fraxinus americana (ash, white)		*		*			*	
F. pennsylvanica lanceolata (ash, green)			*	*				
F. velutina glabra (ash, modesto)					*	*		
Ginkgo biloba (ginkgo or maidenhair tree)		*		*	*	*	*	

Cornus florida

Botanical and Common Name	Conspicuous Flowers	East	North	Great Plains	West	Lower Pacific Coast	South	Lower South
Gleditsia triacanthos (honey locust)		*		*	*		*	
Halesia carolina (silver bell tree)	*	*				*		
Juglans nigra (walnut, black)	*		*			*		
J. regia (walnut, English)				*	*			
Koelreutenia paniculata (golden-rain tree)	*	*			*	*	*	
Laburnum wateri (golden-chain tree)	*	*						
Liquidambar styraciflua (sweet gum)		*		*	*	*	*	
Liriodendron tulipifera (tulip tree)	*	*			*		*	
Malus (crab apple)	*	*	*	*	*	*	*	
Moraine (honey locust)						*		
Nyssa sylvatica (tupelo, pepperidge, or sourgum)		*		*		*		
Platanus occidentalis (buttonwood or sycamore)		*		*	*	*	*	
Populus deltoides (cottonwood)				*	*			
Prunus serrulata (cherry, flowering)	*	*		*	*	*	*	
Quercus palustris (oak, pin)		*		*			*	
Q. phellos (oak, willow)							*	
Q. rubra (oak, red)		*		*	*			

Botanical and Common Name	Conspic-uous Flowers	East	North	Great Plains	West	Lower Pacific Coast	South	Lower South
Stewartia koreana (stewartia)	*	*						
Tilia americana (linden, American)		*	*	*	*			
T. cordata (linden, little-leaf)		*	*	*				
Ulnus parvifolia (elm, Chinese)		*	*	*				
U. pumila (elm, Siberian)								

LIST OF SHRUBS

Botanical and Common Name	Minimum Night Temperature (Fahrenheit)	General Description	Remarks
Abutilon (flowering maple)	Tender	Bell-shaped flowers of paper-thin texture	Give plenty of water and sun; can be espaliered
Aesculus parviflora (bottlebrush buckeye)	−20 to −10	White flowers in July	Good color
Aralia elata	−35 to −20	Small black berries	Prickly
Azalea (see rhododendron)			
Berberis thunbergii (Japanese barberry)	−10 to −5	Bright red fruits	Dozens of uses
Buddleia davidii (butterfly bush)	−10 to −5	Lovely summer flowers	For that special place
Camellia japonica (common camellia)	5 to 10	Handsome flowers in many colors	Another excellent container plant
C. sasanqua (sasanqua camellia)	5 to 10	Mostly small white flowers	Many varieties
Chaeonmeles japonica (Japanese quince)	−20 to −10	Scarlet flowers in spring; many varieties	Outstanding early color

Camellias and rhododendrons are the container plants; assorted evergreen shrubs grow in brick planters and some daisies form one part of the garden. The accent is ground-hugging evergreens at center. (Photograph by Matthew Barr)

Botanical and Common Name	Minimum Night Temperature (Fahrenheit)	General Description	Remarks
Cornus paniculata (gray dogwood)	−30 to −20	Upright in form, with many branches	Fine city tree
C. sanguinea (bloodtwig dogwood)	−30 to −20	Blood-red foliage	Good for winter color
C. stolonifera (red-oisier dogwood)	−35 to −20	Bright red winter twigs	Fine accent

Botanical and Common Name	Minimum Night Temperature (Fahrenheit)	General Description	Remarks
Cotoneaster horizontalis (rock spray)	−20 to −10	Graceful plant	Good filler; takes city abuse
Deutzia scabra ("Candidissima" snow-flake deutzia)	−10 to −5	White double flowers in June	Delicate to grow but handsome
Elaeagnus angustifolia (Russian olive)	−50 to −35	Fragrant flowers	Always good
Euonymus (many varieties)	Check with nursery		
Fatsia japonica (aralia)	5 to 10	Foliage plant with fanlike leaves on stems	Makes bold appearance
Gardenia jasminoides (Cape jasmine)	10 to 30	Dark green leaves and fragrant white blooms	New blooming varieties available
Hibiscus rosa-sinensis (Chinese hibiscus)	20 to 30	Glossy dark green foliage, large flowers	Good performer in tubs or boxes
Hydrangea quercifolia (oakleaf hydrangea)	−10 to −5		Handsome foliage
Ilex crenata (holly)	−5 to 5	Glossy leaves, bright berries	Many good varieties
I. glabra (inkberry)	−35 to −20		Evergreen foliage
Ixora (star flower)	Tender	Small red flowers	Splendid color in white tubs
Juniperus chinensis ("pfitzeriana" Pfitzer juniper)	−20 to −10	Blue-green foliage	Good screen plant
J. communis depressa (prostrate juniper)	−50 to −35	Blue-green foliage	Forms dense mass
Kerria japonica (kerria)	−20 to −10	Yellow flowers	Good color
Lagerstroemia indica (crape myrtle)	5 to 10	Bright flowers in September	Can take city conditions
Lonicera species (honeysuckle)	Check with nursery		Many uses

Azalea

Buddleia

Berberis

Euonymus

Botanical and Common Name	Minimum Night Temperature (Fahrenheit)	General Description	Remarks
Mahonia aquifolium (Oregon grape holly)	−10 to −5	Yellow flowers, black berries	Can take city conditions
Malus sargenti (Sargent crab apple)	−10 to −5	Pure white flowers in May	One of the best
Nerium oleander (oleander)	10 to 20	Dark green leaves and bright flowers	Needs large container and lots of water
Osmanthus ilicifolius (holly olive)	−5 to 5	Glossy leaves on upright stems	Grows fast in tubs
Philadelphis coronarius (sweet mock orange)	−20 to −10	Scented blooms	Favorite city plant
Pieris japonica (Japanese andromeda)	−10 to −5	Showy flowers	Tough to grow, good
Pittosporum tobira	10 to 20	Arching branches	Can be trained to shape
Plumbago capensis (blue phlox)	20 to 30	Small leaves and blue flowers	Robust grower
Podocarpus macrophyllus	Tender	Bright green leaves	Attractive in tubs
Potentilla fruticosa (cinquefoil)	−50 to −35	Yellow flowers in May; many varieties	Fine color
Prunus subhirtella (rosebud cherry)	−10 to 0	A small tree	Excellent for small yards
Rhododendron obtusum amoenum (azalea)	−5 to 5	Superior flowering shrub	Always good
Rosa multiflora (Japanese rose)	−10 to −5	Robust	Always good
R. rugosa (rugosa rose)	−50 to −35	Many varieties	Beautiful accent
Spiraea thunbergii (thunberg spirea)	−20 to −10	Bright white flowers	Fine color
Syringa vulgaris (common lilac)	−35 to −20	Lilac color	Many varieties
Thuja occidentalis (arbovitae)	−50 to −35	Evergreens	Tough plants for untoward conditions

Prunus subhirtella

Viburnum

Viburnum carlcephalum

Philadelphus coronarius

Syringa

Weigela florida

Campsis

Botanical and Common Name	Minimum Night Temperature (Fahrenheit)	General Description	Remarks
Viburnum dentatum (arrowwood)	−50 to −35	Nice autumn colors	Good background
V. lantana (wayfaring tree)	−35 to −20	Good mass	Grows in dry soil
Weigela (many varieties)	−10 to −5	Lovely red varieties	Does well in shade
Wisteria sinensis (Chinese wisteria)	−10 to 5	Floriferous	Beautiful but difficult
Yucca filamentosa (Spanish bayonet; Adam's needle)	−20 to −10	Blue-green, sword-shaped leaves	Dramatic in tubs

LIST OF VINES

Botanical and Common Name	Minimum Night Temperature (Fahrenheit)	General Description	Sun or Shade	Remarks
Akebia quinata (five-leaf akebia)	−20 to −10	Vigorous twiner; fragrant, small flowers	Sun or partial shade	Needs support; prune in fall or early spring
Allamanda cathartica	Tender	Dense, heavy stems and lovely tubular flowers	Sun	Prune annually in spring
Ampelopsis brevipedunculata (porcelain ampelopsis; blueberry climber)	−20 to −10	Strong grower; dense leaves	Sun or shade	Prune in early spring
Amtigonon leptopus (coral vine)	Tender	Excellent as a screen	Sun	Needs light support; prune severely after bloom
Aristolochia durior (Dutchman's pipe)	−20 to −10	High twiner; mammoth leaves	Sun or shade	Needs sturdy support; prune in spring or summer
Celastrus scandens (American bittersweet)	−50 to −35	Light green leaves, red berries	Sun or shade	Prune in early spring before growth starts
Clematis armandii (evergreen clematis)	5 to 10	Lovely flowers and foliage; many colors	Sun	Needs support; prune lightly after bloom
Clytostoma (campsis) *(Bignonia capreolata)* (cross vine; trumpet vine)	−5 to 5	Orange flowers	Sun or shade	Thin out weak branches in spring; clings by disks

Botanical and Common Name	Minimum Night Temperature (Fahrenheit)	General Description	Sun or Shade	Remarks
Doxantha unguis-cati (cat's claw)	10 to 20	Dark green leaves; yellow blooms	Sun	Needs no support; prune severely after bloom
Euonymus fortunei (wintercreeper)	− 35 to − 20	Shiny leathery leaves, orange berries in fall	Sun or shade	Needs support; prune in early spring
Fatshedera lizei	20 to 30	Handsome foliage	Shade	No pruning needed
Ficus pumila (repens) (creeping fig)	20 to 30	Small heart-shaped leaves	Partial shade	Thin plant in late fall or early spring
Gelsemium sempervirens (Carolina yellow jasmine)	Tender	Fragrant yellow flowers	Sun or partial shade	Needs support; thin plants immediately after bloom
Hedera helix (English ivy)	− 10 to − 5	Scalloped, neat leaves; many varieties	Shade	Thin and prune in early spring
Hydrangea petiolaris (climbing hydrangea)	− 20 to − 10	Heads of snowy flowers	Sun or partial shade	Thin and prune in winter or early spring
Ipomoea purpurea (convolvulus; common morning glory)	Tender	White, blue, purple, pink, or red flowers	Sun	Bloom until frost
Jasminum nudiflorum (winter jasmine)	− 10 to − 5	Yellow flowers	Sun or shade	Needs strong support; thin and shape annually after bloom

Botanical and Common Name	Minimum Night Temperature (Fahrenheit)	General Description	Sun or Shade	Remarks
J. officinale (white jasmine)	5 to 10	Showy dark green leaves, white flowers	Sun or shade	Provide strong support; thin and shape after bloom
Kadsura japonica (scarlet kadsura)	5 to 10	Bright red berries in fall	Sun	Needs support; prune annually in early spring
Lonicera caprifolium (sweet honeysuckle)	−10 to −5	White or yellow trumpet-shaped flowers	Sun	Prune in fall or spring
L. hildebrantiana (Burmese honeysuckle)	20 to 30	Shiny dark green leaves	Sun or partial shade	Needs support; prune in late fall
L. japonica "Halliana" (Hall's honeysuckle)	−20 to −10	Deep green leaves, bronze in fall	Sun or shade	Provide support; prune annually in fall and spring
Mandevilla suaveolens (Chilean jasmine)	20 to 30	Heart-shaped leaves and flowers	Sun	Trim and cut back lightly in fall; remove seed pods as they form
Parthenocissus quinquefolia (Virginia creeper)	−35 to −20	Scarlet leaves in fall	Sun or shade	Prune in early spring
Passiflora caerulea (passion flower)	5 to 10	Spectacular flowers	Sun	Needs support; prune severely each fall or early spring

Ampelopsis

Clematis

Lonicera

Jasminum

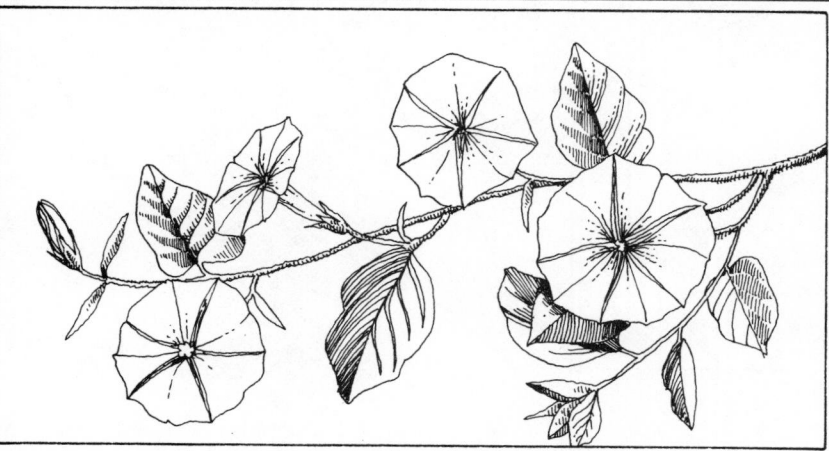

Ipomoea

Botanical and Common Name	Minimum Night Temperature (Fahrenheit)	General Description	Sun or Shade	Remarks
Phaseolus coccineus (scarlet runner bean)	Tender	Bright red flowers	Sun	Renew each spring
Plumbago capensis (leadwort)	20 to 30	Blue flowers	Sun	Prune somewhat in spring
Pueraria thunbergiana (kudsu vine)	−5 to 5	Purple flowers	Sun or partial shade	Provide sturdy support; cut back severely each fall
Rosa	−10 to −5	Many varieties	Sun	Needs support; prune out deadwood, shorten long shoots, and cut laterals back to two nodes in spring or early summer after bloom

Rosa

Wisteria

Botanical and Common Name	Minimum Night Temperature (Fahrenheit)	General Description	Sun or Shade	Remarks
Smilax rotundifolia (horse brier)	−20 to −10	Good green foliage	Sun or shade	Needs no support; prune severely annually
Trachelospermum jasminoides (star jasmine)	20 to 30	Dark green leaves, small white flowers	Partial shade	Provide heavy support; prune very lightly in fall
Vitis coignetiae (glory grape)	−10 to 5	Colorful autumn leaves	Sun or partial shade	Needs sturdy support; prune each fall or spring
Wisteria floribunda (Japanese wisteria)	−20 to −10	Violet-blue flowers	Sun	Provide support; prune annually once mature to shorten long branches after bloom or in winter; pinch back branches first year

BULBS

Bulbs supply a wealth of beauty for little effort. They are planted in containers and covered, and that is that. There is no weeding, no pruning, and generally no battle with bugs. If you want early spring color, plant such dependable bulbs as crocus, narcissus, and snowdrops in the fall. Later in the fall, plant tulips, hyacinths, and

In this backyard city garden lilies, dahlias, and roses are the backbone of planting; the tree in the corner of the garden provides the finishing touch. (Photograph by C. D. Luckhart)

scillas. In the spring plant the summer-flowering bulbs, such as callas and cannas, dahlias and gladiola. Planting this way makes it possible to have some kind of bulb blooming in the garden almost all year.

Mail-order suppliers and growers' catalogs list all plants with fleshy counterparts under the term bulbs. Actually, this catch-all category includes bulbs, corms, tubers, and rhizomes. But no matter how you define them, the makings for the flowers are already in the bulbs, and all you do is plant them.

Many of the most beautiful bulb flowers are winter-hardy and so can be left in containers year after year; they need cold weather to grow. Other bulbs must be replanted each year. The stages of a bulb's life cycle are *blooming, foliage growth,* which is stored in the bulb, and *resting*.

Planting Bulbs

All bulbs need a moisture-retentive but rapidly draining soil composed of high organic matter. Bulbs do not grow as well in clay soil, and few thrive in sandy soil. Dig round holes for bulbs in containers; pointed holes leave an air pocket below the bulb. A 3-inch depth means to plant the bulb's top, not its bottom, 3 inches below ground level. Plant the growing side up; in most cases this is the pointed end or the one showing growth. *Firm* the soil over the bulb; do not leave it loose.

Purchase only top-quality bulbs from reputable dealers and avoid bargains. You are buying an unseen product, so you must trust the dealer to give you healthy, robust bulbs that will bloom for years rather than tired bulbs that may come up "blind" (without flowers).

Most bulbous plants can live off their own storehouse of food for some time, but they should not be neglected when they are in active growth. Water them regularly from the time they start growing until after their flowers fade; then taper off watering gradually. Dormant bulbs do not need any more water than natural conditions provide for them. Spring bulbs can be fertilized once a season; I do not, but some growers recommend it. Summer bulbs can and should be fertilized as soon as growth appears and again in the few weeks before they bloom. Use a balanced feeding mix with a low nitrogen content.

Spring-Flowering Bulbs

Because spring-blooming bulbs bear color in late winter or very early spring and are easy to manage, they are the most popular. These bulbs are left in the ground all year and are called *hardy* bulbs. However, some bulbs that are hardy in one climate may not be in another. Plant most spring bulbs from September until first frost; plant winter aconite and dogtooth violet at the end of August or early September.

Remember that after spring-flowering bulbs bloom, their foliage must ripen for several weeks. Do not cut off the leaves, or the bulb will not be able to regain the strength that went into growing and blooming.

FAVORITE BULBS

Gladiolus (gladiola)

These corms seem to grow in any soil without much attention, but they do need sun. Plants grow quickly, are dependable, and bear flowers 10 to 12 weeks after planting. There are tall varieties and charming small ones in a wide selection of colors. When freezing weather is over, plant the corms 4 to 6 inches deep and about 6 inches apart in a well-cultivated container at least 15 inches deep. Keep plants moist; gladioluses can take copious watering.

When buds appear between the leaves, use a fertilizer. In fall, remove and store the corms if you are in a cold climate; in mild climates leave the corms in their containers. When the foliage turns brown, trim the tops, then dry the bulbs in an airy, shady place for a few weeks. You will see new corms on top of the old dried, withered ones; store the new corms in paper sacks in a dark place at about 40 to 50°F until planting time. The following gladioluses make a welcome addition to any container garden:

G. coviellei are baby gladioluses with white, pink, red, or lilac flowers. They grow in loose spikes on 18-inch stems.

G. hybrida come in many colors and varieties.

G. primulinus, a tropical African species, have yellow flowers.

G. trista are small, with 2- to 3-inch yellow purple-veined flowers.

Lilium (lily)

Lilies are synonymous with grace and beauty, and in recent years hybridists have developed some stellar plants. Easy to grow, lilies may be left undisturbed for years while they increase their display. As soon as you get the bulbs—and buy the best you can afford—plant them, whether it is spring or fall. Give them a rich neutral soil with a pH of 7, which is neither too acid nor too alkaline, and drains readily. Sun is necessary for a

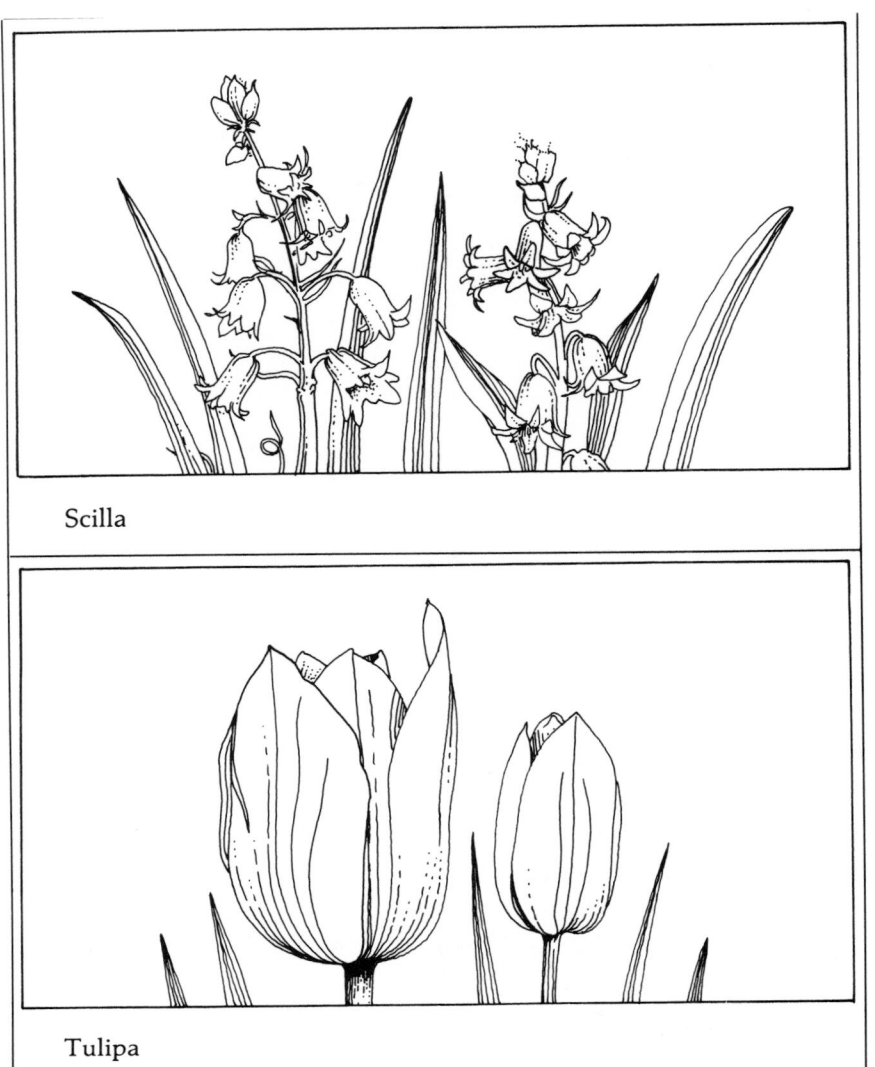

Scilla

Tulipa

bountiful crop of flowers, and thorough soakings are needed to bring them to perfection. Plant lilies at a depth of three times the height of the bulb; use three to five bulbs to a group. Do not worry if plants do not bloom profusely the first year because they are at their best the second and third years.

Eventually they can be divided to increase the number; do this about four weeks after they bloom, and then replant the bulbs after a reasonable length of time. Before or during the blooming season, use a light feeding of 5-10-5, but do not overdo it. Lilies are sometimes bothered by insects and diseases, but a regular spraying or dusting program will solve most problems. Of more concern are mice, which love lily bulbs. Keep your guard up if rodents are prevalent in your area.

Another way to increase the number of plants is to remove four or five outside thick scales of old bulbs at replanting time. Put the scales in soil about 4 inches deep and cover them with sand.

Try these lilies:

L. auratum (goldband lily) grow waxy white fragrant flowers, with spots and golden bands on each segment. They bloom in August or September.

L. candidum (Madonna lily), after producing beautiful white fragrant blooms, die. However, they produce new growth in autumn.

L. longifolium (Easter lily), have fragrant, trumpet-shaped flowers on short stems. Do not grow in severe climates.

Aurelian hybrids are gems that bloom in June and July; flower colors range from white to yellow, with many orange shades. The plants grow 3 to 6 feet tall.

Bellingham hybrids have yellow-orange or orange-red flowers spotted reddish brown in June and July.

Fiesta hybrids are vigorous sun-loving lilies that bloom in July with mahogany, amber, red, burgundy, or lemon-yellow flowers.

Harlequin hybrids have wide-open flowers ranging from ivory white through lilac to violet and purple. The plants grow to 5 feet and bloom in July.

Martagon hybrids develop many flowers to a stem, and the colors include yellow, orange, lilac, tangerine, purple, and mahogany.

Olympic hybrids produce trumpet-shaped flowers in many colors: white, cream, yellow, and pink shaded on the outside with greenish brown. They bloom in July and August and grow 6 feet tall.

Oriental hybrids produce mammoth flowers with segments in white or red, often banded with gold or red and spotted deep red. The sweetly scented flowers bloom in August and September.

Tulipa (tulip)

If you have not looked at the tulip family lately, you are in for a pleasant surprise. The tulip has progressed from an ordinary flower to something extraordinary. There are many varieties, including strains such as fringed, cottage, Darwin, Mendel, and many others. Some tulips are beautiful beyond description, and all are ideal container plants.

Choose the ones that appeal to you. Select early and late ones so you can enjoy the flowers for many months rather than just a few weeks. Give them a sunny place and protect them from strong winds. Use a light well-drained soil; tulips do not grow in very sandy or clay soil.

It is best to plant the bulbs 10 to 12 inches deep because there is less danger of botrytis. Set early-flowering types 4 inches apart, late-flowering ones about 6 inches apart.

Plant bulbs between October and the middle of November. They can be left in their containers. If you remove them, lift them with their roots and leaves, and then keep them in a shady place to ripen. When the foliage turns brown, store the plants in a cool, dry place until planting time. Tulips need cold weather; in a year-round temperate climate you must buy precooled bulbs or store bulbs in the refrigerator for 6 weeks before planting them.

There are numerous classifications of tulips, which basically bloom between the early part of the year through late May. Thus, they are generally described as early, midseason, and late or May-flowering plants. The following are my favorites:

Single (early). These old favorites are easy to grow.

Double (early). These tulips have large, wide-open, long-lasting flowers.

Mendel (midseason). Mendels have lovely shapes and beautiful colors.

Darwin tulips (May flowering). These are the most popular; they are globular in shape and grow to 30 inches.

Darwin hybrids (midseason). These are giants.

Triumph (midseason). The plants are robust, with a good range of colors.

Lily-shaped. Tulips with beautiful reflexed and pointed petals.

Cottage tulips are late-blooming, produce large and almost egg-shaped flowers.

Parrot tulips are late-blooming and have fringed and scalloped flowers.

Double (late). These are peony-type tulips.

Fosteriana are early-flowering, dainty, and have many unusual hybrids.

Kaufmanniana are early-blooming, with large flowers.

Dahlia (dahlia)

Dahlias have tuberous roots and rest between seasons. The next year's flower is produced by the fleshy extension of the old stem. For best results grow dahlias in a sandy soil; give them plenty of water and sun, feed them regularly, and put some bone meal in the soil.

Plant early, but not so early that the plants get chilled. Soak the tubers in water for a day, then plant them 3 to 4 inches deep. Insert a stake next to the plant

Tall dahlias are the background in this city garden; other beds hold succulents and marigolds—it is a colorful urban hideaway. (Photograph by C. D. Luckhart)

Dahlia

because most dahlias need support. Soak well when watering.

As soon as the tops are killed by the first frosts in fall, cut the plants back to about 4 inches above the crown and remove them a few days later. Dry them in a well-ventilated place for a day, then put them in peat moss or vermiculite and store in a cool but not freezing area. In spring, divide the bulbs, allowing one eye or bud to each root, and replant them.

Dahlias have been bred extensively. Before making selections, study all the groups: giant formal, cactus type, sweetheart dahlias, dwarfs, miniatures, pompons, and single-bedding types. They bloom in a rainbow of colors.

Begonia Tuberhybrida (tuberous begonias)

For sheer drama and intense summer color, these plants are star performers. Tuberous begonias today have been bred to near-perfection in flower form, size, and color. The choice is vast. There are more than 10,000 recorded varieties, one seemingly prettier than the other. Some of my favorites include Camelliaeflora, Ruffled, Cristata, Fimbriata, forms of Marginata: *Crispa marginata*, with frilled single flowers, and Double Marginata, with petals lined and edged with bands of contrasting colors. Other forms include Narcissiflora, Picotee, and Rose.

In March, put large tubers in a 2-inch layer of 1 part peat moss and 2 parts sand. Start them in a wood flat or other large container. Set the tubers 2 inches apart and about ½-inch deep, with the dented side up. Cover them with about ¼-inch of the starting medium. Place the container in good light in 60 to 70°F, and keep the tubers just barely moist. Too much water causes rot and not enough curtails growth. Be sure to keep plants indoors. If they develop rapidly and appear to be growing too late before they can go outside, they can be held back by cool temperatures. On the other hand, if they are not growing fast enough, accelerate their growth with more warmth.

After about two weeks, when the sprouts are about 2 inches tall and the danger of frost is past, replant them in containers. Put the containers where there is scattered sunshine. Tuberous begonias will survive some heat during the day, but they need cool nights of 55 to 60°F. Water the plants heavily in bright weather, but not as much when it is cloudy. When they are actively growing, apply a 5-10-5 commercial fertilizer mixed half-strength every second week.

After blooming, when leaves dry and start turning yellow, water plants sparingly; let the growth continue for as long as possible. When the foliage is completely yellow, remove the tubers, wash off the soil, remove stems, and place the plants in an airy, sunny place for a few days. Then store them in a cool, frost-free location until it is time to start them again.

Iris

The bulbous irises are superior cut flowers, and their color and form are highly desirable in the garden. The most popular and frequently grown kinds are the Spanish, English, and Dutch types.

Spanish iris *(I. xiphium)* has narrow and grassy leaves about 12 inches tall. The flowers are of various blue shades. All these irises have the characteristic yellow blotch in the fall. The plants start blooming in May and stop in early June. Spanish irises need good drainage, full sun, and shelter from the wind.

English iris *(I. xiphiodes)* has large leaves, and the large showy flowers are produced in several colors, with blue predominating. They bloom in June and need a moist, acid soil and coolness. They do not respond in heat or drought. *I. reticulata* is another lovely type that blooms early in spring. Plant the bulbs in September or October, 4 to 6 inches apart, in a semishady location. The flowers resemble their Spanish and Dutch iris cousins, but are smaller; these plants rarely grow more than 6 inches.

Dutch irises are hybrids, and although they resemble the Spanish types, they are more robust and floriferous. Colors range from white to yellow to blue. Dutch hybrids need good drainage, sun, and a light soil. They put on their colorful display in March and April.

Plant the Spanish, English, and Dutch irises 4 inches deep and about 4 inches apart. In regions where freezing occurs, mulch over the plants in winter. After foliage ripens, you can remove plants, dry them, and store them in a cool place; leave plants in their containers.

LIST OF SPRING-FLOWERING BULBS

Botanical and Common Name	When to Plant	Depth (Inches)	Sun or Shade	Remarks
Allium (flowering onion)	Fall	3	Sun	Prettier than its common name suggests

Botanical and Common Name	When to Plant	Depth (Inches)	Sun or Shade	Remarks
Chionodoxa (glory of snow)	Fall	3	Sun	Do not disturb for several years
Crocus	Fall	3	Sun	Always dependable
Daffodil (jonquil, narcissus)	Fall	6	Sun	The name "daffodil" is used for all members
Eranthis (winter aconite)	Early fall	3	Shade	Very early bloom
Erythronium (dogtooth violet)	Early fall	6	Shade	Delightful
Fritillaria	Fall	4	Shade	Overlooked but lovely
Galanthus (snowdrop)	Fall	3	Shade	Sometimes blooms during the winter
Hyacinthus (hyacinth)	Fall	6–8	Sun	Protect from wind and mice
Iris	Fall	4–6	Sun	Make good cut flowers
Leucojum (snowflake)	Fall	3	Shade	Flowers last a long time
Muscari (grape hyacinth)	Early fall	3	Sun	Very easy to grow
Ranunculus	Late fall	1	Sun	Lovely cut flowers
Scilla	Fall	2	Sun or light shade	Once established, blooms indefinitely
Tulipa (tulip)	Fall	2	Sun	Many kinds

Crocus

Hyacinthus

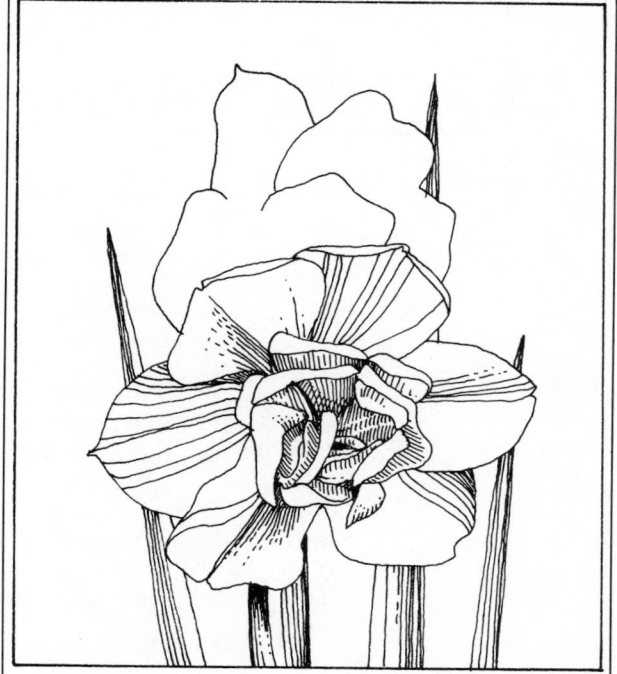

Daffodil

Fritillaria imperialis

Summer-Flowering Bulbs

In most of the United States, summer-flowering bulbs must be removed from their containers over the winter; they can be left in the container only if the temperature does not drop below freezing. Plant these bulbs after all danger of frost is past. When foliage dies down in the fall, remove the bulbs from their containers and let them dry off in an airy place. Trim foliage to about 5 inches. Remove all the dirt from the bulbs and store them in a dry, cool place (50°F) in boxes of dry sand or peat, on open trays, or in brown paper bags.

LIST OF SUMMER-FLOWERING BULBS

Botanical and Common Name	When to Plant	Depth (Inches)	Sun or Shade	Remarks
Agapanthus (flower-of-the-Nile)	Spring/fall	1	Sun	New dwarf varieties available
Alstroemeria	Spring	4	Sun	Good cut flowers
Begonia tuberhybridia (tuberous begonia)	Spring	4	Shade	Wide variety of sizes, colors, and forms
Caladium	Spring	4	Shade	Lovely foliage plants; many varieties

Botanical and Common Name	When to Plant	Depth (Inches)	Sun or Shade	Remarks
Dahlia	Spring	4	Sun	Need sandy soil and lots of water
Galtonia (summer hyacinth)	Spring	6	Sun	Buy new bulbs yearly
Gladiolus (gladiolus)	Spring	4–6	Sun	Need tons of watering
Lilium (lily)	Spring/fall	6–8	Sun	At best in its second year
Polianthus formosissima (tuberose)	Spring	1	Sun	Plant after danger of frost
Sprekelia formosissima (Jacobean lily)	Spring	3	Sun	Ideal container plants
Tigridia (tiger flower)	Early May	2–3	Sun	Exquisite flowers
Tritonia (montbretia)	Early May	2–3	Sun	Overlooked but lovely
Zephyranthes (zephyr lily)	Early spring	1	Sun or light shade	Make good cut flowers

LAWNS

Should you have a lawn in the city? Definitely, yes—if you want one. While many people will tell you that lawns are difficult to maintain, once the green carpet is established, it generally takes care of itself. It is the initial preparation and care that scares most gardeners away. But a lovely green lawn is a prize indeed and adds much to the city garden. It need not be large—even a small lawn is highly decorative in the scheme of things.

You can sow seed and start your own lawn but, as mentioned, this takes time and patience and much care to get the grass growing. I highly recommend using sod. Sod is rolled strips of established grass that fits into place; in this way once the soil is conditioned you can have a lawn in a day. For a few weeks be sure the new lawn is watered evenly. This is vital but once it starts growing—that's it!

No matter what kind of soil exists in the proposed lawn site, recondition it. Break up clods and lumps with a rake or hoe and then be sure the site is level. Add organic matter or humus and then level the area again (I use a metal rake for leveling). Now add 4 to 6 inches of good topsoil; work this into the existing soil you have reconditioned and then level the area again. Topsoil is expensive but the initial expenditure is necessary to provide the lawn with good nutrients—and it only has to be done once.

Sod comes in rectangular sheets 12 inches wide and 12 to 18 inches long and generally about 1-inch thick. Lay the sheets of sod close together, flush with each other. Tamp down or, better yet, roll the sod evenly with a barrel roller. When it is in place, water it almost daily for a few weeks until the grass is growing.

After the initial few weeks of care, routine maintenance is necessary for your lawn; this entails weeding, feeding, and mowing.

Sod is available from nurseries; any appreciable amount is heavy so have suitable muscle on hand the day of delivery.

GROUND COVERS

If the maintenance of a lawn is just too time-consuming for you, consider using ground cover for a special area.

Inpatiens en masse are the garden accent here, with agapanthus in the background and ivy as cover around tree and fence—this combination of annuals, bulbs, and ground cover paint the picture. (Photograph by C. D. Luckhart)

Such plants offer a great deal for little cost and low maintenance. In fact, once these plants are in the ground and watered and fed regularly, that is all there is to it. Ground covers are tough plants that can tolerate abuse if necessary and still survive.

Plants are available in flats of 80 or 100 to a container. Put them into the ground just like regular plants. But do not expect them to thrive in a very poor soil; recondition the soil as for a lawn. Most nurseries will tell you to space ground covers 12 to 16 inches apart. This is a matter of choice rather than a rule. The more closely the plants are spaced, the more rapidly they cover an area. With 12- to 16-inch spacing, it may take almost two years for full coverage.

Every region has its own requirements in ground

Ajuga

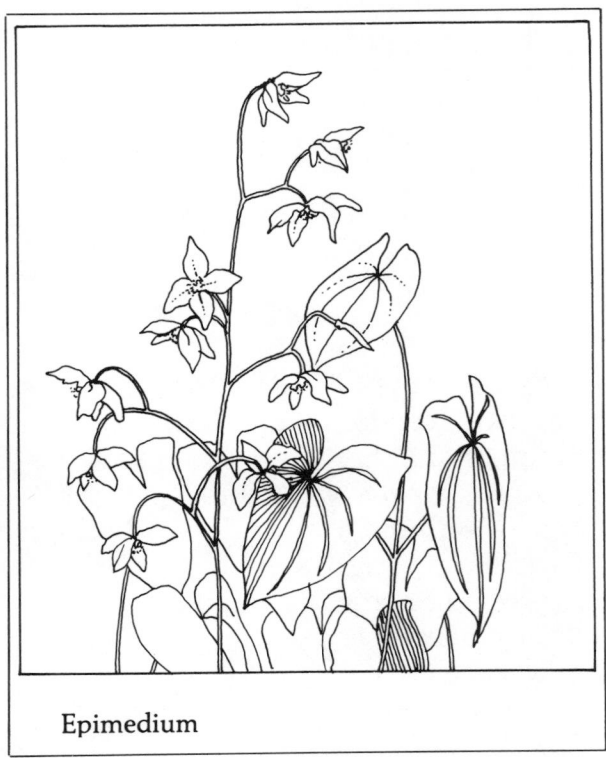

Epimedium

cover plants with respect to climate and soil. The plants offered at your local nursery will be those suitable for your area.

The following list of ground covers are some of the most popular ones:

List of Ground Covers

Aaron's-beard *(Hypericum calycinum)*. Grows to 12 inches. Sun or shade. Tolerates a sandy soil.

Ajuga. Grows to 6 inches; hardy perennial with rosettes of dark-green leaves and spikes of blue spring flowers. Sun or shade. Needs ample moisture.

Chamomile *(Anthemis nobilis)*. Grows to 3 to 5 inches. An overlooked but lovely cover with light green fernlike leaves. Needs sandy soil and full sun; even moisture.

Candytuft *(Iberis sempervirens)*. Grows to 6 inches; dense little bushes with white flowers. Needs sun and rich soil.

Cotoneaster (many). Shrubby, with small leaves and decorative berries. Several good ones.

Dichondra carolinensis. Small dark green leaves form

dense mats. Needs well-drained soil and plenty of water. Tender.

Epimedium. Semievergreen; grows to 9 inches, with glossy leaves and dainty flowers. Likes moist, slightly acid soil and somewhat shady conditions.

English ivy *(Hedera helix)*. One of the most popular ground covers; several handsome varieties. Some have tiny leaves; others, large foliage. Some grow quickly, whereas others take many months to become established. Sun or shade.

Heath *(Erica vagans)*. Grows to 12 inches, with pointed needlelike leaves.

Honeysuckle *(Lonicera japonica* "Halliana"). A tough rampant vine; grows to 6 inches. Sun or shade. Evergreen in the South; semievergreen in the North. Can become a pest unless kept within boundaries.

Ice plant *(Mesembryanthemum)*. A large group of succulent plants; annual or perennial. Recently renamed but still are available at nurseries under the old name. Some have 1- to 2-inch stiff leaves; others grow to 8 inches. All have bright daisylike flowers. Needs sun.

Juniperus (see shrubs).

Liriope muscari. Grows to 12 inches, with grassy foliage forming a dense mat. Sun or shade; any kind of soil.

Manzanita *(Arctostaphylos uva-ursi)*. Grows to 12 inches; evergreen with small, nodding leaves.

Mock-strawberry *(Duchesnea indica)*. Coarsely toothed leaves; good creeper.

Pachysandra terminalis. Grows to 5 to 12 inches. Evergreen for shady areas; slow growing. Has whorls of dark green leaves. Does not do well in sun.

Periwinkle *(Vinca minor)*. Excellent shade-loving evergreen creeper. Dark glossy green leaves and showy white or blue spring flowers.

Hedera helix

Arctostaphylos

Thymus

Hosta

Teucrium

Plantain lily *(Hosta,* or *Funkia)*. Many varieties. Some with large leaves; others with small leaves. Likes water, but will survive a dry situation too. Prefers shade.

Rosemary *(Rosmarinus officinalis* "Prostratus"). Evergreen; grows to 12 inches, with narrow leaves and blue flowers in spring. Needs sun; tolerates poor soil.

Stonecrop *(Sedum amecamecanum).* Low-growing, fleshy, succulent. Spreads rapidly.

Strawberry *(Fragaria chiloensis)*. Small semievergreen leaves and white flowers. Grows rapidly. Sun or shade.

Thyme *(Thymus)*. Low carpet plant. Tolerates hot, dry, sunny places and poor soil.

Wild ginger *(Asarum caudatum)*. Handsome woodlike plant for shady moist areas. Attractive heart-shaped leaves.

Evergreen shrubs predominate in this small city backyard garden. (Photograph by Matthew Barr)

#
Vegetables & Herbs

VEGETABLES

Today vegetables are easy to grow because superior hybridized seeds are available. The vegetables you grow depend upon how much space you have for containers, the climate of the area you live in, and whether your selections are cool- or warm-season vegetables. Some vegetables, tomatoes and squash, for example, need warm weather to grow well, but others, such as beets, spinach, and lettuce, grow best in cooler weather.

PLANNING THE VEGETABLE GARDEN

Ease into gardening. Grow only a few popular vegetables such as lettuce, beets, carrots, tomatoes, and beans the first year; the next year you can zero in on the more exotic vegetables. Do *not* try to grow everything all at

230

A vegetable and herb backyard home garden. (Photograph by Molly Adams)

once. Use your allotted space to its best advantage by planting at properly spaced intervals, described in the table on page 000, and grow climbing plants like cucumbers and squash against walls, fences, or poles. For example, a 10 × 20-foot box garden can accommodate carrots, radishes, tomatoes, cucumbers, eggplant, and squash. Position boxes and planters so there is enough space for you to walk between them and tend the plants. Gardens you have to skip around in are a big bother.

Now let us study the best container vegetables. Note that insects and diseases may attack your food plants; controls and preventatives are discussed in Chapter 10.

Beans

Climbing pole beans and bush-type beans are warm-season plants, easy to grow, and usually yield good harvests. Pole beans typically have more flavor and are more productive than bush beans. Good varieties are Kentucky Wonder and Blue Lake. Grow pole beans against fences or trellises in a rich soil with some compost added. Plant seeds 1½ inches deep after the last frost. Fertilize beans with vegetable food and water generously.

Pole beans produce in about 65 to 70 days and can be picked at various stages of growth; the pods are usually ready about 3 weeks after blooms. If plants are healthy,

you can pick beans every 3 to 5 days. Bush beans are ready for harvesting in about 50 days. Suggested varieties are Tendercrop, Greensleeves, and Bush Romano; good bush-type wax beans are Brittle Wax and Kinghorn Wax.

An arboreal vegetable garden high above the city boasts beans by the dozens—roof gardens are excellent for vegetable growing (Photograph by Bagger)

Beets

Plant seeds ½-inch deep 3 weeks before the last frost is anticipated. When plants are about 2 inches high, thin them so they are about 3 inches apart. When plants reach 8 or 9 inches, thin them again by removing every other plant, leaving 3-inch spaces between plants. Beets need 60 days to grow. Harvest them when they are young because, if they are left too long, they become pithy and lose flavor.

Beets like a cool temperature and dislike excessive heat, so put them in a shady, somewhat cool location, and fertilize lightly. Keep plants evenly moist with buckets of water because beets love water. The best varieties are Early Wonder, Ruby Queen, and Detroit Dark Red.

Broccoli and Cauliflower

Plant these cool-weather plants in spring a few weeks before the last frost and then again in midsummer. With good drainage, these vegetables succeed in almost any soil that has some compost. Sow seeds ¼-inch deep, spacing seeds 18 inches apart in rows 28 inches apart. Or grow prestarted plants, which are sold at nurseries. Water the plants copiously because they should never be dry. Pull cauliflower outer leaves over their heads to blanch them and keep them white. Watch for insects. Good varieties of cauliflower are Early Snowball and Snow King Hybrid; for broccoli try Green Comet and Spartan Early.

Carrots

Carrots need a very open soil and rapid growth, so feed and water the plants frequently. The longer a carrot takes to mature, the pithier it will be. Sow carrot seed in spring or fall. Plant 2 rows of carrots, and thin them out when they are about 2 inches tall. Thin the plants again in about 1 month. (Use the thinnings; tiny carrots are delicious.) Most varieties require about 75 days to mature. You can resow after harvesting if you want more carrots. Suggested varieties are Gold Pak, Imperator, and Chantenay.

Cucumbers

Cucumbers are extremely robust, grow quickly, and produce a good harvest. Sow the midget varieties; insert trellises or stakes into the box or planter so the plants can climb. Add some manure to the soil, and keep in a bright place, although direct sun is not necessary. Water freely.

Cucumbers start bearing in about 40 to 70 days and can be picked at any stage. The tiny young ones are ideal for sweet pickles; larger ones, if you let them mature, are fine for salads. Two good varieties are Bravo Hybrid and Early Surecrop.

Lettuce

The loose-head, leafy types of lettuce are excellent for growing in containers on the ground or in hanging pots. This lettuce is ready for plucking within 45 days. Sow the seed where it is to mature, and protect plants from heat. Cool weather is the secret to good lettuce. If you grow it through the summer, give the crop some shade or use heat-resistant varieties such as Oakleaf and

Salad Bowl. Give the plants light, but sun is not necessary to guarantee a crop. Use a 7-40-6 fertilizer and water thoroughly once the lettuce is growing. When lettuce is mature, harvest the outer leaves along with a few inner ones at each cutting.

Recommended head lettuce varieties are Great Lakes and Salad Bowl; Buttercrunch and Tender Crisp are delightful butterhead varieties; and Oakleaf and Salad Bowl are good leafy varieties.

Peas

Peas like cool temperatures and are a fairly easy crop to grow, especially the low-growing varieties that do not need staking or trellises, such as Mighty Midget, which takes little space and matures in 60 days. Little Marvel, a vine-type variety, also is excellent, maturing in about the same time. Sow seeds in pots or tubs in cool weather, about 15 peas per square foot, and cover with 1 to 2 inches of soil. Germinating peas need plenty of water; later just keep the soil moist.

If temperatures are too hot, the plant will produce all vines, no pods. Watch for aphids, which cause stunted curly leaves, and pick pods regularly or they will become hard.

Peppers

Peppers add an attractive spot of color to any container garden. Peppers need a warm growing period of about 2 months, with night temperatures never below 65°F (19°C). Start planting in April or May, depending upon your region's climate. Frost quickly kills peppers, so be sure weather is stable before you put plants out.

Grow long and slender hot peppers or the succulent

sweet green bell peppers. Frequent harvesting will encourage production through the summer; you can harvest peppers at any size.

Good sweet green peppers are Ace Hybrid and Yolo Wonder; for hot peppers grow Large Cherry or Long Red Cayenne.

Radishes

Radishes are excellent for the rank beginner because no matter how you grow them, they are invariably successful.

Radishes do not like hot weather, so get them going early in spring. Water plants thoroughly for crisp and tender radishes. Fertilize plants when the first young leaves appear. Radishes are ready when they taste crisp and succulent. Try Burpee White or Cherry Belle.

Spinach

Spinach does best in cool temperatures, so grow it in the coolest, shadiest location in the garden. Not as easy to grow as most vegetables, spinach flowers quickly, which stops foliage production. Give spinach plenty of water. Most varieties mature in about 50 days. Plant blight-resistant varieties such as Bloomsdale, America, and Long Standing, and remember to keep plants thinned to 2 inches apart.

Squash

Squash grows so prolifically you often get more than you can consume. A member of the cucumber family, it is generally easy to grow and needs a support such as a trellis. Thin plants or you will have a jungle; try to keep 4 or 5 stout stems per plant. Give plants plenty of sun and buckets of water. Once plants are growing, fertilize sparingly. Pick squash early and often, and watch for borers. Dust plants with rotenone in July or August. Good summer squash varieties are Cocozelle Bush and Crookneck; for winter squash try Gold Nugget and Bush Ebony.

Tomatoes

Tomatoes usually are successful for even the neophyte gardener. They need little more than warm temperatures and as much sun as possible. Very warm temperatures, over 95°F, harm them, so shelter tomatoes from *extreme* sun on very hot days. Keep tomatoes at temperatures above 60°F (16°C) at night or they may not set fruit.

They need plenty of water and a special food sold at nurseries. Keep them growing continuously so you have a good harvest. Fertilize first about 1 week after you transplant the seedlings and again in about 2 weeks. While plants are producing fruit, fertilize every week.

Thin tomato plants by removing the small suckers, the tiny first two or three leaves that appear between the main stem and the foliage, as they appear. Depending upon the variety, tomatoes should bear within 70 to 80 days after seed planting. Watch for hornworms.

Early varieties include Early Hybrid and Spring Giant; midseason ones are Heinz and Marglobe; and small and midget varieties are Red Cherry and Tiny Tim.

PLANTING SCHEDULE FOR VEGETABLES

Vegetable	Planting-Out Time Seeds	Translants	Seed Depth (Inches)	Growing Days Needed in Garden	Comments
Beans, bush	After last frost		1½	50	Material applies to shell beans also, but leave on bush until pods dry
Beans, pole	After last frost		1½	65	Pole limas will be 2 weeks later; trellis required for all
Beets	3 weeks before last frost		½	60	Beet tops are excellent cooked or put in salads
Broccoli and cauliflower	4 weeks before last frost		¼	50 after transplanting	Sow indoors 6 weeks before planting-out time; guard against cabbage loopers, harlequin bugs, and cabbage-family pests
Carrots	2 weeks before last frost or after		½ (3)	75	Late carrots can be kept in ground all winter under mulch
Cucumbers	After last frost		½	40–70	Cucumbers grow well on fences and trellises

Vegetable	Planting-Out Time Seeds	Translants	Seed Depth (Inches)	Growing Days Needed in Garden	Comments
Kohlrabi	3 weeks before last frost		¼	55	Guard against same insects as attack broccoli and cabbage; better than turnip for spring crop in hot summer areas
Lettuce, leaf	5 weeks before last frost		¼	45	Thinnings make excellent early salads; dependable crop
Lettuce, butterhead	5 weeks before last frost		¼	75	May be handled like head lettuce if desired; small, delicious
Lettuce, head	3 weeks before last frost		¼	85	Sow in cold-frame 4 weeks before planting-out time; stands heat better than butterhead type
Onion, sets		Early as ground is prepared	1½–2	45	One-pound average sets should plant about 50-foot row; medium to small sets are better than large ones

Vegetable	Planting-Out Time Seeds	Translants	Seed Depth (Inches)	Growing Days Needed in Garden	Comments
Peas	6 weeks before last frost		1–2	60	May be grown on low trellis
Peppers		After last frost	¼	70	From hot to sweet, all grow on beautiful bushy plants; pick sweet peppers when large; pick hot peppers when fully ripe
Radishes	4 weeks before last frost		¼	25	For prolonged prime supply, make successive sowing 2 weeks apart, spring and fall

Harvesting onions in a city garden. (Photograph by Matthew Barr)

Vegetable	Planting-Out Time Seeds	Translants	Seed Depth (Inches)	Growing Days Needed in Garden	Comments
Spinach	3 weeks before last frost		½	48	A cool-weather crop; goes to seed (bolts) in hot weather
Squash, bush or vine	After last frost		1	Summer types 52; winter types 85–115	Where space is limited, use bush type
Tomatoes		After last frost	½	70 from transplanting	Sow seeds indoors 6 weeks before planting-out date; staked plants may be spaced closer than un-staked ones; late-crop tomatoes may be seeded directly in ground
Turnips	Spring: 6 weeks before last frost. Fall: 10 weeks before first expected frost		½	55	Good fall crop that stores well in a box of sand in a cool spot

HERBS

Herbs are a delightful ingredient in most foods and need no special preparation. They are so easy to grow that this chapter concentrates on general herb information rather than detailed growing instructions. You can buy herbs as prestarts at nurseries, or sow seeds of most herbs as soon as the last spring frost is over.

Basil

This annual plant is a basic ingredient in Italian cuisine. There are many types, ranging from the wide-leaved kinds to the coppery ones, but most people grow sweet basil. Sweet basil grows to about 24 inches and needs really good sun.

Dill

This annual herb is much more vegetable than you might think. Try dried dill on boiled artichokes for a pleasant taste treat. Dill is feathery and ferny in appearance, and its only drawback is that it grows tall, to about 6 feet. The small yellow flowers are borne in clusters. Whenever the weather is warm you can sow seeds; dill will tolerate some shade if necessary.

Marjoram

This is a good herb for salads, fish dishes, and some meats. Marjoram is a perennial plant that generally lives over, but I find it just as easy to seed new plants every year. In spring, when the weather is safely warm, seed marjoram in a sunny place; plants grow to about 20 inches and are rather attractive.

Rosemary

If you have the space to grow it, rosemary will provide a flavorful reward in fish dishes and as a medicinal herb. Plant seed or cuttings, which root easily. Plants grow to about 36 inches. There are both upright and creeping varieties.

Sage

This perennial has gray-green leaves and pretty purple and white flowers. Plants grow in a sunny place, even in poor soil. Although sage is not as popular as most herbs, it has many uses and is especially good in poultry stuffing and pork sausage.

Savory

Summer savory is a delicate-looking plant with a few leaves, and winter savory is big, with dark green leaves and pretty white flowers. Both winter and summer savory need a sunny spot, and both are good for vegetable dishes and poultry stuffing.

Tarragon

This is a favorite culinary herb, but get the right kind of tarragon, *Artemisia dracunculus*. My best tarragon grows in a somewhat shady place, although most herb experts say it does better in full sun. Tarragon is especially good for vinegars and as a sauce with white wine and butter for liver or fish.

Thyme

This perennial plant adds flavor to egg dishes and it can be used to make tea. There are several varieties. Give plants sun.

You can grow a tub of tarragon in any city garden. (Photograph by Matthew Barr)

DRYING HERBS

Gather herbs early in the morning, when plants have just started to bloom, if you want the best flavor. Dry herbs in the sun or in the oven at low heat, or just let them hang in loose bunches in a cool dry attic. When they are dry, strip off the leaves and bottle the herbs in clean, dry, labeled jars.

If you want to overdry herbs, place them on cookie sheets and cover them with waxed paper; heat the oven to 130°F, until the herbs are brittle to the touch. For sun drying, pick a warm dry day and put plants on trays that have ventilation underneath. A screened box is ideal. Make this tray from four pieces of soft wood and some hardware cloth or mesh screen. Turn the herbs a few times so all parts get dry. When herbs are brittle to the touch, strip and bottle them.

For drying herbs in an attic, tie herbs in loose bunches and hang them upside down from rafters or nails in the ceiling. When leaves are brittle, strip them off and bottle the herbs.

Home-grown herbs are more flavorful and tastier than those bought in stores, and there are dozens of herbs that will grow in a garden in the sky. Most herbs need little space—even the tiniest garden can accommodate a

few kitchen herbs. And unlike vegetables, many herbs do not need intense sun or long periods of sun; 2 or 3 hours is fine for most herbs. Grow plants in a well-drained, sandy soil; this is a prime requirement for herbs. Keep the soil evenly moist, and thin plants occasionally to keep them in bounds and to prevent them from crowding out other plants.

Use herbs cut from the plant, for salads and seasonings, or dry them for future use. To dry herbs, put leaves and stems on a baking tin in a 200°F oven with the door open and "bake" them until they are dry. Then strip the stems and leaves and put them in airtight containers. You can also dry herbs by hanging them in bunches from the ceiling in a dark but dry place until it is time to use them.

Sage, tarragon, thyme, basil, parsley, savory, and chives are the easiest herbs to grow. Start annual herbs from seed; buy started plants of perennial herbs at nurseries and set them in soil. Plant basil, chives, parsley, rosemary, sage, and thyme after the last frost, ¼-inch deep.

Tubbed herbs and strawberries in planter boxes are part of this city garden. (Photograph by C. D. Luckhart)

10

Plant
Protection

Because it is usually small, the city garden should present only small insect and/or disease problems. There should never be a great infestation of insects or a plague of diseases if plants are tended regularly and growing well. A healthy plant, like a healthy person, is strong and robust, able to resist invaders.

In roof gardens and balcony gardens, where plants are mainly in pots, there are few plant problems because wind, sun, soot, and pollution rather than insects are likely to adversely affect plants. So remember that if you do see insects on your plants—in ground-level gardens or in container plants—do not buy a barrage of poisons; there are many better ways of eliminating pests.

INSECTS OR CULTURE?

Not all, or even many, plant problems are caused by insects or disease. First look to your care habits. Are

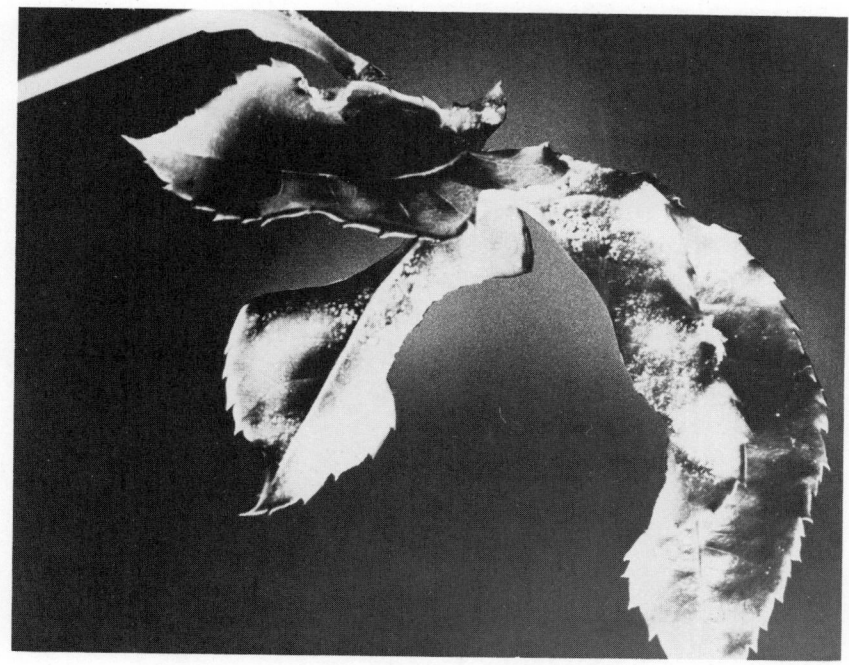

Mildew has desiccated this plant. (USDA photograph)

plants getting enough water and light? Or are they getting too much sun? What about wind; is it harming the plant? Determine just what the problem is before you act. For example:

1. Plants that develop leaves with brown or crisp edges may be getting too much heat and are thus being hindered by fluctuating soil temperatures.

2. If leaves turn yellow, the soil may lack acidity.

3. If leaves develop brown or silvery streaks, plants are getting too much water.

4. If foliage looks limp and wan, plants are not getting enough water.

5. If buds suddenly drop off, fluctuating temperatures are the cause.

It may be the natural tendency of a particular plant to develop yellow leaves that drop off. A plant that does not do well in one place should be moved to a different location; sometimes this makes all the difference in the world.

If your cultural conditions are good and plants are still suffering, look for insects. Most common garden pests are recognizable on sight. It is important to know what you are fighting before you do battle. In most cases, even if plants do have insects, poisonous sprays are not necessary. Old-fashioned methods and new biological controls can eliminate most of the culprits.

INSECT PREVENTATIVES

One of the best ways to avoid plant problems is to prevent them before they start. Observe plants frequently to see if they are growing—new shoots and leaves—or just existing. In the city, soot and dust accumulation on leaves can cause more damage than insects because they close plant pores and make transpiration impossible. Wash and hose plants frequently. When you hose down plants, aim the spray at the bottom of leaves, leaf axils, and hard to get at places where soot and insects can congregate. There are many hose-attachment devices suitable for this; some spray, some create a fine blast of water, and others mist plants. Use the one that best suits your needs.

If you see a few aphids or mealybugs, you can eradicate them quickly without much trouble. But once insects get a foothold you are in trouble; sprays, chemicals and other means will be necessary to save vegetables, so watch closely for the first appearance of bugs.

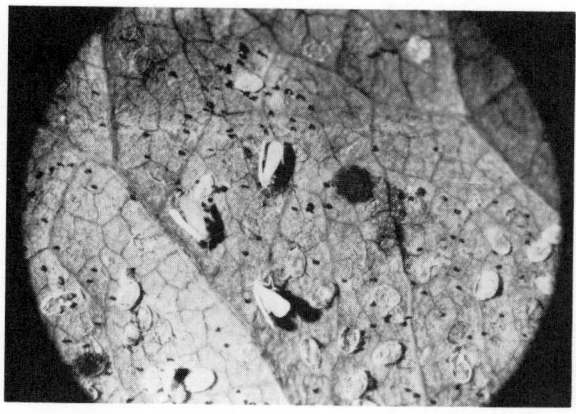

Whitefly in the garden can cause damage to plants. (USDA photograph)

Spider mites affect all kinds of plants; here a chrysanthemum is seriously injured by the pests. (USDA photograph)

Aphids are tiny, oval, soft-bodied pests; mealybugs are cottony masses, and scale are hard-shelled insects that attach themselves to plants and somewhat resemble apple seeds. All these insects are easy to see and easy to get rid of if you catch them early. Laundry soap and water deters aphids; alcohol on a cotton swab makes mealybugs disappear. Scrape off scale with a stiff toothpick dipped in soapy water. Picking off insects by hand is a good control also. The one insect you will not be able to see that is liable to attack vegetables is the spider mite; all you can do is hope that your plants are not attacked by this culprit.

Vegetables attract other unwanted visitors. Various chewing insects love leafy vegetables, so keep rotenone insecticide on hand. *Hookworms* and *cutworms* may appear on tomatoes. Hand pick and destroy the pests, or use one or two applications of sevin. Cucumber beetles are easily discouraged from squash and cucumbers by regular applications of rotenone or pyrethrum. If you are growing beans, watch for *bean leaf beetles* or *Mexican bean beetles* and use sevin.

Squash borers can wipe out a good crop. If you see them, dust with rotenone, especially in early June to about mid-July. Snails and slugs love vegetables, so use snail and slug bait. Corys is the best if you can find it, but if not, try Bug-Geta, which is in the form of pellets that you sprinkle on the soil.

Use these chemicals and all insecticides with care, and only as detailed on the package. It is most important in any type of vegetable garden to follow instructions on the label about discontinuing use a certain length of time before harvest.

INSECT CONTROL METHODS

Persistent Poisons

The ecologists' main concern today is not how poisonous a chemical is, but how persistent and accumulative it is. Researchers have discovered that many years after their application, hydrocarbon chemicals such as lindane, aldrin, chlordane, DDT, and dozens of others are still found in living organisms—virtually everywhere on earth. Avoid any chlorinated hydrocarbons.

Biological Control

This is a valid control because it is fighting nature with nature and uses natural predators instead of poisons. Ladybugs, praying mantes, and lacewing bugs are all part of biological control. This method also involves planting onions, marigolds, chrysanthemums, and other plants that naturally repel insects. Birds too are part of the defense. Swallows are excellent insect-eating scavengers, as are purple martins. Another group of beneficial birds is from the flycatcher family, of which the kingbird is a member. Its diet consists mainly of insects. Wrens, titmice, and bush tits are still other friendly birds that help keep your garden insect-free. The Baltimore oriole consumes caterpillars, pupae, and even adult moths. To attract birds to your garden, plant berry bushes such as pyracantha and have water available for the birds because they love water and congregate wherever there is a supply, whether it is from a garden fountain, in a bird bath, or from the mist of a water sprinkler.

Systemics

Systemics are poisons such as Di-Syston and Meta-Systox-R. This is a popular way of killing insects because it is easy and takes little time. Still, it is highly toxic and cumulative, and the persistent effects have not yet been studied thoroughly, so proceed with caution. Poison comes in granules (there are also liquids) that are sprinkled on the ground; the ground is then watered. Poison is absorbed by the plants' roots, and all parts of the plant become toxic to some insects for a period of 4 to 6 weeks. However, systemics control only a few insects—aphids, leafhoppers, and mealybugs—and any careful gardener can surely control these without dubious chemicals.

Organic Chemicals

These insect deterrents are made from plants: chrysanthemums, rotenone, quassia, and others. They are nonpersistent and harmless to warm-blooded animals. They are excellent controls, although several applications may be necessary. Organic controls are being used increasingly in combination with other, more lethal poisons. So check the labels on cans and packages carefully to be sure of the contents.

As mentioned, the ecologists' main concern is not how poisonous a chemical is but how persistent and accumulative it is. The preventatives now listed, although poisonous, are considered nonaccumulative at this time. Note that first we present preventatives for nonfood plants.

INSECT PREVENTION CHART

Insects	Appearance	What They Attack	What They Do	Control
Aphids	Green, black, pink, yellow, or red soft-bodied insects	Almost all plants	Stunt plants, deform and yellow leaves by sucking juices	Malathion, rotenone
Beetles	Usually brown or black; wingless	Flowers and beans	Eat leaves and flowers	Hand pick if possible
Caterpillars (includes bagworms, cutworms, cankerworms, tent caterpillars)	Easily recognized	All kinds of plants	Defoliate plants	Rotenone, Diazinon, Malathion

Insects	Appearance	What They Attack	What They Do	Control
Grasshoppers	Familiar insect	Plants, trees	Eat leaves	Sevin
Lacebugs	Small bugs with lacy wings	Azaleas, oaks, birches, hawthorns, other plants	Mottle leaves	Malathion
Leafhoppers	Wedge-shaped insects that hop	Many plants	Turn leaves pale or brown; stunt plants	Malathion
Mealybugs	White cottony insects	Many plants	Stunt plants so they do not grow	Sevin, Diazinon
Mites	Minute sucking insects	Almost all plants	Discolor leaves	Systemics
Nematodes	Microscopic worms	Many plants	Stunt plants so they die	Sterilize soil
Scale	Tiny, hard, oval insects	Many plants	Yellow leaves or cause them to be lost	Diazinon
Snails, slugs (not insects but common pests)	Easily recognized	Many plants	Eat foliage	Snare-all without metaldehyde
Springtails	Tiny black jumping bugs	Some plants	Pit leaves	Malathion
Thrips	Tiny winged insects	Few plants	Make leaves silvery	Malathion
Wireworms	Hard, shiny, coiled worms	Flowers, vegetables	Kill seedlings; work underground	Diazinon

Source: Much of the above data is taken from the Thoughtful Gardener's Guide, in "Cry California," *Journal of California Tomorrow,* vol. 4, no. 3, Summer, 1969.

INSECT SPRAY SCHEDULE FOR VEGETABLES

Vegetable	Pest/Appearance	Preventative	When to Spray
Beans	Mexican bean beetles. Orange to yellow, with black spots on back. Fuzzy larvae, ⅓-inch long. Feed on pods and underside of leaves	Rotenone	When larvae or adult begins to feed. Repeat once at 7- to 10-day intervals.
Beets	Leaf miners. Slender, gray, black-haired flies, ¼-inch long. Pale green larvae make blotches on leaves	Diazinon, Malathion	When first blisters appear on leaves. Repeat once at 7- to 10-day intervals.
Broccoli	Maggots. Yellowish white, legless worms, less than ½-inch long. Tunnel in foods.	Diazinon	Transplanting time.
Cauliflower	Cabbage loopers. Pale green worm to 1½ inches long. Chew holes in leaves.	Sevin, Malathion	When young worms begin to feed. Repeat every 5 to 7 days until 1 week before harvest.
Cucumbers	Cucumber beetles, flea beetles, leafhoppers. Eat foliage	Sevin	At 7- to 10-day intervals when insects appear. Avoid spraying open blossoms.
Lettuce	Aphids. Suck juices causing leaves to yellow.	Malathion	When insects appear, and weekly as needed.
Onions	Thrips. Tiny, yellow or brown, winged insects. Larvae white, wingless. Suck juices, causing white blotches on leaves.	Malathion	When leaves begin to scar. Repeat two to three times.

Vegetable	Pest/Appearance	Preventative	When to Spray
Peas	Aphids and weevils. Brown with white or black markings, ⅓-inch long. Larvae white, small, to ⅓-inch.	Malathion, rotenone	Insects appear when plants blossom and before pods form.
Spinach	Leaf miners and aphids.	Diazinon, Malathion	When plants are young, before leaves curl; discontinue 7 days before harvest.
Squash	Cucumber beetles, flea beetles, leafhoppers.	Same as cucumbers	Same as cucumbers
Tomatoes	Cutworms. Dull gray, brown, or black worms. Hornworms. Large green worms, to 4 inches.	Sevin, diazinon	Apply pesticide to soil surface around plants when setting them. Use every 7 days when pests appear.
	Aphids and mites.	Sevin, Malathion, Kelthane	

When using any insecticide or fungicide, check the label to determine when to stop using before harvest. It is generally 1 to 2 weeks.

PLANT DISEASES

Bacteria, fungi, and viruses are the cause of several plant diseases, but none are especially severe or likely to attack many plants. Diseases are generally named for their dominant symptoms (blight, canker, leaf spot) or for the organism causing the disease (rust, powdery mildew). These diseases may be prevalent in the rural garden, where there is much more space and more plants, but in the city garden they are rare. However,

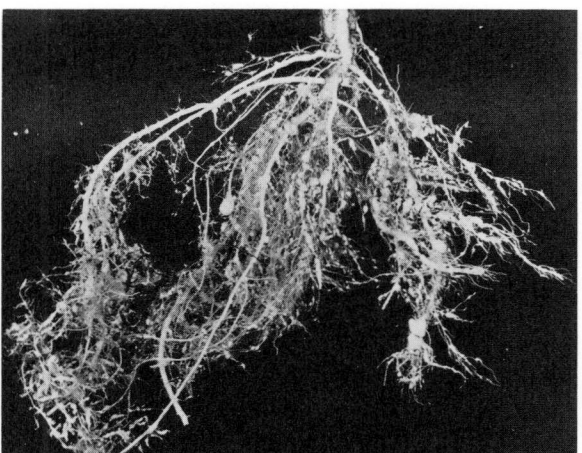

Blister rot infects many trees and can cause damage; it should be treated accordingly. (USDA photograph)

Nematodes attack plant roots and can devastate all kinds of plants. (USDA photograph)

Gall is another plague of some trees and can cause damage. (USDA photograph)

There are several kinds of cankers that attack plants. Left unchecked they can cause serious damage to a garden. (USDA photograph)

unfavorable conditions and poor cultural practices open the way for these agents to cause trouble. Excessive moisture is particularly important because it is necessary for the germination of the disease organism's spores. Several insects too carry diseases from one plant to another.

Three common causes of plant disease are fungi, bacteria, and viruses. Fungi are familiar to us because we have seen it on stale bread, fruit, and mushrooms. There are thousands of different kinds of fungi, some of which can cause serious plant damage. Rot, wilt, rust, and powdery mildew are basically caused by specific fungi.

Human diseases are caused by bacteria, and so are several plant ailments. Bacteria are microscopic organisms that survive in soil or plant parts and cause blight, rot, galls, or wilting. Bacteria are the causative agents of fire blight and iris rhizome rot.

Many of the most serious diseases of ornamental plants are caused by viruses. We are still trying to decipher viruses in humans, and they are as much a mystery when they attack plants.

Other plant diseases that may strike plants occur rarely:

Powdery mildew is a white or gray growth, usually appearing on the surface of leaves, branches, or fruit. Leaves are powdery, with blotches, and sometimes curled. Plants are often stunted. Control with a hose spray or heavy rain.

Leaf spot can extensively damage ornamental plants, resulting in defoliation. Leaves have distinct spots with brownish or white centers and dark edges. The disease is rarely fatal, but affected foliage should be cut off. Control by spraying with Zineb or Ferbam.

Wilt is caused by various organisms and can affect mature plants and seedlings. Usually wilt organisms live in soil. Cut away infected parts. There is no known chemical control.

Cankers are lesions on woody stems, with fungi entering through unbroken tissue. To control, cut away infected parts.

DISEASE CONTROL FOR VEGETABLES

Plant diseases have favorite crops they like to attack. Many vegetable varieties are disease-resistant; look for

VEGETABLE DISEASE CHART

Disease	Vegetable Attacked	Damage
Anthracnose	Beans Cucumbers Squash	Sunken, reddish brown to blackish spots; red areas on leaves
Aster yellows	Carrots	Inner leaves stunted, yellow
Bacterial blight	Beans	Water-soaked spots on leaves
Bacterial spot	Tomatoes Peppers Eggplant	Scabby spots on fruit
Blight (many kinds)	Many crops	Leaves affected in three main ways: spot, ring, and streaks
Bosaic	Beans	Mottled leaves
Verticillium and/or Fusarium yellows	Cucumbers Squash Tomatoes	Red areas on leaves
Fusarium yellows	Cauliflower Broccoli Cucumbers Squash	Leaves turn yellow
Leaf blight	Carrots	Outer leaves turn yellow
Powdery mildew	Peas	White to grayish coating on leaves
Viruses	Many crops	Leaves mottled or spotted in patterns
Wilt	Peas Tomatoes	Yellow, dwarfed plants; plants stunted

them when buying seeds, especially tomatoes, because they are certainly worth the search.

The following chart summarizes what you should know about diseases that attack vegetables. Once you identify the specific disease, buy the remedy at the local nursery. The remedies are sold under various trade names; there are too many names to list, so ask someone at the nursery for a good brand.

APPENDIX:
Some More City Garden Plans

The following plans are suggested landscapes for various types of city gardens—they are to give you ideas for your own gardens. In these plans I have used specific plants; these may be found at mail order suppliers or, in some cases, local nurseries. Or you can substitute plants of your own tastes depending on your preference for color.

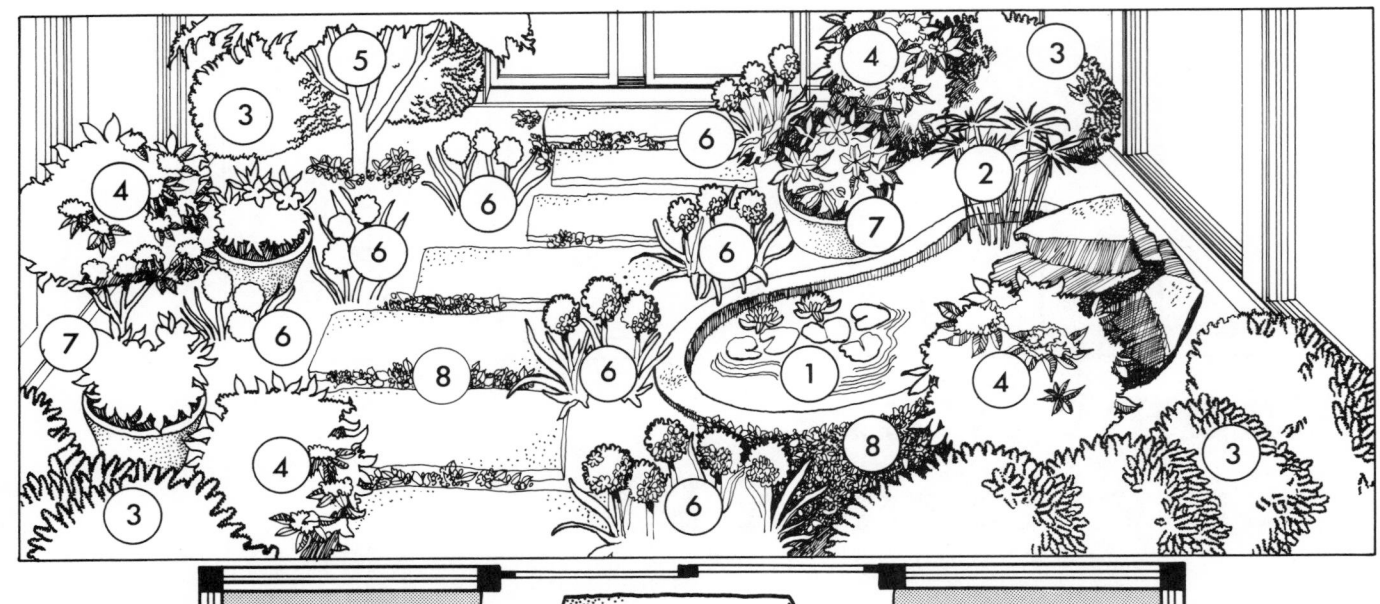

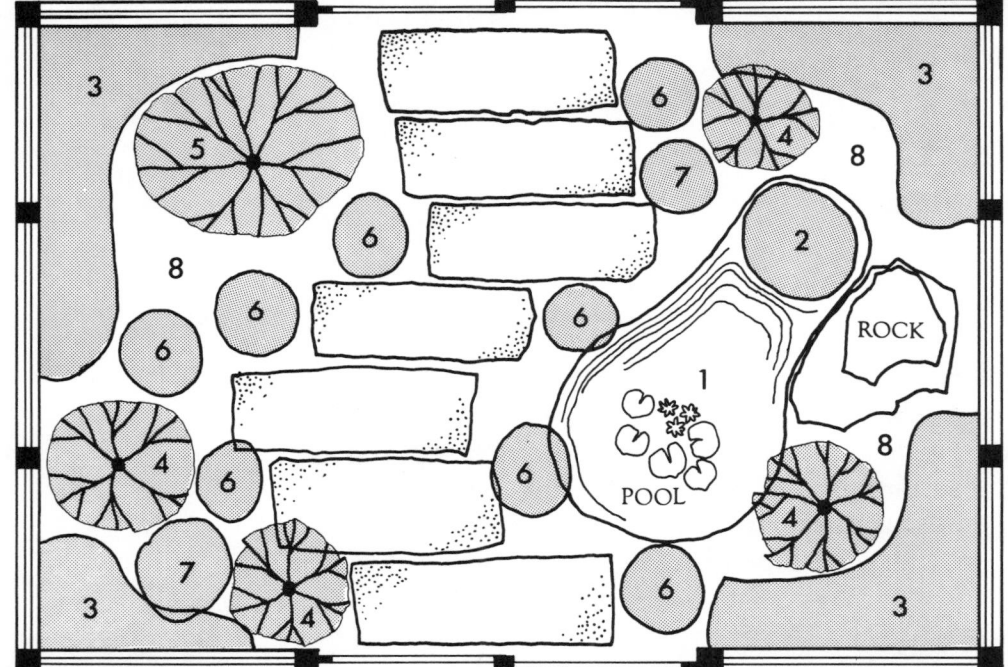

Atrium Garden

1. Nymphaea 'Rose Arey'

2. Cyperus alternifolius

3. Picea abies 'Repens'

4. Azalea 'Helen Curtis'

5. Acer palmatum

6. Armeria maritima

7. Browallia

8. Ajuga genevensis

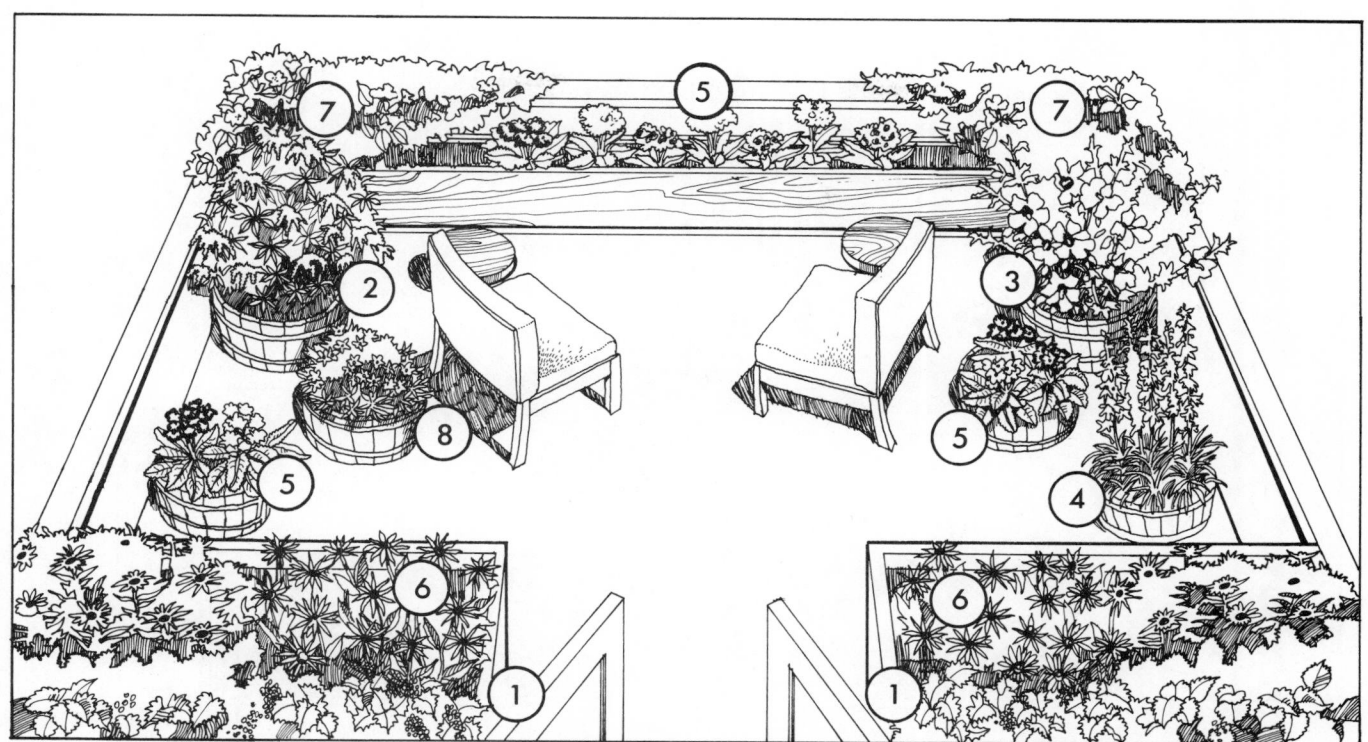

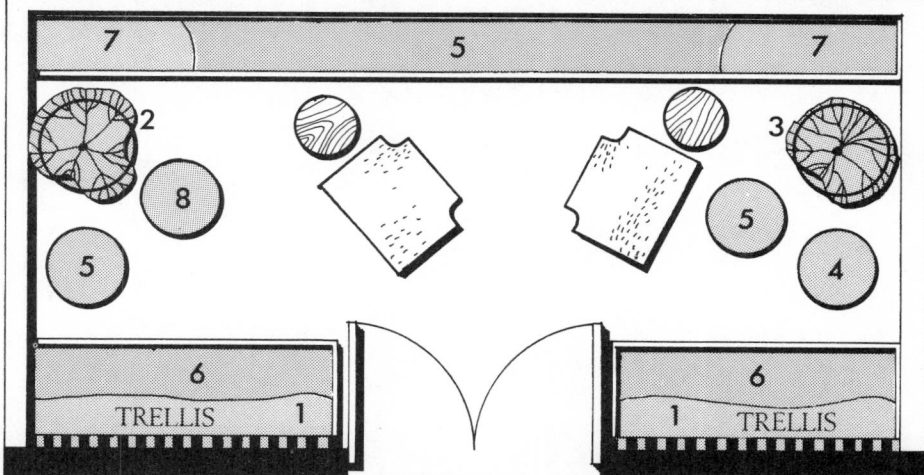

Balcony Garden

1. Ampelopsis brevipedunculata

2. Pieris japonica

3. Althaea

4. Lobelia cardinalis

5. Polyanthus

6. Echinacea

7. Campsis tagliabuana

8. Lithospermum diffusa

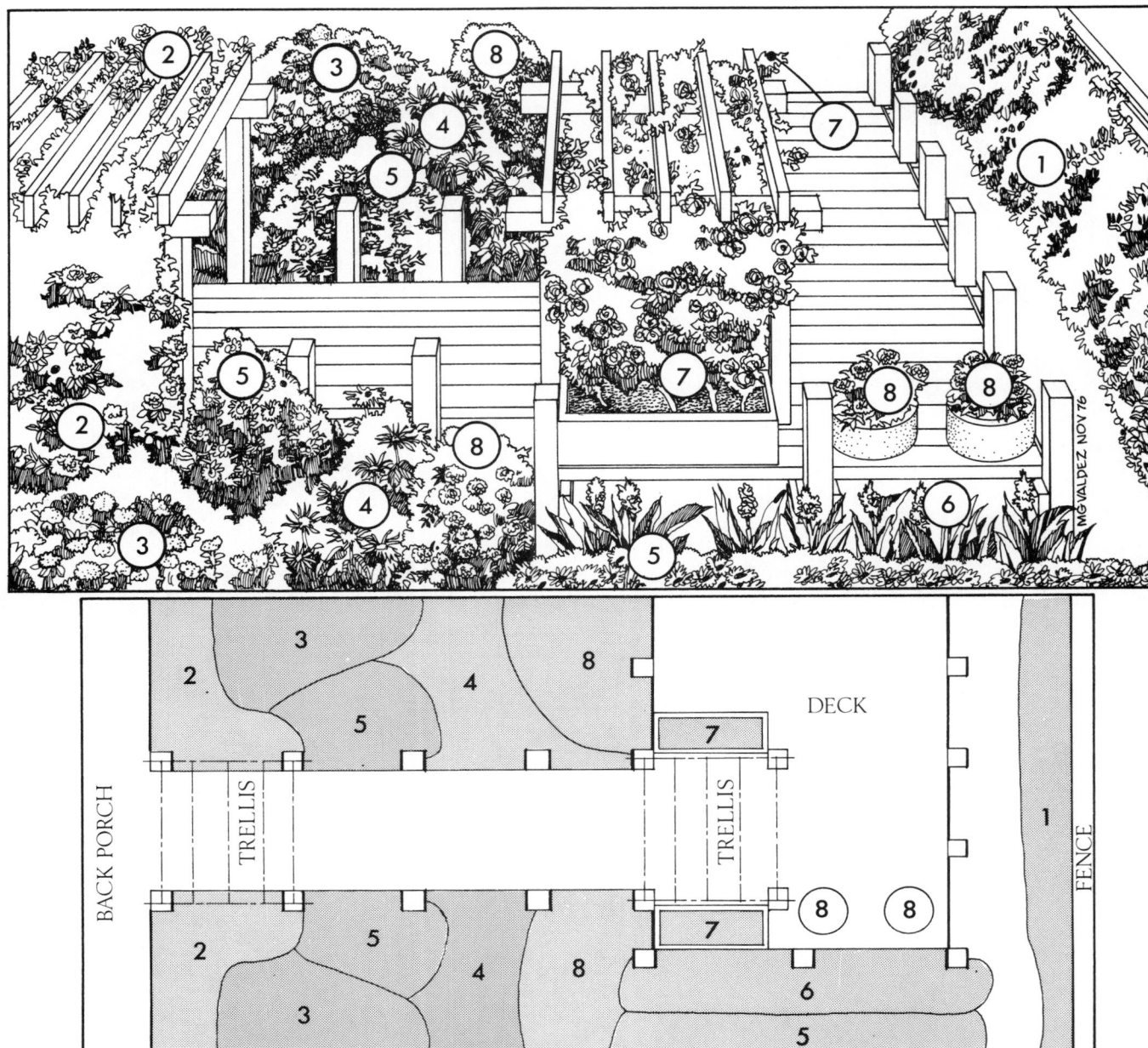

Backporch Garden

1. Lonicera sempervirens	5. Chrysanthemum
2. Rosa	6. Canna
3. Viburnum carlcephalum	7. Rosa
4. Monarda didyma	8. Dahlia

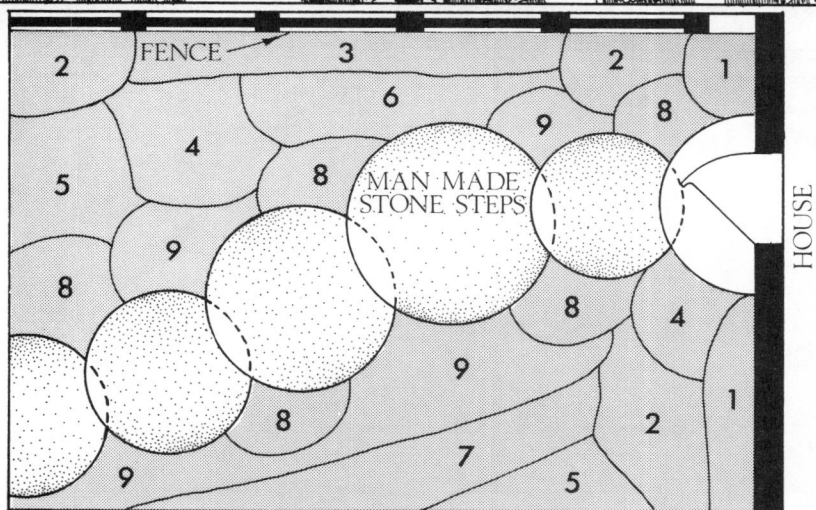

City Garden (low maintenance)

1. Campsis tagliabuana

2. Montbretia c ocosmiiflora

3. Rosa

4. Hemerocallis

5. Helenium

6. Hypericum calycinum

7. Tagetes

8. Antirrhinum

9. Gaillardia

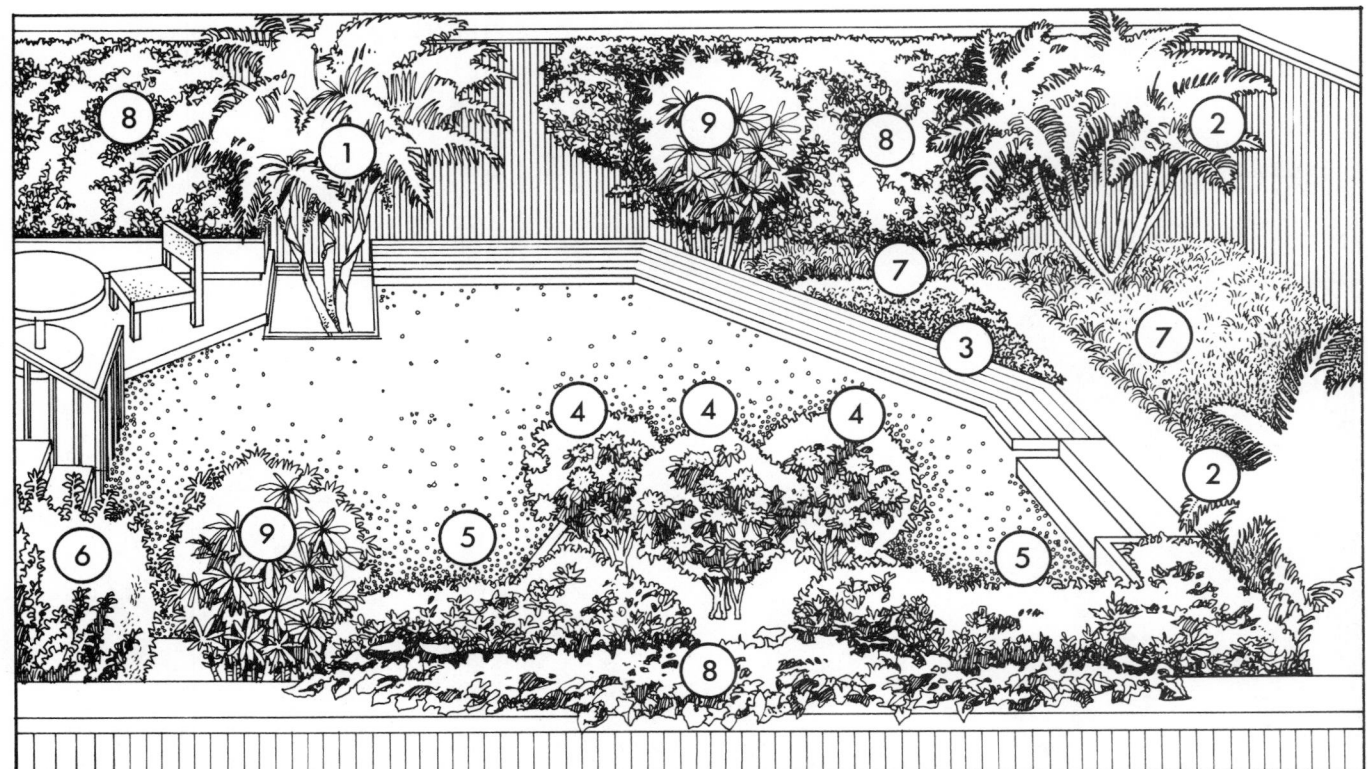

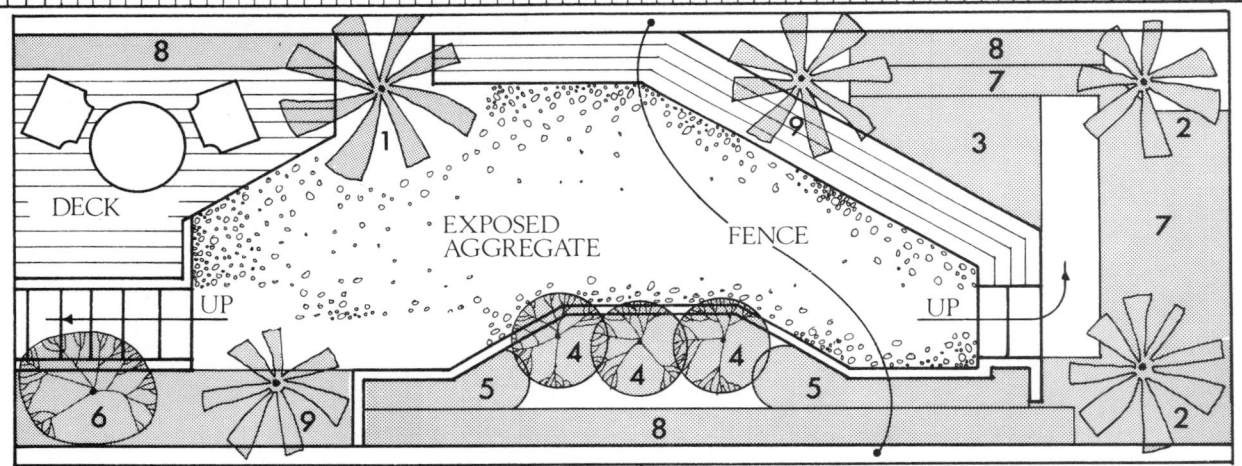

City garden [narrow lot]

1. Chrysalidocarpus lutescens

2. Dicksonia antarctica

3. Hedera helix

4. Azalea

5. Veronica spicata

6. Ilex cornuta

7. Ophiopogon japonicus

8. Hedera canariensis

9. Livistona chinensis

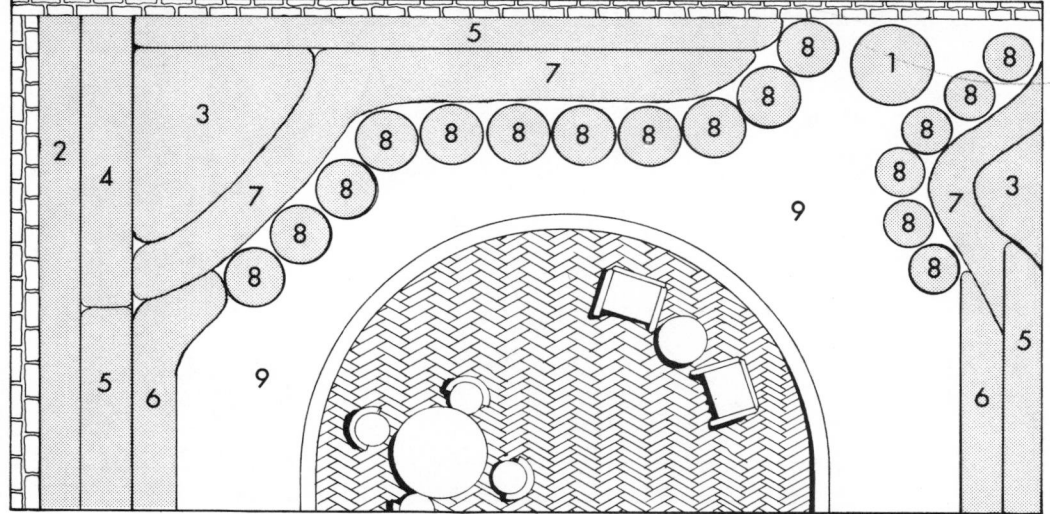

Courtyard Garden

1. Acer rubrum

2. Euonymus fortunei radicans

3. Caryopteris clandonensis

4. Helianthus multiflorus

5. Chrysanthemum

6. Plumbago capensis

7. Chrysanthemum

8. Chrysanthemum

9. Begonia

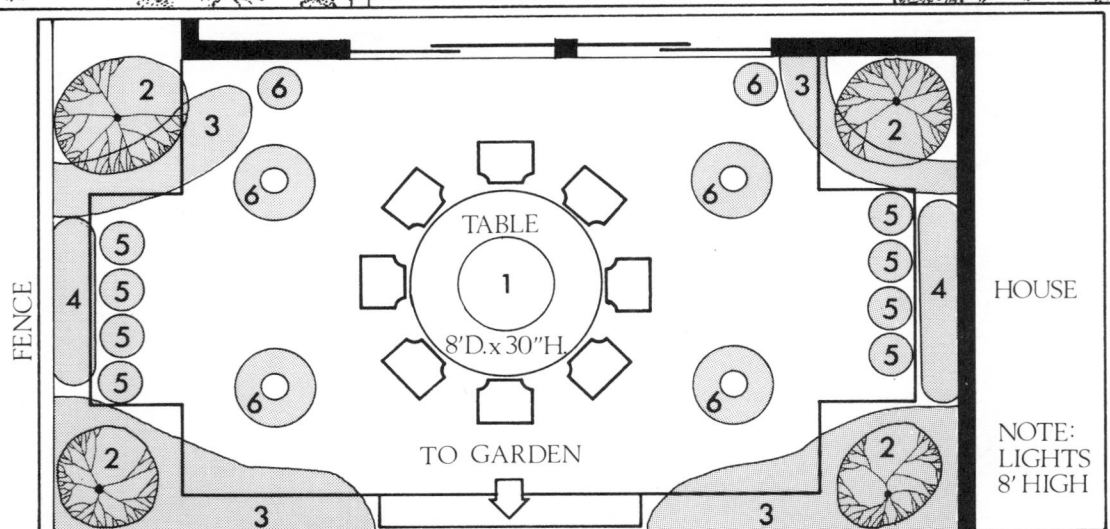

Patio Garden

1. Zinnia

2. Rhamnus frangula

3. Lantana nana compacta

4. Rosa

5. Tagetes

6. Salvia

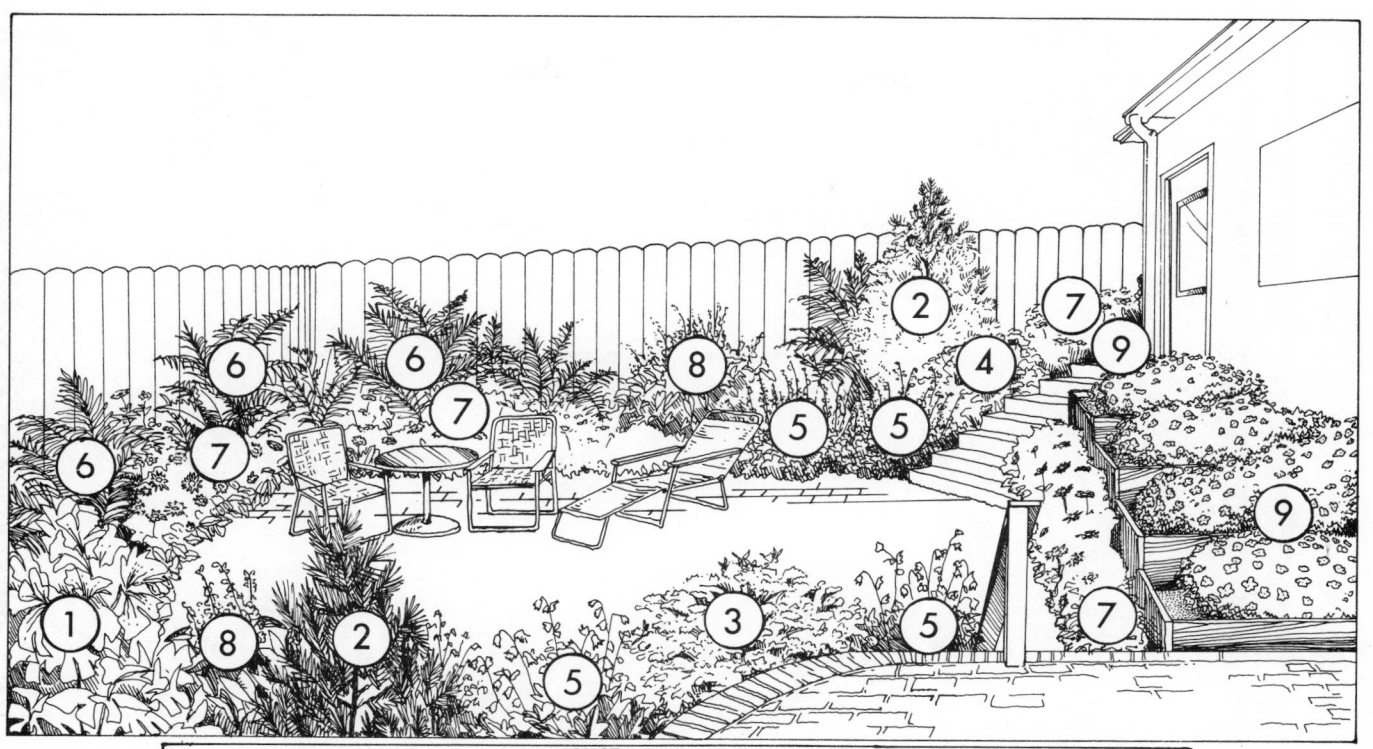

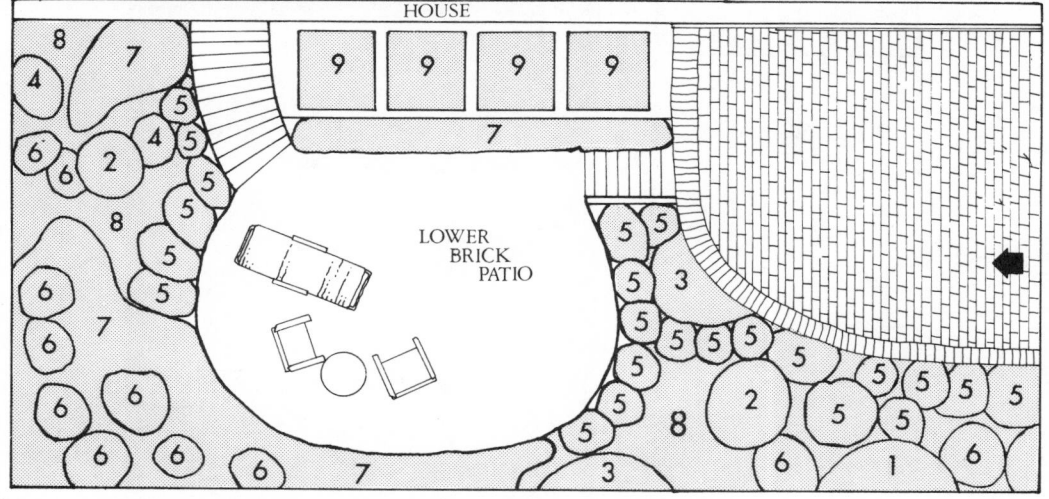

Patio Garden (multi-level)

1. Gingko bilobs

2. Pinus stroba

3. Viburnum rhytidophyllum

4. Cornus florida

5. Heuchera bressingham

6. Dennstaedtia punctilobula

7. Epimedium pinnatum

8. Impatiens

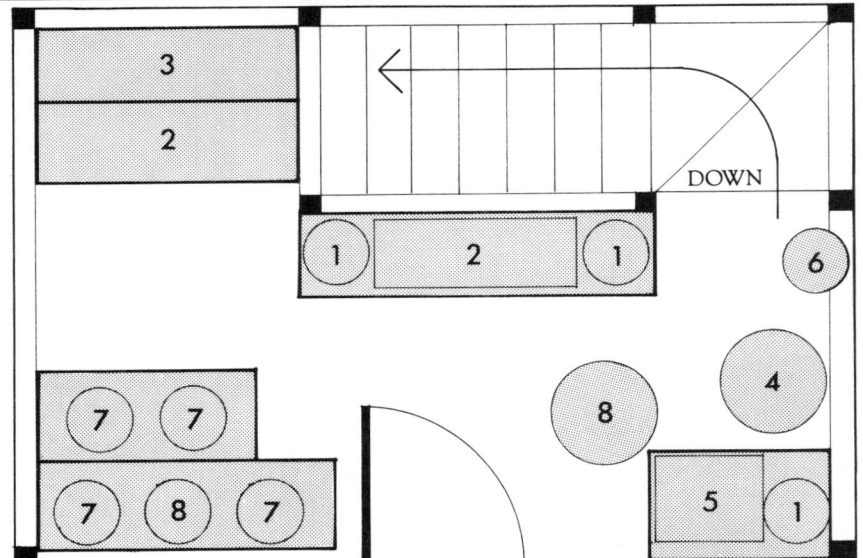

Porch Garden

1. Ipomoea purpurea 'Heavenly Blue'

2. Geranium (Double-dip type)

3. Tomato 'Small Fry'

4. Squash 'Diplomat'

5. Allium schoenopraesum

6. Begonia pendula

7. Begonia tuberhybrida

8. Fragaria vesca 'Baron Solemacher'

Rooftop Garage Garden

1. Buddleia davidii 'Empire Blue'

2. Cotoneaster apiculata

3. Caryopteris clandonsis 'Heavenly Blue'

4. Calendula 'Sunny Boy'

5. Aubrieta deltoidea

6. Iberis

7. Petunia

8. Chrysanthemum 'Diener's Double'

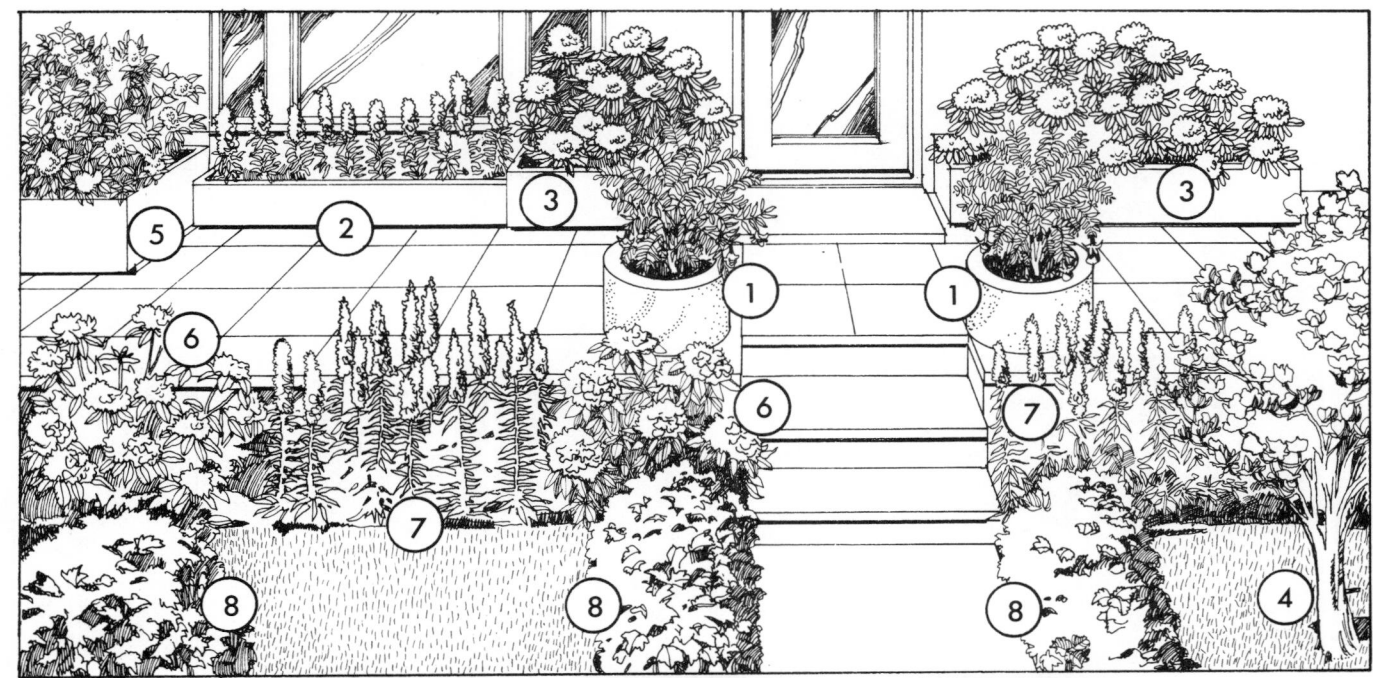

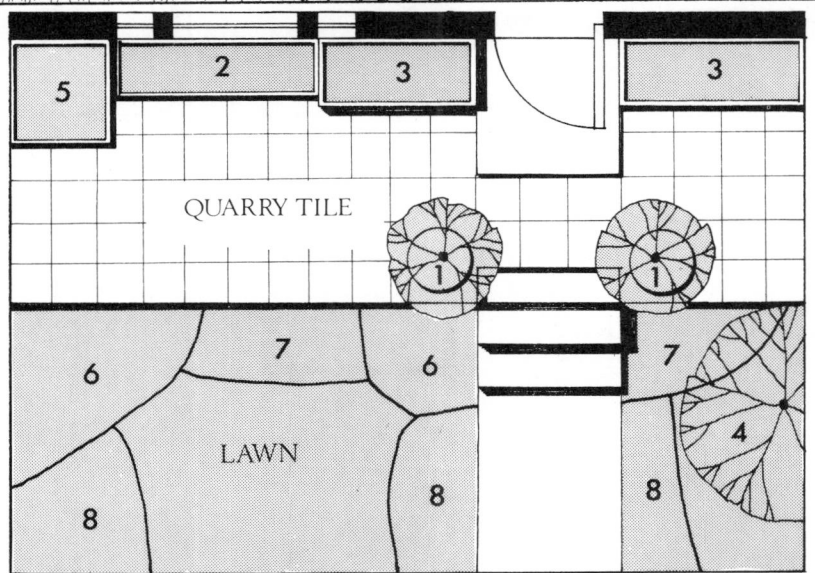

Terrace Garden

1. Punica granatum

2. Mathiola incana

3. Daphne cneorum

4. Magnolia soulangiana

5. Syringa laciniata

6. Rhododendron carolinianum

7. Lythrum 'Morden's Pink'

8. Viburnum opulus

Where to Buy Plants

The following is a list of suppliers where you can purchase plants. The list is by no means complete, and although no endorsement is implied by the listing here, I have dealt with the following companies through the years and found them to be reliable, and always willing to answer questions and give information about their plants.

PLANTS FOR THE GARDEN

Burgess Seed & Plant Co., Inc.
67 E. Battle Creek St.
Galesburg, MI 49053

Shrubs and trees; perennials, fruit trees, vegetables.

W. Atlee Burpee Co.
Philadelphia, PA 19132
Clinton, IA 52732
Riverside, CA 92502

Shrubs and trees; perennials and annuals, fruit trees, vegetables.

Henry Field Seed &
Nursery Co.
Shenandoah, IA 91601

Shrubs and trees;
vegetables, perennials.

Inter-State Nurseries
Hamburg, IA 51640

Shrubs and trees,
perennials, vegetables.

Musson Forests, Inc.
Indima, PA 15701

Trees and shrubs.

George W. Park Seed Co.
Greenwood, SC 29646

Perennials, annuals, trees
and shrubs.

Wayside Gardens
Hodges, SC 29695

Shrubs and trees;
perennials and annuals.

White Flower Farm
Litchfield, CT 06759

Perennials and annuals.

Books for Further Reading

Brett, William S., and J. E. Grant White. *Small City Gardens*. New York: Abelard-Schuman, 1967.
Bush-Brown, James, and Louise Bush-Brown. *America's Garden Book*. New York: Scribners, 1979 (revised edition).
Dietz, Marjorie. *Concise Encyclopedia of Favorite Flowering Shrubs*. Garden City, N.Y.: Doubleday, 1963.

Eckbo, Garrett. *Art of Home Landscaping*. New York: McGraw-Hill, 1980 (paperback).

Kramer, Jack. *Complete Book of Patio Gardening*. New York: Putnam, 1970.

Schuler, Stanley. *Gardening in the East*. New York: Macmillan, 1969.

White, J. E. Grant. *Designing a Garden Today*. New York: Abelard-Schuman, 1966.

Wyman, Donald. *Ground Cover Plants*. New York: Macmillan, 1956.

———. *Shrubs and Vines for American Gardens*. New York: Macmillan, 1970.

———. *Trees for American Gardens*. New York: Macmillan, 1969.

Zion, Robert L. *Trees and Architecture in the Landscape*. New York: Litton Educational Publishing, Reinhold, 1969.

INDEX